Is it rational to be moral? Can moral disputes be settled rationally? Which criteria determine what we have a good reason to do? In this innovative book, Logi Gunnarsson takes issue with the assumption made by many philosophers faced with the problem of reconciling moral norms with a scientific world view, namely that morality must be offered a non-moral justification based on a formal concept of rationality. He argues that the criteria for the rationality of an action are irreducibly substantive, rather than purely formal, and that assuming that morality must be given a non-moral justification amounts to a distortion of both rationality and morality. His discussion includes substantial critical engagement with major thinkers from two very different philosophical traditions, and is notable for its clear and succinct account of Habermas' discourse ethics. It will appeal to anyone interested in practical reason and the rational credentials of morality.

LOGI GUNNARSSON teaches philosophy at the Humboldt-Universität zu Berlin. Among his publications are *Wittgensteins Leiter: Betrachtungen zum Tractatus*, and a number of articles in journals including *Journal of Philosophical Research*, *Deutsche Zeitschrift für Philosophie* and *Dialektik*.

CAMBRIDGE STUDIES IN PHILOSOPHY

General editor ERNEST SOSA

Advisory editors
JONATHAN DANCY *University of Reading*
JOHN HALDANE *University of St. Andrews*
GILBERT HARMAN *Princeton University*
FRANK JACKSON *Australian National University*
WILLIAM G. LYCAN *University of North Carolina, Chapel Hill*
SYDNEY SHOEMAKER *Cornell University*
JUDITH J. THOMSON *Massachusetts Institute of Technology*

MAKING MORAL SENSE

Beyond Habermas and Gauthier

LOGI GUNNARSSON
Humboldt-Universität zu Berlin

PUBLISHED BY THE PRESS SYNDICATE OF THE UNIVERSITY OF CAMBRIDGE
The Pitt Building, Trumpington Street, Cambridge, United Kingdom

CAMBRIDGE UNIVERSITY PRESS
The Edinburgh Building, Cambridge CB2 2RU, UK   www.cup.cam.ac.uk
40 West 20th Street, New York, NY 10011–4211, USA   www.cup.org
10 Stamford Road, Oakleigh, Melbourne 3166, Australia
Ruiz de Alarcón 13, 28014 Madrid, Spain

First published 2000

Printed in the United Kingdom at the University Press, Cambridge

Typeset in Bembo 10.5/12pt   System 3b2   [CE]

A catalogue record for this book is available from the British Library

Library of Congress Cataloguing in Publication data
Gunnarsson, Logi.
Making moral sense: beyond Habermas and Gauthier/Logi Gunnarsson.
p.   cm. – (Cambridge studies in philosophy)
Includes bibliographical references and index.
ISBN 0 521 78023 3
1. Ethics. 2. Reason. I. Title. II. Series.

BJ1012.G86 2000
170–dc21   99–086800

ISBN 0 521 78023 3 hardback

For my parents,
Gunnar Ólafs and Ingibjörg Lúðvíksdóttir

Contents

vii

Contents

Preface

Das Schwere ist hier, nicht bis auf den Grund zu graben, sondern den Grund, der vor uns liegt, als Grund zu erkennen.

The difficult thing here is not to dig down to the ground; no, it is to recognize the ground that lies before us as the ground.
> (Wittgenstein, *Bemerkungen über die Grundlagen der Mathematik*, VI.31. Trans. G. E. M. Anscombe.)

When it comes to the justification of moral views, philosophers tend to think that they need to "dig down to the ground", to find a secure non-moral foundation for morality to stand on. This is a fundamental mistake. The substantive reasons we have regarding morality lie before us; the difficulty is to recognize them as reasons which do not need a non-moral foundation. The task of this book is to help us recognize the reasons that lie before us as reasons.

I have worked on the issues in this book in two main stages. My attempts to formulate my ideas found a preliminary ending with the submission of my dissertation at the University of Pittsburgh in 1995. Since then I have been thoroughly rethinking my theses and arguments and this work presents my current thoughts.

In writing this book, I have benefited from the generous advice of many people. My greatest debt is to John McDowell. Not only is this work deeply influenced by his writings, but as my dissertation advisor he was an invaluable source of inspiration and criticism in our numerous enjoyable philosophical conversations. Annette Baier, Robert Brandom, David Gauthier and Nicholas Rescher were also members of my dissertation committee and I am grateful to all of them for reading my work so carefully and for the many helpful discussions we had. Since Gauthier's work is under criticism in this book, he deserves special credit for invariably receiving my arguments in the spirit that philosophy lives from criticism. Although James Conant was not on my committee, we discussed my work on many occasions, and I owe him gratitude for those fruitful conversations.

Jürgen Habermas I thank for responding fairly and vigorously to my criticisms of his theory in the discussions we had during my stays at the J.W. Goethe-Universität in Frankfurt (1989–1990 and the winter term of 1992–1993). He also kindly invited me to join his doctoral colloquium and sponsored my research fellowship from Deutscher Akademischer Austauschdienst, which I thank for its support.

Many other people read my work during the years 1992–1995. I have benefited not only from extensive discussions with Joel Anderson, Felmon Davis and Matthias Kettner but also from the comments of these people: Bruce Basara, Donald Bruckner, Raymond Geuss, Bennett Helm, Friedrich Kambartel, Angelika Krebs, Hans-Peter Krüger, Jonathan Mandle, Eric Marcus, Jennifer Whiting, Lutz Wingert, and Iris Young.

The second stage in the development of the ideas in this book began in 1996 with a grant I received from the Icelandic Research Council to work on this project. This grant was renewed for 1997 and I am very grateful to the Council for its support. Since 1996, I have profited from trying my ideas on audiences in many different places. In particular, I want to mention the insightful comments given by Neera K. Badhwar and Bernard Gert, who were my commentators at the 1997 Pacific and Eastern meetings of the American Philosophical Association, respectively.

Of the people who have read, criticized and commented on my work in the last few years, I owe special gratitude to two persons. From the time I joined the Humboldt-Universität in 1997, Jay Wallace has been an especially inspiring and challenging philosophical interlocutor. His penetrating criticisms and resourceful constructive comments have led me to reformulate my arguments and ideas in many places. Mikael M. Karlsson was my teacher at the University of Iceland and has been a philosophical companion since then. Here I not only want to thank him for being an endless source of ideas and objections over the years, but also for his acute and rich constructive criticism of recent drafts of this book.

Since 1996, I have also been helped greatly by comments from the following persons: Róbert Haraldsson, Ulrike Heuer, Jeffrey

Honnold, Kristján Kristjánsson, Martin Löw-Beer, Katja Vogt, and two anonymous readers for Cambridge University Press. My editor at Cambridge, Hilary Gaskin, I thank for showing interest in the project in the first place and for her professional and competent advice along the way. Likewise, I am grateful to the copy-editor, Leigh Mueller, and the production controller, Caroline Murray, for their careful editorial work.

Material in chapters 8–9 is based on Gunnarsson 1995a and material in chapter 12 on Gunnarsson 1997a. It appears here with the publishers' kind permission.

Although this book is done, I am afraid that I won't be able to stop working on the issues in it. One might say that the book is an attempt to employ practical reasons to recommend a certain way of thinking. About this pragmatic bend and other aspects of this work, I have – ever since I started talking about these topics – been engaged in a continuing dialogue with Eva Klingenstein and I do not expect it to stop. I thank her for reading my material and for her skeptical enthusiasm.

PART I

Problems

1

The justificatory crisis of morality

We are honest and truthful, we pay our debts and keep our promises. We are caring and concerned, yet impartial and just. We are sensitive, friendly, merciful, forgiving, generous, thankful, loyal, and self-sacrificing. We are politically conscious and active, and we are respectful of people's rights whatever their gender, race, or sexual orientation. And lately we have even started recycling. In short, we are just great.

Unfortunately, accompanying this feeling of greatness is the nagging worry that we are simply being stupid. The fear is that the very source of our pride is actually a sign of our stupidity: that being moral is, in the final analysis, fundamentally irrational.

There are plenty of reasons to suspect that we are indeed being irrational. I will mention three. The most obvious reason is that being moral often requires us to sacrifice our interests or to act against our desires. We keep our promise to meet somebody for dinner even though we would much rather do something else. We divide the cake fairly though we want all of it, and we even save our enemies while rather wanting to see them dead. Now if being moral requires us systematically to act against our desires in this way, how can it be rational?

The second reason for being suspicious about morality does not as such have anything to do with a possible conflict with the satisfaction of desire. It depends on the obvious fact that the morally evaluative vocabularies which we use to guide our lives represent only one possible way of evaluating. Other moral or non-moral evaluative vocabularies would lead us to evaluate our lives quite differently. For example, instead of striving to treat others fairly and congenially, a person could set it as her ideal to treat them ruthlessly or indifferently, or she could give herself high marks for being cool rather than concerned, or original and independent rather than loyal and

3

thankful. Given the obvious possibility of conflict between these different ways of evaluating, it is by no means clear that it is rational to let our current moral evaluative scheme dominate our lives or to use it at all.

The third doubt concerning our self-satisfaction about our moral virtues is rather different. Here the question is not whether in acting morally we are doing what is rational *for us*. We do not employ a moral vocabulary only to guide our own lives, but also to criticize others. Here the worry is that our criticism of others does not amount to rational criticism but that it is rather a way of exercising power over others under the guise of moral comment. In other words, in morally criticizing others, we are not interacting with them rationally but rather abusing them. Underlying this worry is the question whether it can ever be rationally settled who is right: we or they. If it cannot be rationally settled, then our criticism can only be abuse in disguise.

This problem becomes particularly pressing when the criticizer and the criticized are members of two radically different cultural communities. It could be argued that the critic inevitably relies upon the practices of her community and that she can only be shown to be right if these practices are rationally superior to the practices of the other community. However, the argument goes, it is impossible to show the practices of one of two radically different cultural communities to be more rational than the other. I do not think that this argument is good or that the problem is insoluble, but it is a problem which needs to be resolved before we may assume that our criticism of other cultural practices can be a piece of *rational* criticism.

These worries all present a problem about *the rationality of morality*. For the sake of convenience, this problem may be divided into two fundamental subproblems: (1) *The basic choice problem*: is it rational to be guided by moral considerations at all? (2) *The moral alternatives problem*: is it rational to be guided by one particular moral view as opposed to others? These are the two main problems which I shall discuss in this work.[1] Notice that it is certainly possible to answer

[1] Although I shall also discuss other problems, I use the distinction between these two problems to structure my discussion. A third subproblem should be mentioned here. This is *the problem of priority*: is it rational to give moral reasons priority over other reasons? (Cf. Scanlon 1998, 148.) This problem must be distinguished from the basic choice problem. Even if it is rational to take moral considerations into account in rational deliberation, it still needs to be asked whether moral reasons can be overridden

only the first question positively. In that case, one would suppose that it is rational to be guided by some moral view or other, but think that the choice among different moral perspectives is not a matter of rationality.

It is extremely tempting to think that the only possible solution of these problems is to offer a *non-moral* justification of morality. Such a justification would demonstrate the rationality of morality on entirely non-moral premises. This is tempting because it seems that any other kind of justification would be question-begging and would not have the necessary independence from morality to provide criteria for deciding which moral view is the most rational.

One central thesis of this work is that it is entirely misguided to think that morality needs a non-moral justification. This thesis distinguishes the work from the writings of both the friends and the foes of non-moral justifications of morality. The former are busy constructing such justifications, whereas the latter occupy themselves with tearing them down or with giving *a priori* arguments to the effect that such justifications are bound to fail. Thus, even the foes of non-moral justifications seldom call into question the assumption that morality would be unjustified if such a justification cannot be given. This, however, is precisely the assumption which I want to call into question. I shall argue that *even if* there are flawless non-moral justifications of morality, it is a mistake to think that morality *needs* such a justification. In fact, I argue that to proceed on the assumption that morality needs such a justification distorts our view of rationality, morality, and the relationship between the two. Thus, it is not my aim to argue that non-moral justifications are impossible, but rather that — even if possible — they are not an ideal against which the success of justifications of morality and moral views should be measured.[2]

One powerful motivation for non-moral justifications of morality is at the same time a reason for thinking that these justifications must be purely *formal*. The thought here is that doubts about the rationality of morality arise precisely because moral thinking relies heavily upon *substantive* intuitions. For example, actions are taken to be morally

by other reasons, and if they can, how it is to be decided when they are overridden. This issue of overridingness is the problem of priority.

[2] This means that *rational* justifications of morality and moral views neither are to be equated with nor need to be supported by *non-moral* justifications.

wrong because they are *cruel* or right because they are *considerate*. However, so the argument goes, it can always be asked whether it is rational to guide one's life by such substantive considerations. And in order to show this to be rational, it won't help to appeal to other substantive considerations. The problem is not that these considerations are moral but that they are substantive. No actions are rational or irrational on account of some substantive features but rather on account of formal ones. Thus, in order to solve the justificatory crisis of morality, it is not enough to offer a non-moral justification of morality. The justification must also be purely formal.

According to this view, morality needs a formal non-moral justification. I call a theory *"rationalistic"* if it aims to deliver such a justification. In this book, rationalism will be my main target of criticism. As an alternative to it, I present another justificatory ideal which violates not only the rationalistic requirement that the justification of moral views must be formal but also that it must be non-moral: I argue that a justification of moral outlooks based on *substantive* reasons which *cannot be purified of moral content* is an adequate justification and is preferable to a rationalistic justification.[3]

Although it is widely assumed that morality needs a rationalistic justification, only a few philosophers actually offer a *purely* rationalistic justification. The works of these philosophers will be the focus of the argument that my substantive approach should be favored over rationalism. If I did not undermine the actually existing rationalistic positions, my argument would remain unconvincing. After criticizing these few, selected positions, I then go on to explain why I think that other rationalisms have the same flaw. In this way, I hope to deliver arguments which are convincing in their specificity while at the same time indicating how they have a general application.

There are two basic kinds of rationalism, depending upon whether the concept of rationality employed is "Hobbesian" or "Kantian". I

---

[3] It should be noted that the alternative to rationalism that I offer is also to be contrasted with theories which attempt to justify morality from a *substantive, non-moral* starting point. In favoring my alternative, I shall be defending the idea of giving justifications which have neither a non-moral nor a formal starting point. In other words, my approach is to be contrasted with the idea of giving a justification of the ethical life from an Archimedean point outside it, whether that point is understood in terms of a substantive notion of well-being or a formal notion of practical reason (see Williams 1985, chs. 2–4). In chapter 5, section 2 (hereafter 5.2), I explain how I plan to deal with theories which offer substantive non-moral justifications.

will focus on the work of the two contemporary philosophers who have perhaps done the most in recent years to develop these two conceptions of reason: David Gauthier and Jürgen Habermas. Gauthier's contractarianism is an impressive attempt to provide a rigorous Hobbesian justification of morality with the help of the tools of rational choice theory; while with his theory of communicative reason, Habermas has surely made one of the most important contributions to the development of a Kantian concept of reason in recent decades.[4]

Because of the deep differences between these two thinkers, and because Gauthier tends to be studied by "analytic" philosophers and Habermas by "Continental" thinkers, the common rationalistic core of their theories has been overlooked. It is sometimes noted in the literature that they are both, broadly speaking, contractarians.[5] However, this book does not criticize them as contractarians. For this reason, I shall not discuss at any length the theory of the other, perhaps most prominent, contemporary defender of a Kantian approach to moral and political theory – namely John Rawls. Rawls is a contractarian and a Kantian, but he is not, in my sense, a rationalist.

To see that Rawls – as opposed to Gauthier and Habermas – is not a rationalist, we need only to consider briefly the attitude of these thinkers to "reflective equilibrium" justifications. Contrary to Rawls, Gauthier and Habermas both distance themselves from the idea of a reflective equilibrium as the ultimate justification of moral and political norms.[6] Roughly speaking, a moral judgment has been given a reflective equilibrium justification if it has been shown that this judgment is in reflective equilibrium with our moral principles and considered moral judgments. A state of reflective equilibrium has been reached if the process of modifying our moral principles in the

---

[4] In this work, I shall only be concerned with contemporary versions of rationalism. Another recent work which explicitly defends a Hobbesian rationalism is Danielson 1992. Different kinds of Kantian rationalism are offered in Apel 1973; 1988c; Gewirth 1977; Kuhlmann 1985; and Korsgaard 1996.

[5] See Heath 1995, 80–82.

[6] Habermas 1988d, 89 [78–79]; 1988e, 127 [116]; Gauthier 1986, 5, 269. Rawls, in contrast, is happy to see it as the ultimate justification; see Rawls 1993, 28, 51–53. I briefly compare Rawls and Gauthier in 6.2, and Rawls and Habermas in 8.2. (In citing texts which appear in my bibliography under their original German title, I first give the reference to the German text and then, in square brackets, to an English translation.)

light of our considered moral judgments and vice versa has been completed in the sense that no further adjustments seem proper.[7] The point to notice here is that reflective equilibrium justifications remain firmly *within* morality: moral principles are justified in terms of other *moral* principles and considered *moral* judgments. This immediately raises doubts as to whether such justifications can meet skeptical worries about the rationality of morality. According to rationalism, in order to dissolve these skeptical worries, one must give a justification of morality which – contrary to reflective equilibrium justifications – does not rely on any moral intuitions.

The appeal of rationalism is obvious. To appeal to moral intuitions to demonstrate the rationality of morality seems viciously circular. To rely on other substantive intuitions seems just as hopeless, since it seems that the rationality of following such intuitions can always be called into question. And, in contrast to scientific theses, there seems to exist no empirical confirmation of moral principles.[8] Thus, it seems that the only possible savior of morality would be a *formal non-moral* justification. It is the task of this work to undermine this rationalistic justificatory ideal and to replace it by my substantive approach.

In the next chapter, I shall give a fuller and more precise account of rationalism and sketch my own alternative to it.

---

[7] For a more detailed discussion of reflective equilibrium justifications, see chapter 15.
[8] According to Alan Gewirth, empirical facts serve to test the correctness of the factual statements of natural science. These empirical facts are an "independent variable" that serves to determine the correctness of factual statements. Gewirth believes that such an "independent variable" seems – on the face of it – to be missing in the case of moral statements and that in the absence of such an "independent variable" no answer can be given to moral skepticism. His rationalism is supposed to solve this problem by demonstrating the existence of an "independent variable" for the case of morality (without assuming any metaphysically suspect moral facts or assimilating morality to natural science) (Gewirth 1977, 4–9, 78, 175–177, 365).

2

Alternative resolutions of the justificatory crisis

I SUBJECTIVIST RATIONALISM

It is Gauthier's declared aim in *Morals by Agreement* to argue that "[m]orality . . . can be generated as a rational constraint from the non-moral premisses of rational choice."[1] One way of interpreting the project of starting from non-moral premisses – and this is indeed how Gauthier understood it in this work – is that the goal is to show that "agents lacking all moral concerns . . . would rationally introduce morality into their interactions in order better to achieve their nonmoral ends."[2] In his more recent article "Value, Reasons, and the Sense of Justice," Gauthier has outlined another justification that can also be understood as relying only on non-moral premisses. There, the idea is not to show that moral sensibility – or, more specifically, the sense of justice which is the focus of Gauthier's discussion in this article – is a "mere instrument for our nonmoral gratification."[3] Rather, the aim is to show that the sense of justice is of value to agents "whatever their particular aims and concerns."[4] It is on account of this idea, as will be explained, that I take Gauthier to be a rationalist. This idea can be captured by saying that "justice is a necessary instrumental value."[5] To show justice to be a *necessary instrumental* value is, in my terminology, to give a *subjectivist rationalistic*

---

[1] Gauthier 1986, 4.
[2] Gauthier 1993a, 201.
[3] Gauthier 1993a, 201.
[4] Gauthier 1993a, 199. This claim must be qualified. For example, it does not hold for "an agent whose life-plan is focused on the destruction of his fellows, who lives to kill." Strictly speaking, it holds only for "those persons whose overarching life-plans make them welcome participants in society" (Gauthier 1993b, 188, 189) (see 6.3).
[5] Gauthier 1993a, 199.

justification of justice.[6] The subjectivism is reflected in the instrumentality of the value and the rationalism in the necessity.

What does it mean to say that something is of necessary instrumental value? To say that something is of *instrumental* value is to say that it is valuable as a means to something else that is valuable. This is where Gauthier's subjectivism surfaces. Practical reason is strictly instrumental: it is silent on which ends we should have and can only tell us how best to pursue our ends, where these ends are taken as subjectively given.[7] To show that something is of *necessary* instrumental value is to show that it is valuable – in the instrumental sense – whatever our ends may happen to be.[8]

Gauthier's justification of morality is thus *formal* in two senses. First, reason is understood instrumentally and it is thus silent on which ends we should pursue. Second, morality is supposed to be rational for the agent no matter what the substantive contents of her goals are.

By showing that morality is of necessary instrumental value, Gauthier wants to solve two problems he sees morality confronted with. The first problem is a variation on the problem of the *rationality of morality* which I mentioned in the last chapter. For Gauthier, this problem takes the following form: since for him instrumental rationality is the only notion of practical reason there is, morality cannot survive a conflict with the deliverances of instrumental reason. However, according to Gauthier, in order to show that it is rational for a person to be moral, it is not enough to show that she must be moral in order to achieve the (moral or non-moral) ends that she happens to have. Gauthier wants to be able to say that actions may be irrational even if they are the best fulfillment of the ends that the agent *happens to have*. Having those ends – for example, to be kind to one's fellow humans – may stand in the way of the person's reaping some benefits which she might otherwise be able to enjoy. Now since instrumental reason is incapable of evaluating the agent's ends

---

[6] I do not assume that Gauthier thinks that we can, or need to, show that all of what we ordinarily think of as morality can be shown to be of necessary instrumental value. In showing in *Morals by Agreement* that the rational constraints on actions are moral constraints, his concern is really with showing that these constraints are *just*. The principle of interaction justified in that work is a principle of justice (Gauthier 1986, 6, 150–156, 208–223, 233–267).

[7] Gauthier 1986, 24–26, 46–55.

[8] Gauthier 1993a, 198–199.

directly, morality cannot be shown to be rational by establishing that it helps the agent to fulfill certain rationally privileged ends. Thus, the only possible way of demonstrating the rationality of morality consists in establishing that it is instrumentally rational to be moral *whatever* the agent's ends are, i.e., in showing that morality is of *necessary* instrumental value.[9]

The second problem Gauthier wants to solve concerns the *"categorical force"* or *"unconditionality"* of morality. He takes morality as presenting us with unconditional demands because "[f]rom the standpoint of the agent, moral considerations present themselves as constraining his choices and actions, in ways independent of his desires, aims, and interests."[10] This does not just mean that moral requirements sometimes conflict with our self-interest. According to Gauthier, morality has a "prescriptive grip" which cannot be explained entirely (as a Humean might think) in terms of our sympathetic feelings, since morality speaks to those "hard cases" where even our sympathetic feelings would not move us to act in accordance with what morality demands of us. Morality operates somehow independently of our affections, including our sympathetic concern for the well-being of our fellows.[11] The problem is that instrumental reason seems – at first sight – to be unable to deliver morality's unconditional demands.[12] Since what is instrumentally rational for an agent depends on her contingently given ends, it seems that unconditional demands can never be shown to be instrumentally justified. By showing that morality is of necessary instrumental value, Gauthier would solve this problem: if morality is indeed of necessary instrumental value, it is rational to be moral not just if one happens to have certain goals but whatever one's goals are.[13]

Before defining rationalism, a misunderstanding of Gauthier's claim that morality is of necessary instrumental value must be dismissed. It might be thought that Gauthier's point is simply that it is in the long-term interest of the straightforward instrumental reasoner

---

[9] Gauthier 1986, 11; 1988b, 386–389; 1991a, 18–25; 1993a, 180–183, 189, 197–204. For a more elaborate discussion of this point, see 6.2.

[10] Gauthier 1991a, 16.

[11] Gauthier 1991a, 17–18.

[12] This problem does not coincide with the problem of the rationality of morality. One surely does not need to assume that morality speaks to us in unconditional demands in order to question the rationality of morality.

[13] Gauthier 1991a, 20–25, 29–30.

to behave morally. This would not mean that the instrumental reasoner reasons morally. Rather, each time this instrumental reasoner has to decide what to do, the question comes up whether she should follow the moral course of action, and each time her reasoning will be instrumental: even though it is generally in her interest to behave morally, it may sometimes be in her long-term interest to act immorally, and then she has a good instrumental reason to do so. In other words, in the case of such a conflict between morality and instrumental reasoning, instrumental reasoning is overriding.

Gauthier, however, does not want to show that morality is of necessary instrumental value only in the way just described. Rather, he wants to show that there is an instrumental rationale for ceasing to reason exclusively instrumentally and starting to reason *morally* as well. The agent should cease to be a straightforward instrumental reasoner and become a *constrained* instrumental reasoner: more specifically, an instrumental reasoner constrained by morality. This means that in order to show that one should do something it is not enough to show that instrumental reasoning would tell one that it is in one's (long-term) interest to do that. There exists an instrumental rationale for reasoning morally – as opposed to exclusively instrumentally – and if moral reasoning were to tell one not to do a particular action, it might be that one would have an overriding reason not to act in this way. Morality (that is, the morality for which there is an instrumental rationale) is a direct source of reasons for the morally constrained instrumental reasoner, whereas this is not so for the straightforward instrumental reasoner.[14]

What exactly makes Gauthier's theory rationalistic? I understand rationalism as a theory which addresses itself to a moral skeptic and aims to refute the skeptic on the skeptic's own terms. This moral skeptic has a purely formal understanding of rationality and wants to be rational in this sense. She thinks, however, that being rational in

---

[14] Gauthier 1986, 167–170; 1993a, 197–199; 1993b, 185–191; 1996, 20–28. There is a second way in which Gauthier's claim could be misinterpreted. One might suppose that he wants to show that there is an instrumental rationale for becoming a morally constrained instrumental reasoner, where this is understood as an instrumental rationale for becoming irrational and making irrational choices. This is not Gauthier's understanding of it. He thinks that the morally constrained instrumental reasoner is rational and that the choices that she makes based on morally constrained instrumental reasoning are themselves rational. See Gauthier 1986, 184–187; 1994.

this way does not require her to accept any moral norms.[15] In Gauthier's case, this means that the skeptic is a person who aims to be a fully rational instrumental reasoner and thinks that being rational in this way does not require her to start to reason morally. Gauthier's theory is rationalistic because it is meant to establish that the formal rationality which the skeptic herself accepts requires her to respect certain moral principles. I accordingly define rationalism as follows:

> A theory is rationalistic if and only if it (1) addresses itself to a moral skeptic who has a formal understanding of rationality and (2) aims to show that this moral skeptic cannot be rational in this sense unless she respects certain specific moral norms.

As I already mentioned, in trying to show that the skeptic cannot be formally rational unless she accepts certain moral norms, rationalism is aiming to refute the skeptic *on the skeptic's own terms*. A distinction of Robert Nozick's can be usefully employed to illustrate this point. He distinguishes between the foreign and domestic relations of a subject's system of beliefs. According to Nozick, one way in which a subject could respond to a skeptic who questions the possibility of knowledge is to try to *convince* the skeptic by showing that in the light of some of the skeptic's other beliefs the skeptic herself must think that knowledge is possible. This is a task of the foreign relations department of the subject's belief system, since the topic is how *the skeptic's* beliefs fit together. The bureau of internal affairs has another job. The subject has accepted some of the things that the skeptic points out and this presents the subject with a problem as to how knowledge is possible. The goal is not to convince the skeptic, but rather to explain how knowledge is possible in light of the problem presented. Since the skeptic may not accept all the statements on which the explanation depends, the explanation is a matter for the subject's domestic relations department.[16] Applying this terminology to the present case, we can say that rationalism is engaged in foreign relations. Its goal is not simply to show that the

---

[15] It should be noted that this is a very special form of moral skepticism. For example, my skeptic has a purely formal understanding of rationality. Other moral skeptics might not. When I speak of "*the* moral skeptic" in this work, I have in mind the kind of skeptic described here, without assuming that there are no other forms of moral skepticism. I focus on this kind of moral skepticism because it is the form which rationalism speaks to.

[16] Nozick 1981, 15–17.

moral skeptic is irrational, but to show that she is irrational even by her own standards.

Attention should be drawn to the fact that rationalism, as I have defined it, is committed to showing that it is rational to respect *certain specific* moral norms. This does not mean that rationalists such as Gauthier and Habermas agree on what norms it is rational to accept. It just means that all rationalists aim to justify *some* specific moral norms. If rationalism were to show successfully that a rational skeptic must indeed accept certain specific norms, then rationalism would have solved the problem of the rationality of morality in both of its versions: both the *moral alternatives problem* (the problem *which* morality it is rational to accept) and the *basic choice problem* (the problem whether it is rational to be moral *at all*). My aim is to show that it is not necessary to refute the moral skeptic on her own terms to solve either of these problems (see 11.4).

2 INTER-SUBJECTIVIST RATIONALISM

I understand Habermas as a rationalist because he offers a transcendental-pragmatic or universal-pragmatic justification of certain moral norms.[17] Let me thus start by explaining briefly what it means to give such a justification.

Transcendental-pragmatic or universal-pragmatic justifications (for short, "up-justifications") are *transcendental* in the sense that they work by asking what makes a certain activity, e.g. doubt, possible. The idea is that by answering this question we will discover what makes doubt possible in the first place and will thereby discover what cannot be doubted itself. The sense in which an up-justification is

---

[17] Habermas is not the only philosopher to offer such justifications. For example, Karl-Otto Apel and Wolfgang Kuhlmann also do. Habermas prefers to call his justifications "universal-pragmatic" rather than "transcendental-pragmatic" in order to stress that he – contrary to Apel and Kuhlmann – does not understand them to be delivering *a priori* knowledge but rather empirical–philosophical knowledge of the presupposition of our current concept of reason, a concept that might itself change (Habermas 1984c, 379–385 [21–25]; 1988d, 104–108 [94–98]; 1991f, 190–195 [80–84]). Despite this difference, the justifications offered by all three philosophers are rationalistic: they all offer a non-moral formal justification of morality. Thus, though I will not discuss Apel and Kuhlmann explicitly in the text, in the discussion of the views which I think they share with Habermas I also include footnote-references to their work. For a longer discussion of the central differences between them relevant to our topic, see the Appendix.

pragmatic is best explained by considering a notion central to it, the notion of *pragmatic (or performative) self-contradiction*. Consider an example of a person who asserts "I do not exist." One could argue that this person has by the very act of asserting this involved herself in a pragmatic self-contradiction. If her assertion is to be successful, certain presuppositions must be fulfilled. If these presuppositions are not fulfilled she will not have succeeded in asserting anything. Presumably, one of the presuppositions is that she exists. Now, this presupposition of the assertion contradicts the propositional content of the assertion ("I do not exist"). In other words, this is a case of a *pragmatic* self-contradiction for the following reason: the contradiction is between a presupposition of an assertion as a performance or action (the assertion in its pragmatic sense) and the propositional content of the assertion. This pragmatic self-contradiction shows that one cannot coherently doubt one's own existence.[18]

Up-justifications of moral norms are just one instance of this general form of justification. The goal is to show that a radical moral skeptic – a skeptic who asserts "There is nothing irrational about rejecting moral norms" (or something equally radical) – gets caught in a pragmatic contradiction, since there is a contradiction between the propositional content of this assertion and the conditions of possibility of the assertion considered as a contribution to a rational argumentation.

No contribution to rational argumentation may contradict the conditions of the possibility of rational argumentation. According to Habermas, one such condition is that nobody be excluded from the argumentation. If somebody were excluded from participating, then the form of interaction between the participants would not be rational argumentation, properly speaking. In fact, it would not be argumentation at all. The implicit end of argumentation is to resolve rationally some question which is under discussion. To exclude somebody from the discussion is a threat to the rationality of the answer. Thus, the assertion "Smith should be excluded from the argumentation" cannot count as a contribution to a rational argumentation, since it serves to undermine the very conditions that make rational argumentation possible (the presuppositions of rational argumentation): there is a contradiction between the propositional content of this assertion and

---

[18] Habermas 1988d, 90–91 [79–80]; Apel 1975, 262–269; Kuhlmann 1985, 88–89. It should be noted that all of these authors give credit to Hintikka 1962.

15

the conditions that must be fulfilled if it (as performance) is to count as a contribution to rational argumentation.

Habermas would argue that the moral skeptic's assertion of "There is nothing irrational about rejecting moral norms" is similarly problematic. He believes that among the presuppositions of rational argumentation are some norms with moral content. Thus, as a participant in a rational argumentation about the question "Is there anything irrational about rejecting moral norms?" the moral skeptic (who thinks that the answer is negative) must presuppose that certain moral norms are being respected. If they are not respected – given that they are presuppositions of rational argumentation – the discussion of this question cannot count as rational argumentation. This means that these moral norms cannot be rationally rejected, since they must be respected if there is to be any such thing as rational argumentation. The impossibility of rationally rejecting these norms is crystallized in the pragmatic contradiction between the propositional content of the skeptical assertion "There is nothing irrational about rejecting moral norms" and the presuppositions of this assertion considered as a contribution to rational argumentation (where these presuppositions include the one that certain moral norms cannot be rationally rejected).[19]

If this kind of up-justification of moral norms is successful, it seems to solve the problem of the *rationality* of morality.[20] It seems that since it is the rationality of morality itself that is at stake, appeal to moral intuitions will beg the question against the moral skeptic. Up-justifications are constructed so as not to depend on the acceptance of any moral intuitions. Up-justifications of moral norms amount to an analysis of the presuppositions of *rational argumentation as such* rather than the presuppositions of moral argumentation: the skeptic does not engage in moral argumentation but only in "meta-moral" argumentation about the question whether it is irrational to reject moral norms. Since the up-justifications rely on an analysis of the presuppo-

---

[19] Habermas 1988d, 96–103 [86–93]; Apel 1988c, 352–357; Kuhlmann 1985, 181–215.

[20] I mention here only the problem of the rationality of morality, since it seems to me that Habermas does not want to account for the unconditionality of morality in a rationalistic way (Habermas 1991f, 132–137, 186–192 [31–35, 77–81]). Apel and Kuhlmann, in contrast, do want to give a rationalistic account of the unconditionality of morality; see Apel 1973, 415–417 [270–271]; Kuhlmann 1992b, 154–157; 1985, 227–239.

sitions of argumentation of the latter kind, the question against the skeptic is not begged. Thus, by showing – without relying on any moral intuitions – that only if certain moral norms are respected is rational argumentation possible, up-justifications reveal that rationality itself – incorporated in rational argumentation – has a moral dimension. And if rationality itself has a moral dimension, radical skepticism about the rationality of morality is refuted.[21]

As already explained, I count Gauthier's theory as a kind of *subjectivist* rationalism. I understand Habermas' up-theory as a species of *inter-subjectivist* rationalism. According to Habermas, there is, besides instrumental reason, another form of reason occupying the practical sphere. The up-justifications of morality serve to explicate this other concept of rationality. These explications amount to an analysis of the presuppositions of rational argumentation, the rationality of which is not instrumental. If it turns out – as up-theorists think – that this rationality requires the acceptance of certain moral norms, then these moral norms have been shown to be *directly inter-subjectively* valid in the sense that their validity does not depend on an instrumental relation to subjectively given ends. Indeed, the validity of moral norms will turn out not to be subjective at all, not even in the derivative sense – as subjectivist rationalism would have it – of being dependent on necessary instrumental values.[22]

The distinction between subjectivist and inter-subjectivist rationalisms emerges clearly in the difference between the structure of Gauthier's theory and Habermas' up-theory. Gauthier admits only one fundamental concept of reason, instrumental reason. Habermas offers an additional concept – the concept of communicative reason – and this is the one central to moral justification and to the justification of morality itself. For Gauthier, any reasoning about moral ends is suspect until it can be validated in terms of instrumental reason. According to Habermas, communicative reason enables us to reach inter-subjectively valid conclusions about moral ends – universaliz-

---

[21] Habermas 1988d, 86–104 [76–94]; 1991f, 185–192 [76–81]; Apel 1989, 52–59 [153–157]; Kuhlmann 1992c, 197–204. Apel and Kuhlmann think that with his up-justifications Habermas is unable to establish the rationality and unconditionality of morality; see Apel 1989; Kuhlmann 1992c, 187–189. For Habermas' response to this sort of criticism, see Habermas 1988d, 104–108 [94–98]; 1991f, 190–199 [80–88].

[22] Habermas 1987a, 28–40 [10–19]; Apel 1990, 39–52 [47–54]; Kuhlmann 1992b, 154–162.

able interests – and no further validation is called for. This feature of his up-theory comes out in his two-level approach to moral theory.[23] Some moral norms are justified by up-justifications, which can be understood as *explications of the concept* of communicative reason. Other moral norms are justified in moral discourses in which the conclusions are not justified by up-justifications. Nevertheless, communicative reason is *employed* in those discourses, and this is what makes it possible for direct reasoning (in discourse) about moral ends to produce results that are inter-subjectively valid and stand in no further need of validation.[24]

Habermas' idea is to show that certain moral norms are necessary presuppositions of something. According to Habermas, in order to show, without begging the question, that even the most radical skeptic must *necessarily* accept these moral norms, the starting point of the argument must be characterized in such a way that it provides common ground between the skeptic and the up-theorist – a common ground acceptable even to the most radical moral skeptic. In this sense, that which is supposed to have moral norms as presuppositions must itself be characterized *non-morally*.

Now although the moral skeptic does not engage in moral argumentation, she is willing to engage in rational "meta-moral" argumentation about the question whether moral disputes can be settled rationally. The skeptic wants to respect the rationality inherent in the rules of rational argumentation, and she understands this rationality in a purely *formal* way. This makes it possible to specify a starting point for the up-argument which both the skeptic and the up-theorist accept: they both want to respect the formal aspect of rationality. The difference is that the up-theorist thinks (and it is the aim of the up-justification to show) that one cannot be rational in that way without respecting certain moral norms.

According to Habermas, the aspect of rationality which the skeptic wants to respect cannot be understood adequately except as a manifestation of a concept of rationality that must be understood in moral terms. In other words, what the skeptic aspires to have cannot be conceived of in a *purely* formal way. The up-argument is meant to

---

[23] For a more detailed discussion of the two-level approach, see chapter 8.
[24] Habermas 1988d, 75–86, 103–104 [65–76, 93–94]; 1991b, 11–20 [196–203]; Apel 1973, 424–426 [277–278]; 1988b, 199–203, 210–211; Kuhlmann 1985, 246–253; 1992c, 200–201.

uncover the moral dimension of the rationality inherent in rational argumentation. In other words, the argument is meant to make explicit that there never was any non-moral and purely formal rationality for the skeptic to stand on. It just appeared so to the skeptic.[25] Habermas himself is not a formalist, but the moral skeptic to whom his up-argument is addressed is.[26] Therefore, Habermas' theory fulfills both of the conditions of the definition of rationalism:

> A theory is rationalistic if and only if it (1) addresses itself to a moral skeptic who has a formal understanding of rationality and (2) aims to show that this moral skeptic cannot be rational in this sense unless she respects certain specific moral norms.

Even though Habermas' and Gauthier's theories both fulfill the conditions of this definition, they do so in a different way. The moral skeptic aspires to be rational and believes that this does not require being moral. In his debate with the skeptic, Habermas does not accept the skeptic's purely formal notion of rationality as the final court of appeal. Rather, he wants to demonstrate that the rationality of rational argumentation cannot be understood purely formally.[27]

For Gauthier, in contrast, the final court of appeal is a purely formal concept of reason: instrumental reason. The very point of his theory is to give an *instrumental rationale* for reasoning morally. On Gauthier's story, the conclusion that we should abandon our exclusive commitment to instrumental reasoning (or any other conclusion concerning practical reason) must be substantiated by a purely formally understood instrumental reason.

This means that Habermas and Gauthier differ as to whether the skeptic's understanding of rationality – mentioned in condition (1) of the definition – articulates an intelligible concept of reason. Accord-

---

[25] Habermas 1988d, 88–104 [78–94]; 1991f, 133–134 [31–32]; Apel 1988c, 352–357; Kuhlmann 1992c, 181–182, 197–204.

[26] I do not mean to suggest that there is not another sense in which Habermas would count as a formalist. The important point here is that he thinks that reason cannot be understood purely formally in the way that the moral skeptic wants to understand it.

[27] Habermas' universal-pragmatic justification of the universalization principle has two premises from which a conclusion is supposed to follow (Habermas 1988d, 92–93 [82]; 1991f, 133–134 [31–32]). For this reason, it does not have the structure of a transcendental justification by analysis of presuppositions (even though the justification of one of the premises does) in the sense defined in the beginning of this section. Nevertheless, since it fits my definition, it is a rationalistic justification. For a further discussion of this justification of Habermas', see 8.3–5.

ing to Habermas, it does not. There is no *purely* formal concept of rationality on which an argument for the acceptance of moral norms can be based. According to Gauthier, the skeptic articulates a perfectly intelligible concept of reason, and Gauthier's argument is based on this concept. The skeptic simply has an imperfect grasp of what the correct applications of this concept require of her. They require, per condition (2), that the skeptic respect certain specific moral norms.

3 THE SUBSTANTIVE APPROACH

In this book, I shall argue that a justification of moral outlooks based on *substantive reasons* which *cannot be purified of moral content* is an adequate justification and is preferable to a rationalistic justification. To argue this is to defend what I call "*the substantive approach.*" In this way, I aim to show that morality does not face a justificatory crisis in the absence of a rationalistic justification.

The substantive approach relies on the notion of a *substantive reason*, a notion which has not been given much attention in contemporary moral philosophy. Accordingly, the second main ambition of this work will be to develop and defend a substantive account of practical rationality. Since the bulk of the book deals with practical justification as it pertains to morality, this account will mostly be developed and tested in that context. However, I by no means intend only to defend substantive justifications as justifications of moral outlooks. I mean to offer a substantive account of practical rationality itself – an account which I call "*substantivism.*" According to substantivism, actions can be rational or irrational on account of substantive considerations, whereas *formalism* maintains that a formal test alone decides whether an action is rational or irrational. While rationalism is an attempt to defeat on her own grounds a moral skeptic who aspires to be rational in a purely non-moral and formal way, formalism is a theory about practical reason according to which rationality must be understood purely formally.[28]

It might now be said that the definitions of the four positions I have introduced so far (rationalism, the substantive approach, substantivism, formalism) will be meaningless unless I explain what I

---

[28] Of course, the acceptance of formalism does not commit one to rationalism. Formalists must assume that all reasons are, in the final analysis, formal reasons, but they need not assume that moral reasons must be based on *non-moral* formal reasons.

mean by the pairs "formal/substantive" and "moral/non-moral." To this I have two responses. First, it is not my responsibility to explain the meaning of "formal" and "moral." It is the rationalist who thinks that morality needs a justification which is both formal and non-moral. I defend a justification which the *rationalist* would count as neither formal nor non-moral, and this is what makes it an alternative to rationalism. Thus, I do not need a general characterization of what makes something formal or non-moral. My thesis is simply that a justification which the rationalist would count as neither formal nor non-moral is superior to the rationalist's own justification. If others would count the justification I offer as formal and non-moral, I would have no problem with that. Similar remarks apply to the formalist.

My second response is to give examples of reasons which I count as substantive. I think that, at least in some cases, a good reason for an action may be that it is adventurous and a reason against an action that it expresses contempt for another person. Now the formalists known to me would not accept these reasons as good reasons unless they can be shown to be based on reasons they count as formal. I shall argue, however, that in some cases these can be good reasons in their own right. These reasons would be counted by the formalists as substantive reasons, and indeed it seems to me that they should be. To give a reason for an action by saying that it is adventurous is to support the action by reference to its *content* rather than by subsuming it under a *formal rule*: it is sometimes taken to speak in favor of an undertaking that it is *adventurous* and perhaps *risky* rather than *boring* and *safe*. Such descriptions of actions in terms of their content provide us with extremely subtle and nuanced ways of supporting and criticizing actions. We support and criticize them by describing them as bold, boring, brave, and bigoted, contemptuous, comic, conscientious, and convoluted, daring, devilish, diligent, dull, and so on. If the reasons for actions are in fact captured by such descriptions, I think they are indeed appropriately called substantive reasons.

It should be stressed that I take *subjectivism* about practical reason to be a formalistic theory. According to subjectivism, the rationality of actions is relative to the agent's desires, and rationality puts no constraints on the content of the agent's desires. This theory is formalistic because it counts actions as rational if they help to fulfill the agent's desires *no matter what the content of these desires is*. Of course, in order to figure out whether an action helps to satisfy a desire, we need to know the content of the action and the desire. But the rationality of the action depends on the formal relationship between these contents, irrespective of what they are. According to substantivism, however, rationality sometimes depends directly on the content of an action or a desire.

In the next chapter, I shall offer a more precise characterization of subjectivism. Many philosophers proceed on the assumption that morality only appears to us to face a justificatory crisis if we accept a subjectivist notion of practical reason. Thus, they assume that in order to dissolve the crisis it is enough to show that subjectivism is false.[29] I think that this assumption is deeply mistaken. I shall argue that even if subjectivism is rejected, a rationalistic justification of morality will still appear to be a justificatory ideal which needs to be satisfied in order to save morality from a justificatory crisis.

[29] This is perhaps not an assumption which, if it were made explicit, people would acknowledge that they accept. However, a great deal of philosophers proceed *as if* they were making this assumption. I have here in mind contemporary authors who neither are rationalists in my sense nor think that morality faces a justificatory crisis. Their discussion of the justificatory status of morality tends to have the following structure: after having produced lengthy arguments against subjectivism, they immediately draw the conclusion that there is no problem about the justificatory status of morality (one example is the transition from chapter 5 to chapter 6 in Smith 1994). I do not mean to suggest that they assume that there is *no* more work to be done after subjectivism has been refuted. However, they seem to assume that, while subjectivism presented a fundamental threat to morality, after its demolition there is no such *fundamental* threat left.

3

Subjective reasons

I understand subjectivism as a specific form of what may be called "the internal reasons model of practical reason." The internal and external reasons models amount to two different interpretations of statements of the form "Agent A has a reason to φ" and "There is a reason for A to φ." Is the statement "Agent A has a reason to φ" falsified by the lack of something in A's "subjective motivational set" which would support the performance of the action in question by A?[1] A positive answer to this question amounts to the internal reasons model – the view that all practical reasons are internal reasons – and a negative answer amounts to the external reasons model – the view that there are external reasons.[2]

The distinction between the internal and the external reasons model is drawn in terms of the notion of the agent's subjective motivational set. What, though, is in the agent's subjective motivational set? One might suppose that it is composed of the agent's current desires. This is not how Bernard Williams understands it. According to Williams, the content of the set is *not* exhausted by the agent's *desires*. Rather, the subjective motivational set "can contain such things as dispositions of evaluation, patterns of emotional reac-

---

[1] It should be emphasized that I understand the internal and external reasons models as offering different interpretations of what it means to say that an agent has a *good* reason to φ rather than of what it means to say that an agent has a reason *motivating* her to φ. The two positions differ in their views concerning the relation between motivation and the good reasons an agent has, but their object of analysis is what it means to say that an agent has a good reason to φ.

[2] Williams 1981, 101–102. The two positions are sometimes called "internalism" and "externalism". I decided not to call them that in order to keep this issue distinct from other contemporary debates using these terms; for a characterization of these different debates, see Parfit 1997, 99–109.

tion, personal loyalties, and various projects, as they may be abstractly called, embodying commitments of the agent."[3]

In addition, Williams assumes that the contents of the subjective motivational set are *not statically given*, but are affected by the agent's deliberations. Imagination plays a role in deliberation and its use can result in both addition to the subjective motivational set and subtraction of elements from it.[4] This has important consequences for the way in which the internal reasons model is to be understood. According to the internal reasons model, all reasons are relative to the agent's subjective motivational set: the agent can have a reason to ϕ only if her ϕ-ing is supported by an element in her subjective motivational set. However, it is not always possible to identify *prior to* deliberation an element in the subjective motivational set which supports ϕ-ing. The relevant element may itself be a *result* of the deliberative process. Thus, even though the agent does not have an internal *reason* for ϕ-ing unless ϕ-ing is appropriately related to an element in the agent's subjective motivational set, not all *deliberations* consist of relating an antecedently *given* element of the set to an action. Although all deliberations start from the agent's subjective motivational set, the deliberative process is not always confined to figuring out a suitable connection between actions and given elements in the set, but may also add to or subtract from the set. To answer the question "Does agent A have an internal reason to ϕ?", we must ask whether A's ϕ-ing is suitably related to an element in A's subjective motivational set, as it occurs as a result of her deliberations, rather than prior to deliberation.

Taking account of these remarks about deliberation, the distinction between the internal and external reasons models may now be formulated as follows: according to the former, it is only by virtue of the presence of an element of the subjective motivational set – the presence of which is either "psychologically given" or the result of a deliberative process starting from the subjective motivational set – that A can count as having a reason for ϕ-ing.[5] In contrast, the external reasons theorist holds that A may have a reason to ϕ even

[3] Williams 1981, 105.
[4] Williams 1981, 104–105.
[5] This does not mean that, in order to have an internal reason for ϕ-ing, A must in fact be able to conduct the deliberation starting from the relevant member of her set and leading to the motivation to ϕ (Williams 1995a, 188).

though such an element is absent from A's subjective motivational set. What is required for A *actually* to have an external reason to φ – even though the requisite element is absent from the subjective motivational set – is that in coming (that by failing) to believe that something constitutes a reason for φ-ing she is coming to *consider the matter aright* (she is failing to *consider the matter aright*).[6]

In addition to saying that deliberation does not only consist in relating possible actions to given elements of the subjective motivational set, Williams says: "There is an essential indeterminacy in what can be counted as a rational deliberative process. Practical reasoning is a heuristic process, and an imaginative one, and there are no fixed boundaries on the continuum from rational thought to inspiration and conversion."[7] Nevertheless, he must assume that there is a difference between a change of mind as a result of rational deliberation and one as a result of conversion. Otherwise, no sense can be made of the distinction between cases in which an agent already has an internal reason to φ and manages to make this clear to herself (via rational deliberation), and cases in which an agent, who previously did not have an internal reason to φ, acquires such a reason (via conversion). Even if the boundary between the two categories is not sharp, Williams' employment of the notion of rational deliberation to explain what an agent has an internal reason to do clearly assumes that there is a distinction between the two.

In spelling out how rational deliberation differs from conversion, Williams would have to steer between two extremes. On the one hand, rational deliberation cannot be the arbitrary addition of a new element to the agent's set (or subtraction from it), since that is surely what conversion would be. On the other hand, in rational deliberation, the agent may not be responding to an external reason. Thus, in order to distinguish rational deliberation from both conversion and a response to an external reason, the addition (subtraction) of an element from the set must somehow be grounded in the agent's current set. The agent must in some sense be drawing a "rational implication" of her current set. One may distinguish two different

---

[6] Williams 1981, 109; McDowell 1995a, 72–73. According to Williams, to say that an agent has an external reason to φ also means that if the agent deliberates rationally she will – *whatever her subjective motivational set* – come to be motivated to φ (Williams 1981, 109). McDowell takes issue with this additional gloss on what it is to have external reasons (McDowell 1995a, 70–76); see 4.1.

[7] Williams 1981, 110; see also Williams 1995b, 38.

ways of steering between the two extremes; these correspond to two different interpretations of the internal reasons model.

The subjectivist interpretation

It is commonly assumed that a person may be mistaken about her desires. For example, she may think that she would rather go to the movies than spend the evening at home. However, it might actually be the case that she would rather stay at home, and, if fortunate, she might *discover* this. Prior to reflecting on it, she already really preferred to stay at home and simply had to discover this.[8]

This idea of a discovery can be used to interpret the notion of rational deliberation. In some cases, the deliberating agent simply discovers elements of the set that were unknown to her: she just did not notice them.[9] In other cases, where the imagination adds elements to the set, this may also be understood as a kind of discovery. Such cases can be thought of in analogy with cases in which a person discovers facts about her desires by trying things out. If a person has never tried either spring rolls or dumplings, she will need to try both to find out which she prefers. She had previously no encounters with these food items and thus there was in her subjective motivational set no preference one way or the other. Nevertheless, it may be said that experience makes clear to the person her subjective disposition: she had a disposition for, say, dumplings all along and that has now been discovered. Analogously, the person can use her imagination to discover her subjective disposition. The use of her imagination may result in the addition of members to the set, but these are really just manifestations of the subjective disposition that has been discovered.

This interpretation of rational deliberation makes sense of Williams' inclusion of such things as dispositions of evaluation and patterns of emotional reaction in the set: when the imagination adds members to the set it does so simply as a response to such dispositions or patterns. Thus, in adding members, it is merely responding to a discovery of facts about given members of the set.

By drawing on this notion of discovery, we can now distinguish

---

[8] This is not to say that there are not other cases in which a person acquires a preference or a desire in the course of reflection.

[9] Williams 1981, 103.

between "practical" and "theoretical" deliberation and show that neither of them counts as a case of conversion or response to external reasons. It is the business of "theoretical" rationality to determine correctly the facts about the agent's surroundings and the contents of her subjective motivational set. Taking these facts as a starting point, "practical" rationality has two tasks: (a) to recommend the addition (or subtraction) of elements to the set in order to achieve "coherence" among the elements of the set (also taking account of the elements brought to light in "theoretical" deliberation), and (b) to recommend actions supported by elements in the subjective motivational set.[10]

By this account of rational deliberation, conversion differs from rational deliberation in that in the case of conversion the agent simply adds members to the set that were neither to be discovered there nor to be added on the basis of considerations of coherence. Rational deliberation is also not a response to external reasons. In "theoretical" deliberation, the agent discovers facts about her surroundings and her subjective motivational set, but no facts about what she has reason to do.[11] Her "practical" deliberations deliver recommendations based on relations with members of her subjective motivational set, including members brought to the surface in "theoretical" deliberation.

This interpretation of rational deliberation can now be used to define subjectivism. According to subjectivism, there are no *non-relative* rational requirements about what must, may or may not belong to the agent's subjective motivational set. The lack or presence of a particular element in a person's set does not make her subject to rational criticism, unless a *relative* criticism can be given of its lack or presence – unless its lack or presence can be criticized *in the light of other elements already present in the set*. Accordingly, I define subjectivism as follows:

A theory is subjectivistic if and only if it holds (1) that there are only

---

[10] It can now be seen that there are two senses in which the elements of the set are not *statically given*: on the one hand, "theoretical" reason may discover the implications of the agent's subjective dispositions; on the other hand, considerations of coherence may recommend the addition or subtraction of elements.

[11] For a discussion of the question of whether it is possible to distinguish between facts about what an agent has a reason to do, on the one hand, and facts about her surroundings and something like her subjective motivational set, on the other, see Karlsson, forthcoming.

internal reasons and (2) that there are no non-relative rational constraints on the content of a person's subjective motivational set.

The non-subjectivist interpretation

It could be maintained that without certain elements in her subjective motivational set, a person would simply not be a rational person. According to this position, certain elements are thus *constitutive* of rationality. Since this position would count the absence of these elements as itself a sign of irrationality, it must reject (2). Thus, it is a *non-subjectivistic* position.

If this position nevertheless accepts (1), it would be a version of the *internal reasons model*. A defender of this position might explain the compatibility of the acceptance of (1) and the rejection of (2) as follows: (2) is rejected because certain elements are constitutive of rationality. A person, however, never has an external reason to add any of these elements (or any other elements) to her subjective motivational set. The presence of at least some of these elements is a *precondition* of having reasons at all. Only a person whose subjective motivational set has some of these elements can count as rational and as having reasons at all, but the reasons she has will be relative to her set. In other words, they will be internal reasons.[12]

I mention this non-subjectivistic internal reasons model here only in order to clarify the bone of contention between my position and subjectivism. I shall only dispute clause (2) of the definition of subjectivism.[13] Clause (1) – which subjectivism shares with the non-subjectivist internal reasons model – will be left untouched.[14] Thus, although I am about to state my own substantivist position in terms of

[12] This may be the position defended in Korsgaard 1986. It must be emphasized here that the defender of the non-subjectivist internal reasons model need not have a narrow interpretation of the notion of rational agency: some may want to understand rational agency in narrowly formal terms, while others may take certain substantive constraints to be constitutive of rational agency.

[13] In chapter 10.

[14] Even though both interpretations of the internal reasons model go beyond anything that Williams says, I think that the subjectivist interpretation is a natural elaboration on his view. He wants to resist the view that any rational agent as such must acknowledge certain requirements (Williams 1981, 110). Although he means this as a resistance to the external reasons model, I believe that he would also resist it in its internal reasons interpretation. He seems to recognize the non-subjectivist interpretation as a "limiting case" of the internal reasons model (Williams 1995a, 220 [endnote 3]), but to reject it as false.

external reasons, it could, as far as my arguments against subjectivism are concerned, also have been stated as a development of the non-subjectivist internal reasons model.

Substantivism maintains that some reasons are substantive. As I understand it, to say that somebody has a *substantive reason* to do something has two components. It means (a) that the person has an external reason to do it and (b) that the considerations which speak in favor of doing it are irreducibly substantive. A person can say either about herself or about somebody else that the relevant person has a substantive reason to do something. If she says this about herself, she must also assume that she has an internal reason to do it: in saying that she has a reason to do something, she must count something she accepts as speaking in favor of the action. However, in saying that she herself has a substantive reason to do something, the person must assume that she has an external reason to do it: even if something in her subjective motivational set does in fact speak in favor of doing it, she must assume that she would have had a reason to do it even if this had not been so. Thus, when I say that a person thinks that she has a substantive reason, that a person relies on a substantive reason or employs a substantive reason, I mean that she makes assumptions (a) and (b) about herself.[15]

In contrast to substantivism, subjectivism maintains that there are only subjective reasons, where a *subjective reason* is understood as an internal reason which is only supported by elements in the agent's subjective motivational set which are themselves not supported by any non-relative rationality constraints.

2 SUBJECTIVISM AND THE JUSTIFICATORY CRISIS

Subjectivism creates problems for morality, with respect to both its presumed unconditionality and its rationality. Consider first its un-conditionality: morality apparently presents people with demands that they should heed, whatever their interests happen to be; moral requirements are not conditional on people's subjective constitution.

[15] In order to prevent misunderstanding, it should be stressed that the substantive features on which a substantive reason is based may concern a person's feelings. For example, the fact that a person *enjoys* doing something might give her a good substantive reason to do it even though nothing in the person's subjective motivational set supports doing it (in fact, the person's dispositions might strongly oppose doing what she enjoys doing). Cf. Scanlon 1998, 42–47.

If subjectivism is true, it seems that the presumption of such unconditional demands could not possibly be well founded. There simply
would be nothing to account for the unconditionality. According to
subjectivism, all reasons are relative to the agent's subjective motivational set and there are no rational restrictions on the contents of that
set. If the agent happens to be disposed to acting morally, she may
have a reason to do so. That she is so dsposed, however, is certainly
no unconditional requirement. If the disposition fades away, so does
the reason to act morally.

Subjectivism presents no less of a problem for the rationality of
morality, and the source of the difficulty is the same. According to
subjectivism, the most fundamental form of justification consists of
relating actions to elements of the agent's subjective motivational set.
There are no non-relative rational constraints on the contents of
agents' subjective motivational sets. Thus, if an agent's subjective
motivational set opposes the demands of morality, it is rational to act
against these demands. It must therefore be concluded that though it
might be rational for some people to behave morally sometimes, it is
quite doubtful that it is rational for most people most of the time.

Now philosophers keep trying – starting with a subjectivist notion
of rationality – to show that it is rational to accept certain moral
principles. I shall suggest in chapter 7, however, that the subjectivist
conception of reason is simply not thick enough to establish that it is
rational for all or most people to accept certain moral principles. If
that is true, it would seem that subjectivism not only creates a
problem for the unconditionality and rationality of morality, but also
imposes restrictions on the concept of rationality that make it unable
to solve the problem that it creates.

This makes it clear that, in order to solve the justificatory crisis of
morality, subjectivism must be refuted. Now it might be argued that
for the solution of the crisis it is not only necessary but also sufficient
to reject subjectivism. In fact – so the argument goes – it is only
because of false subjectivist assumptions that morality appears to face a
justificatory crisis in the first place. Once these assumptions have been
rejected, the appearance that it faces a crisis will dissolve all by itself.
After all, if subjectivism is false, then what is rational for a person does
not simply depend on what happens to be in her subjective motivational set. And so, once subjectivism is rejected, there is no special
reason to think that it is not rational for a person to be moral even if

being moral cannot be justified in terms of her subjective motivational set. In particular, there is no reason to think that morality needs a rationalistic justification. If subjectivism is false, then the moral skeptic may well have a good reason to be moral, even if there is no good justification of morality which can be based on the skeptic's subjective motivational set. So why should we think that a justification of morality must be acceptable on the moral skeptic's own terms?

As I shall argue in chapter 5, to show that morality does not face a justificatory crisis, it is not enough to refute subjectivism. Rationalism itself presents a justificatory ideal with great attractions. According to this ideal, morality must be shown to be acceptable to a moral skeptic on the skeptic's own terms. If it cannot be shown to be acceptable in this way, then – assuming that we still hold on to this justificatory ideal – morality must appear as a superstructure entirely without rational support. Under these circumstances, it would indeed be appropriate to speak of a justificatory *crisis* of morality: given the rationalistic justificatory ideal and the absence of a successful rationalistic justification of morality, morality appears as a human construction cut off from any rational foundations.[16]

I think that the appearance of a justificatory crisis needs to be taken very seriously: as I shall argue in chapter 5, rationalism does indeed present an extremely appealing justificatory ideal. Thus, the main task of this work becomes to show that we should not measure the success of justifications against this ideal. Once it has been shown that this ideal should be rejected, then it can be seen that it was a mistake to think that morality faces a justificatory crisis in the first place. I shall replace the rationalistic ideal by the ideal presented by the substantive approach. Once we accept the substantive approach, we can see that there are reasons for taking up a moral stance which do not need rationalistic underpinning. Thus, even in the absence of such a rationalistic foundation, morality is not a superstructure without rational support. In this sense, morality does in fact not face a justificatory *crisis*.

This does not make it a foregone conclusion that rationality comes down in favor of morality at the end of the day. According to the substantive approach, in considering the rationality of taking up

[16] The term "justificatory crisis" is meant to be an allusion to Gauthier who speaks of a "foundational crisis" (Gauthier 1991a, 15).

moral stances, we may appeal to all the substantive reasons we have, moral and non-moral. It cannot, however, be said in advance what we have reason to do, *all things considered*. In this work, I shall not attempt to show that, all things considered, it is rational to be moral. I want to show that we should reject the rationalistic justificatory ideal and thus that morality does not face a justificatory *crisis*. The significance of this conclusion lies partly in the fact that, because – as I shall argue in chapter 5 – the rationalistic justificatory ideal is so appealing, morality does indeed appear to face a serious justificatory crisis. Even more importantly, this conclusion shows that the real task with respect to morality is not to try to give it a rationalistic justification, but to enter into a serious deliberation about the various substantive reasons we have for and against the different moral stances.

Before elaborating on the appeal of the rationalistic justificatory ideal, I must, in the coming chapter, discuss John McDowell's external reasons model. McDowell is perhaps the most important contemporary critic of this ideal and has delivered some important arguments necessary to undermining it. In chapter 5, I will then show why McDowell's arguments nevertheless do not suffice to undercut this justificatory ideal. That will set the stage for my own argument in the rest of the book.

4

Substantive reasons

I EXTERNAL REASONS AS REASONS INTERNAL TO ETHICS

How do we critically assess whether an ethical external reasons statement is true, whether coming to believe it is really coming to see matters aright? According to McDowell, in order for the statement to pass critical scrutiny, it is not necessary to show that anybody who counts as a rational person must – on pain of violating the principles of some reasoning process – come to believe it.[1] It is not necessary to show that, starting from reasons external to ethics, there is an argument demonstrating the correctness of the ethical reasons. Rather, in order to establish the correctness of an ethical outlook, an ethical evaluation of ethical reasons is required.[2] Of course, this does not mean that whatever it takes to become a rational person is irrelevant to the evaluation of an ethical outlook. It just means that the evaluation cannot be done entirely from a standpoint outside of an ethical sensibility:[3] "[e]thical external reasons are not external to ethics."[4]

These remarks on ethical justification are of particular relevance to my goals in this book. The aim of rationalism is to address the rational moral skeptic on her own grounds and show that the skeptic's commitment to a formal notion of rationality also commits her to accepting certain specific moral principles. This is precisely the sort of

---

[1] McDowell 1995a, 75–76, 78–79. R. Jay Wallace argues that the external reasons theorist must say more about the way in which an agent comes to be motivated by the external reasons she has, and he supplies such a story himself (see Wallace Ms., ch. 3). Since I am not here concerned with the connection between motivation and reasons, I leave such difficulties of McDowell's account aside. I am interested in other objections to his account.

[2] McDowell 1995a, 73, 80–82.

[3] McDowell 1995b, 171–174; 1998, 165–166.

[4] McDowell 1995a, 80.

33

move that McDowell wants to resist. The moral skeptic may be a rational person and nevertheless miss the ethical external reasons that she has.[5] In this, I agree with McDowell. However, as I will argue in 5.1, I think that his arguments do not suffice to show that morality does not need a rationalistic justification. Thus, I shall be offering other arguments for the conclusion that morality does not need such a justification.[6]

Doesn't this distinction of McDowell's between the irrationality of persons and insensitivity to external reasons make it mysterious how the cogency of external reasons (for instance, ethical external reasons) can be tested? Williams supposes that the external reasons theorist must assume that any rational agent, as such, must acknowledge the requirements for which there are external reasons.[7] McDowell himself suggests that this mistaken supposition about the external reasons theorist is rooted in the idea that otherwise the testing of external reasons would be rendered metaphysically suspicious. McDowell explains this idea, with which he takes issue, in the following way:

> [T]he notion of truth or objectivity, implicit in the appeal to "considering the matter aright" which the external reasons theorist needs, requires beliefs to be capable of being formed either under the causal control of the circumstances that render them true or as a result of exercising rationality, conceived in purely procedural terms, as something that can be compelling without need of substantive presuppositions. Beliefs about values or obligations had better not fall under the first of these disjuncts, on pain of a weird metaphysics; so, according to this line of thought, they would have to fall under the second.[8]

This line of thought amounts to an important motivation for

---

[5] In my text, I use the terms "ethical" and "moral" interchangeably. I do not want to dispute that a meaningful distinction might be drawn between the ethical and the moral. However, it is not my concern to draw any such distinction. I use both of these terms to refer to that area of our activities which the rationalist thinks needs a rationalistic basis.

[6] In addition, I do not think that his arguments suffice to show that we are justified in assuming that there are external reasons. Thus, I shall offer my own argument also for this conclusion (see 10.5).

[7] Williams 1981, 108–110. In a response to McDowell 1995a, Williams says that the external reasons theorist must not suppose that those who do not acknowledge the requirement in question are *irrational* (Williams 1995a, 191–192).

[8] McDowell 1995a, 81.

rationalism: only by starting from a *formal* concept of rationality can one hope to demonstrate the rationality of morality. Any justification of morality that started with substantive reasons – underived from formal reasons – would make the justification of moral principles mysteriously metaphysical. Thus, the rationalist concludes, if the justificatory crisis of morality is to be solved, morality must be given a rationalistic justification.

If the necessity of a rationalistic justification is to be called into question, then this line of reasoning must be undermined. In my view, McDowell himself has satisfactorily answered this argument, and the next section sketches his answer.[9]

2 THE METAPHYSICAL OBJECTION

The idea that there are external reasons crucially involves the assumption that the person accepting the external reasons statement is *considering the matter aright*. Alternatively, we might say that the person holds the *truth* about this matter. Let us consider a person who comes to think that she has an external reason to laugh because a joke is funny.[10] How could it be shown that she has such a reason?

It must be shown that in finding it funny she is considering the matter aright.[11] Here two ways of showing this suggest themselves.

---

[9] Since, here, I merely want to indicate how this rationalistic argument can be answered, McDowell's response is only presented in its barest outlines. In order to explain why I think that his answer is compelling, much more would need to be said. In particular, it would have to be explained how McDowell's position is compatible with a sound *naturalism*. For McDowell's most complete discussion of this issue, see McDowell 1995b; see also McDowell 1996, Introduction and Lecture IV.

[10] It should be noted that in my discussion I do not assume that the fact that something is funny actually gives us an external reason to laugh. The discussion is merely supposed to show that there is nothing metaphysically dubious about this assumption.

[11] Of course, this is not enough. It must also be shown that the fact that it is funny gives her an external reason to laugh. In this context, two versions of the accusation of a metaphysical mystery may be distinguished: (1) it is metaphysically dubious to assume that there are *evaluative facts* (e.g., about what is funny); (2) it requires dubious metaphysics to assume that a *fact about reality* (e.g., the fact that something is funny) can *by itself* give an agent a *normative reason to do something* (e.g., to laugh). Both versions are possible interpretations of J. L. Mackie's argument from queerness (see Mackie 1977, 38–42). In my text, the emphasis will be on (1). It should also be noted that in McDowell 1998, the discussion of the funny is about valuations concerning what is funny, not about external reasons judgments based on those valuations. Nevertheless, as I shall explain in footnote 23, I think that McDowell also answers the accusation in version (2).

On the one hand, it could be argued that it only needs to be shown that she, or most people, are disposed to laugh about such a joke. The problem with this proposal is that something may not be comic even if people are disposed to laugh about it. On the other hand, it might be argued that the only possibility of showing it consists in drawing on the concept of the funny itself. It will not do to say that we are disposed to laugh; instead we must explain what is funny about something and why something else is not funny. According to McDowell, only in this way could we show that something is really funny.[12]

However, as McDowell points out, there is no guarantee that by employing this second method, we will succeed in showing that there is a truth of the matter about what is funny and what is not. It cannot be excluded in advance that there is not enough substance to the reasons for and against things being funny for us to conclude that there is a right and a wrong about what is really funny. This can only be determined by actually examining these reasons.[13]

Now a similar question to the one about the comic can be raised about ethical thinking as a whole: can one ethical stance be shown to be rationally superior to another?[14] Here McDowell's answer is analogous to his solution for the comic. We must rely on the ethical concepts we employ, in order to determine whether there is a way of seeing matters aright with respect to ethical issues:

> The threat to truth is from the thought that there is not enough substance to our conception of reasons for ethical stances. When we try to meet this threat, there is no reason not to appeal to all the resources at our disposal, including all the ethical concepts that we can lay our hands on, so long as they survive critical scrutiny; and there need be no basis for critical scrutiny of one ethical concept except others, so the necessary scrutiny does not involve stepping outside the point of view constituted by an ethical sensibility.[15]

If we in this way actually succeed in showing that there is "enough

---

[12] McDowell 1998, 157–161.
[13] McDowell 1998, 160–162.
[14] See McDowell 1998, 155–156.
[15] McDowell 1998, 162. According to McDowell, this critical scrutiny, like any critical scrutiny, will be Neurathian in that it needs to hold certain things fixed as a basis for the critical examination of others. Nevertheless, he thinks that such critical reflection can be radical and open-ended and can also rely on non-ethical resources (see McDowell 1995b, 168–176).

substance to our conception of reasons for ethical stances," then McDowell says that "truth in ethics" has been "earned from within ethical thinking."[16] We have *earned* it because we have shown this by evaluating the reasons there are for the different ethical stances. And we have earned it *from within* ethical thinking because these reasons were evaluated by relying on concepts which are themselves ethical.

The objection raised at the end of the last section can now be formulated in the following way: the attempt to earn truth from within the ethical amounts to relying on ethical concepts which have not been substantiated in terms of a formal concept of rationality. If the ethical concepts are in this way to be the ultimate basis of justification, then it must implicitly be assumed that they correspond to objective properties of a reality independent of human sentiments. If they are not assumed to correspond to such properties, then they are incapable of serving as the basis of justification. However, to suppose that the ethical concepts correspond to objective properties amounts to dubious metaphysics.

McDowell argues that the story of earning truth from within does not require such suspicious metaphysical presuppositions. If we have indeed earned truth from within for the comic, then we must suppose that in finding something funny, the subject is reacting to something which is true whether or not the subject thinks it is. In this way, there is no difference between the property of being comic and, say, the property of being rectangular. However, there is still a difference. We can only understand the funny by relating it to a human sensibility: we cannot understand the funny without knowing that it merits *amusement*. The rectangular, we may assume, can be perfectly understood without thus relating it to human sentiments.[17] The similarity and dissimilarity between the funny and the rectangular are the keys to the answer to the charge of dubious metaphysics. The similarity shows that we can sensibly say that in finding something

---

[16] McDowell 1998, 162.

[17] Rectangularity differs from redness in a similar way: what it is for something to be red cannot be adequately explained without appealing to the fact that it looks red in the right circumstances, whereas that something is rectangular can be adequately explained without appealing to the fact that it looks rectangular in the right circumstances (see McDowell 1996, 29–34; 1985, 110–118). Nevertheless, there are important differences between redness and the funny; for, in order for something to be funny it must *merit* (and not only cause, in the right circumstances) amusement. And McDowell does not suggest that amusement is phenomenal in the way that the experience of redness is (see McDowell 1985, 118–120; 1998, 160–161).

funny we are considering matters aright. The dissimilarity shows that in assuming this we are not assuming that the funny is a property in a reality independent of human sentiments.[18]

What possibilities, however, does the denial that the funny is a property in a reality independent of human sensibilities leave open? Does it leave open that the funny is a *projection* of human sentiments on a reality which does not contain the funny as a property?[19] According to McDowell, it does not. If the funny were such a projection, it would not make sense to assume that truth can be earned from within.[20] Assuming that truth has been earned from within for the funny, the response to the funny – amusement – can only be explained and made sense of as a response to objects that merit amusement. However, the sense in which they merit amusement is not accounted for in terms of something external to the concept of the comic. Rather, these objects merit amusement because they are funny. But if this is to be the explanation of amusement, then we cannot assume that the funny is a projection on a reality which contains no property of being funny.[21] Thus, the funny is no less a property of reality than the rectangular is; it is just that the latter can be understood without assuming that it is a property which merits a certain subjective response.[22]

The remarks about the funny can now be extended to a story

[18] McDowell 1998, 157–162; 1995b, 167–171; 1985, 117–120.
[19] By speaking here of projection, I am alluding to Simon Blackburn's projectivism about value and morality. For Blackburn's views, see Blackburn 1981; 1984, chs. 5–6; 1993; 1998, esp. chs. 3–4 and 8.
[20] McDowell 1998, 154–155, 160–161. Blackburn seems to disagree. He argues that the projectivist understands questions such as "On what does the wrongness of cruelty depend?" as "internal" questions (rather than as "external" questions) which demand a *moral* answer (Blackburn 1993, 172–174). This suggests that the projectivist can allow that truth in ethics can be earned from within moral thinking (see also Blackburn 1998, 48–51, 256–261). I agree with McDowell that Blackburn's projectivism cannot allow this (see footnote 29 in ch. 10).
[21] I have applied here to amusement and the funny what McDowell says about fear and fearfulness in McDowell 1985, 119. In his discussion of the funny in McDowell 1998, he argues that projective accounts of something would be undermined "if we cannot home in on the subjective state whose projection is supposed to result in the seeming feature of reality in question without the aid of the concept of that feature" (p. 158). In the discussion of fear in McDowell 1985, he is willing to grant that it might be possible to thus home in on fear. He then goes on to make the point about fear and fearfulness which I have explained here with the example of amusement and the funny.
[22] McDowell 1985, 115–121; 1995b, 167–170, 174–176; 1998, 163–165.

about ethical external reasons. For example, we can explain how the fact that something is *demeaning* may give us an ethical external reason not to do it. Assuming that truth can be earned for the demeaning, the fact that something is demeaning merits a certain response. Part of this response is that we should not do what is demeaning.[23] Thus, we may say that the fact that something is demeaning gives us an ethical external reason not to do it. This story about the justification for not doing what is demeaning differs from empirical justifications. Contrary to empirical justifications, this justification does not rest on the assumption that we have established perceptual contact with a reality independent of human sentiments.[24]

This dissimilarity between ethical and empirical inquiry does not mean that McDowell thinks that truth needs to be earned only in the first case. As I understand McDowell, there is no kind of inquiry for which truth does not need to be earned. In order to be entitled to treat an issue as something about which there is a way of considering the matter aright, we must be able to give a justification for thus treating it. Such justifications are what earn us the right to treat it in this way. If we could either by-pass such justifications or move beyond them by directly contacting an unconceptualized reality, then we would not need to earn the right to treat something in this way:

[23] As mentioned in footnote 11, one version of the accusation of metaphysical dubiousness is the following: it requires dubious metaphysics to assume that a *fact about reality* (e.g., the fact that something is demeaning) can *by itself* give an agent a *normative reason to do something* (e.g., not to perform demeaning acts). In my opinion, McDowell's view – that the relevant feature of reality (e.g., demeaningness) must be understood as something which calls for a certain subjective response – shows that there is nothing metaphysically dubious about this assumption. Of course, this does not show that substantivism rather than subjectivism offers the correct account of reasons. It only shows that there is nothing metaphysically dubious about substantivism. (For McDowell's answer to the objection that *awareness* of a fact about reality cannot *by itself* give rise to a *motivating* reason, but must be supplemented by a *desire*, see McDowell 1978 and McDowell 1979.)

[24] See McDowell 1995b, 167–171; 1998, 153–154, 160–162. The difference between empirical and ethical justification raises the issue of whether the terminology "earning *truth*" is a happy one for ethical sensibilities. The issue can be raised precisely because ethical and empirical reasons are different and because, without investigating the matter, it cannot be excluded that there is something special about the concept of truth which connects justifications of truth-claims specifically to empirical rather than ethical reasons. Since my interest is in the question of how to show that something is an ethical external reason, I can leave this issue aside. Whenever I talk about earning truth for a sensibility, what I am interested in is the possibility of earning the right to think that there are external reasons for the sensibility to be sensitive to.

we would acquire this right for free via a conceptually unmediated contact with reality. Since McDowell thinks that this idea of a conceptually unmediated contact with reality does not make sense, he must deny that the metaphor of unearned truth has application to any field of inquiry.[25]

In order to explain McDowell's position adequately here, more would need to be said. Since further elaboration would distract too much from my topic, I let this suffice. The important point is that McDowell denies that ethical inquiry differs from empirical inquiry in that only in the former does truth have to be earned.[26] This philosophical move of McDowell's is of importance in his reply to the "bootstrapping objection," to which I now turn.

3 THE BOOTSTRAPPING OBJECTION

The thesis that truth in ethics can be earned from within is open to a bootstrapping objection: if the soundness of an ethical outlook is to be demonstrated by ethical reasons, then those who do not share that outlook cannot be *argued into* accepting it. If, however, the soundness of the ethical outlook is to be demonstrated by reasons that persons will only accept once they share the outlook to a sufficient degree, and they cannot be argued into sharing it, then the demonstration smells of suspicious bootstrapping. McDowell discusses this objection in his Critical Notice of Williams' *Ethics and the Limits of Philosophy*. Williams argues that science has a hope of representing the world in a way that is not perspectival whereas there is no such hope in ethics, and he takes this to undermine the objectivity of ethics.[27] McDowell responds:

[25] As far as I know, McDowell never says this directly about the metaphor of unearned truth. Given the views defended in McDowell 1996, however, I think that this must be his position. What I have said in this paragraph is meant to allude to McDowell 1996 (esp. Lectures I–II). Here McDowell shows how we can think of the relationship between mind and world without thinking of reality either as the creation of the mind or as something outside the conceptual sphere. For another way of showing how it is possible to think of the relationship in this way, see Abel 1993 and Abel 1999.

[26] Insofar as the idea of earning truth is taken to require a contrast with unearned truth – which was certainly Blackburn's idea in introducing the idea of earning truth (Blackburn 1984, 170–171, 195–196) – McDowell's own view would perhaps be better stated without using the idea of earning truth at all.

[27] Williams 1985, 134–140.

[D]oes science really contrast with ethics in the right way to be immune to all suspicion of bootstrapping, and thus to yield an exemplar of objectivity of which ethics must seem to fall short? Ethical thinking is local in two ways: first, its characteristic concepts are not intelligible independently of particular cultural perspectives; and, second, it aims (explicitly or implicitly) to be directed by standards of good and bad arguments, and the standards available to it are not independent of its own substantive and disputable conclusions. Williams gives eloquent expression to a view of science as aspiring, with considerable success, to transcend localness of the first sort. But it is surely the second that gives rise to the air of bootstrapping. So if a feature of science is to bring out a way in which whatever ethical thinking can achieve falls short of genuine objectivity, it would surely need to include freedom from localness of the second sort. In that case, to suppose that Williams's point about the non-localness of science establishes what is needed is to suppose something like this: that by affirming the perspective-freedom of scientific concepts, one shows that the correct application of those concepts is simply dictated by the world itself, rather than needing to be judged by standards of reasoning that are not independent of scientific knowledge as it stands, a human construction at a particular juncture in its historical development. This is a picture of science as a mode of inquiry in which the facts can directly imprint themselves on our minds, without need of mediation by anything as historically conditioned and open to dispute as canons of good and bad scientific argument. But this picture embodies a philosophical fantasy of truth, and of science as an approach to truth. The point about causation makes no difference to this: it would be an illusion to suppose that when a body of belief is such as to warrant a causal gloss on the idea of facts impressing themselves on us, it thereby contrives to prise itself apart from the province of reason.[28]

We can use this passage to pull together McDowell's response to the rationalist challenge introduced at the end of §1. The second localness means that truth needs to be earned from within both in ethics and in science. This means that the bootstrapping objection against earning ethical truth from within cannot be limited to ethical truth but must be extended to scientific truth. However, the objection will only seem a threat to scientific truth if our view of real truth

[28] McDowell 1986, 380; see also McDowell 1995b, 168–169, 175–176.

"embodies a philosophical fantasy of truth." Having given up that fantasy, we may suppose that, in both ethics and science, we rely on substantive reasons that are not substantiated by a conceptually unmediated contact with the world itself or by a formal notion of rationality.[29] Rather, these reasons are informed by the specific conceptual machinery that is at work in empirical experience and in ethical sensibilities when we discover that things are thus and so.[30] Thus, there is no reason to suppose that just by virtue of being substantive (and not substantiated in terms of a formal notion of rationality) ethical reasons lack something that enables substantive scientific reasons to count as bona fide reasons. Nevertheless, since the ethical case is to be compared with the cases of the funny, to suppose that truth is earned from within in both ethics and science is not to assimilate ethical and scientific reasons.

I think that McDowell has indeed shown that justifications of ethical outlooks based on substantive ethical reasons, which are not substantiated in terms of a formal concept of rationality, can be rendered metaphysically unmysterious without assimilating them to empirical justifications. In showing that it is a mistake to think that morality needs a rationalistic justification, I shall be relying on this conclusion of McDowell's. However, I do not think that he has succeeded in neutralizing the bootstrapping objection. He is right in pointing out that the comparison between ethics and *science* does not give rise to a compelling bootstrapping objection to the conception of external reasons as reasons internal to ethics. As I shall argue in the next chapter, however, the rationalist can still employ a bootstrapping objection to argue that morality needs a rationalistic justification. The task of the next chapter is also to outline my own argument in the rest of this work.

[29] Williams would presumably object that he does not invoke the idea of a conceptually unmediated contact with reality. Rather, the difference between science and ethics is that only in the former case is there "convergence on how things (anyway) are." Science gives us the hope of an "absolute conception" of reality which consists of "nonperspectival materials" and "could nonvacuously explain how itself, and the various perspectival views of the world, are possible" (Williams 1985, 139–140). For McDowell's answer to this strategy of Williams', see McDowell's remarks in McDowell 1983 on Williams' more elaborate discussion of the absolute conception in Williams 1978; see also McDowell 1986, 380–381.

[30] See McDowell 1996, esp. Lectures I–II and §IV.7.

5

Overcoming rationalism

As explained at the end of chapter 3, it could be argued that, if subjectivism is rejected, then there will no longer be any reason to suppose that morality faces a justificatory crisis. I think that this argument is mistaken. I shall argue that, even assuming that McDowell's rejection of subjectivism should be accepted, and assuming that McDowell's model neither assimilates ethical reasons to empirical reasons nor renders them metaphysically weird, he has not thereby shown that the appearance of a justificatory crisis of morality is a mere illusion.

McDowell argues, in my opinion successfully, that the comparison with science does not undermine the idea of supporting an ethical outlook by substantive ethical reasons. However, it seems that the comparison between substantive and rationalistic justifications can present a threat to the soundness of any ethical outlook. There seems to be no guarantee that substantive and rationalistic justifications do not produce conflicting results: a substantive justification might recommend a particular ethical outlook, whereas a rationalistic justification might recommend a conflicting one. In the case of such a conflict, it seems extremely tempting to conclude that favor must be given to the rationalistic justification. By definition, rationalistic justifications start with premises that even a moral skeptic could accept. In other words, they seem to start on a firmer basis than substantive justifications. Obviously, in the extreme case, one can imagine that a rationalistic justification would in fact validate the moral skeptic in her skepticism.[1] Thus, rationalism seems to present morality with a potential crisis. It also seems, however, to be morality's only possible

---

[1] Strictly speaking, this is not compatible with rationalism as I have defined it, since, as defined, its aim is to refute moral skepticism. It is easy, however, to change the defini-

savior: as just suggested, a substantive justification would be overruled by a conflicting rationalistic justification. Therefore, only a successful rationalistic justification in *favor* of morality could undermine the threat presented by potential rationalistic reasons *against* it.[2]

Substantive ethical justifications of ethical outlooks face two problems which seem to show that they would be overruled by conflict with rationalistic justifications. They face *the bootstrapping problem*: since such justifications rely on ethical considerations, it seems that they are simply question-begging. Since rationalistic justifications are addressed to the moral skeptic, they do not have this problem. Substantive ethical justifications also face what we may call "*the controversiality problem*." Here the problem is not that such justifications of ethical outlooks are question-begging, but rather that their premises are essentially controversial. It seems that each substantive moral consideration can be reasonably doubted by a rational person. Since rationalistic justifications are based on premises which not even the moral skeptic can question, they do not face this problem. Their basis is secure.[3]

These arguments for the conclusion that morality needs a rationalistic justification rest on the claim that rationalistic justifications compare favorably to substantive ethical justifications. Thus, to answer these arguments and to show that the support for ethical outlooks is indeed to be sought in substantive rather than rationalistic reasons, we need to *compare* explicitly substantive and rationalistic reasons. This is what I will do in part III.[4]

---

tion so as to keep it the same except to leave it open whether the result is to be a refutation or a confirmation of moral skepticism.

[2] This is essentially Gauthier's line of reasoning in Gauthier 1991a, 18–22. I have abstracted from the subjectivist details of his argument to lay bare its rationalistic core.

[3] In my view, these problems are also left unresolved by David Wiggins, who defends the same basic approach to valuations as McDowell (see Wiggins 1991c).

[4] Due to the lack of such a comparison, Lovibond 1983 also fails to meet the rationalistic threat to morality. In her book, Lovibond argues that there is no reason to draw a metaphysical fact/value distinction or to suppose that only the propositions of science as opposed to the propositions of ethics are capable of truth. Nevertheless, moral discourse may be more subjective than scientific discourse but not in the sense that it falls on the subjective side of a metaphysical fact/value gap. Rather, she invites us to picture a "fact/value continuum" on which discourses are ordered according to how extensive the role of "intellectual authority relations" is in them, according to how strong their "pull toward objectivity" (Quine) is. Determining the strength of their pull is a "phenomenological question" whose answer we get by "describing language-games" (Wittgenstein; Lovibond 1983, 42–43, 58–68). If one were to use this picture to undermine the rationalistic threat, then it would not be enough to compare *phenom-*

Here it may be argued that, in supposing that a comparison of substantive and rationalistic justifications is needed, I am forgetting a line of reasoning which could be used to show that the rationalistic justifications themselves are subject to substantive constraints. The starting point of this line of reasoning is a "Davidsonian" idea invoked by McDowell in response to Williams' contention that the external reasons model cannot account for the explanatory role of reasons statements.[5] McDowell points out that Williams himself acknowledges that a person may not have an internal reason to φ, even though the person falsely believes that φ-ing would satisfy a desire of hers and is thus motivated to φ.[6] According to McDowell, by acknowledging this, Williams is making room for the "Davidsonian" thought that "the explanatory power of reason-giving explanations depends on there being a critical dimension to the concept of rationality."[7] As discussed in 3.1, Williams uses the notion of practical deliberation to put a distance between that which the critical exercise of rationality would give a person a reason to do and that which the person happens to be motivated to do. McDowell questions whether this puts the *right* distance between the two. He maintains that we cannot derive claims about theoretical reason from an independent account of the workings of the mind. On the contrary, theoretical reason itself places both formal and substantive constraints on the intelligible attribution of belief. The same must hold of the relationship between practical reason and desires. What is practically rational cannot depend on the workings of antecedently intelligible desires; on the contrary, practical reason places constraints on what can count as an intelligible desire in the first place.[8]

Whatever its merits as an argument against subjectivism, this

enologically the "pull" of substantive and rationalistic reasons (which Lovibond does not do). What we would need to know is whether we have a good reason to employ substantive reasons rather than rationalistic reasons, and that demands an *evaluative* comparison.

[5] Williams 1981, 106–111.

[6] Williams 1981, 102–103.

[7] McDowell 1995a, 76. As McDowell points out, this is a thought emphasized by Davidson (he refers to Davidson 1980, esp. Essays 11 and 12; McDowell 1995a, 83–84 [endnote 10]).

[8] McDowell 1995a, 77–80; McDowell refers here to G. E. M. Anscombe's doubts about the intelligibility of a desire for a saucer of mud which is not based on what might be desirable about a saucer of mud (see Anscombe 1957, 70–71). In Part I of Hurley 1989, similar "Davidsonian" considerations are employed to undermine subjectivism.

argument about the necessity of substantive constraints does not suffice to undermine rationalism. The rationalist might accept the fundamental point – some substantive constraints are needed in order for something to be a recognizable exercise of practical reason – but take the scope of the substantive constraints to be much more limited than McDowell suggests. She would go on insisting that all justifications must be given in terms that the moral skeptic can accept. She would then argue that the substantive constraints that must be placed on the moral skeptic's beliefs and preferences if the skeptic is to count as a rational person are very thin (remember that McDowell allows that a rational person may miss some of her own external reasons). The rationalist would insist that the only point of the constraints is to render the moral skeptic – at least initially – an *intelligible* person, and for that purpose the substantive constraints will be only minimal. While accepting that some minimal constraints must be imposed, the rationalist keeps to her ideal of a justification: we start with a person who is minimally rational or intelligible and argue that anybody who aspires to be rational *in that way* would also accept some moral principles.[9] According to the rationalist, any form of justification that does not live up to this ideal of thus drawing substantive principles out of a minimal notion, but rather imposes further substantive restraints that are themselves not underpinned by the minimal notion,[10] would fall prey to the problems of bootstrapping and controversiality.

I conclude that the argument about the necessity of substantive constraints does not show that we can get around explicitly comparing substantive and rationalistic reasons: to show that we should give up the rationalistic justificatory ideal, we must indeed compare the merits of these different kinds of justification.

In carrying out this comparison, I will be employing a method which differs from the methods of most contemporary philosophers.

[9] This is compatible with giving the rationalistic argument in terms of instrumental rationality. Although such a rationalist would be rejecting extreme subjectivism – by allowing some substantive restriction on the content of the subjective motivational set – she could offer her argument in the following form: for someone who is minimally rational in this way, it is instrumentally rational to accept principle X.

[10] Although the up-theorists think that the moral skeptic has an imperfect grasp of the notion of reason, their aim is still to draw her acceptance of moral principles out of her commitment to a formal notion of rationality, rather than to introduce those moral principles as independent substantive constraints.

Most of them assume that the issue between philosophical positions should be settled by conceptual analysis. They offer analyses of, say, "our concept of reasons" and argue that their own theory "better accounts for" this concept than the other theories. I will employ some arguments which have this structure. For example, I shall argue that substantivism can "better account for our concept of reasons" than subjectivism can. In other words, I shall argue that substantivism better represents how we actually understand ourselves and our reasons for action. However, it is open to the subjectivist to retort that our self-understanding and understanding of reasons must be revised. This is where the contemporary discussion of the subject gets stuck. Both subjectivists and their adversaries seem to offer us a coherent way of understanding ourselves. In my view, the way out of this deadlock is to argue that there are good *practical reasons* for favoring substantivism. I do not expect a philosophical position only to help us understand ourselves, but also to help us *lead a good life*. Therefore, my case for substantivism and the substantive approach against the alternatives will, in the final analysis, rest on the practical argument that my views enable us to lead a better life.

It should be noted that the practical arguments I shall offer will themselves rely on substantive reasons and, at least sometimes, on ethical reasons. This means that on the "meta-level" – in the dispute between the different philosophical positions – I employ just the same kind of reasons as I recommend we see as operative on the "object-level." For example, I recommend (for the "object-level") that we see the rationality of ethical standpoints as being dependent on substantive ethical reasons rather than rationalistic reasons, and I employ (on the "meta-level") substantive ethical reasons to support this recommendation. In chapter 12, I shall further explain and defend the philosophical method of this work.

2 OVERVIEW

One of my central ambitions is to show that morality does not need a rationalistic justification. It could be argued that this result is of merely academic interest if there is indeed a successful rationalistic justification of morality. If there is such a justification, hasn't rationalism simply solved the justificatory crisis of morality, and why should we bother asking whether we would have needed such a justification?

Now it seems to me that this is not the situation we are in. I think there are no successful rationalistic justifications. If that is so, it becomes quite important to show that we do not need such a justification. Thus, in Part II I shall argue that the rationalistic justifications of Gauthier and Habermas are not successful. The lesson of these arguments is that rationalistic premises are simply too weak to deliver any substantive moral results.

In Part III, then, I go on to show that morality does not need a rationalistic justification and that rationalism distorts our view of rationality and morality. As I have already said, I will do this by comparing rationalistic and substantive justifications and arguing that the latter are preferable.

As I already explained, rationalism relies on a formalistic account of practical reason,[11] whereas the substantive approach assumes substantivism. This means that, though Part III completes the comparison with rationalism, more needs to be said to complete the defense of the substantive approach. If we call those theories which offer a non-moral justification of morality "foundationalist" and those which do not "non-foundationalist," then the substantive approach could also be called "*non-foundationalist substantivism.*" The argument for the conclusion that the substantive approach should be favored over rationalism still leaves open two possibilities: that *non-foundationalist* formalism should be favored over substantivism (see Fig.1) and that *foundationalist* substantivism should be favored over the substantive approach.

Fig. 1. Formalisms

	subjectivist	inter-subjectivist
foundationalist	*subjectivist rationalism*	*inter-subjectivist rationalism*
non-foundationalist	*non-foundationalist subjectivist formalism*	*non-foundationalist inter-subjectivist formalism*

It is the task of Part IV to exclude these two possibilities. I exclude

[11] Or more precisely: rationalism is addressed to somebody who accepts formalism – namely, to a moral skeptic who has a purely formal understanding of rationality.

the first possibility by giving a general argument to the effect that substantivism should be favored over formalism. The argument against the second possibility is less straightforward. Before explaining its structure, let me first make explicit what kind of a position foundationalist substantivism is. Foundationalist substantivism accepts substantivism as a theory of practical reason and it offers a *substantive non-moral* justification of morality.[12] Even though the argument of Part III shows that morality does not need a *formal* non-moral justification, it leaves it open whether morality needs a *substantive* non-moral justification. This is the possibility I must exclude.

The key to the argument against this possibility is a distinction between two kinds of substantivism. I argue against what I call "*list-substantivism*," which is, roughly, the view that there exists a list of certain basic reasons and that all other reasons must be based on these. Instead I defend a view which I call "*particularist substantivism*." According to this theory, something can be a reason in a particular case, even if it cannot be based on any basic reason.

Given the distinction between list-substantivism and particularist substantivism, on the one hand, and between foundationalist and non-foundationalist theories, on the other, four kinds of substantivism are possible: foundationalist list-substantivism, non-foundationalist list-substantivism, etc. (see Fig. 2). Although the mere rejection of list-substantivism does not undermine the motivation to offer a non-moral justification of morality, I shall argue that the reasons I offer against list-substantivism are at the same time reasons to doubt that morality needs a substantive non-moral justification. Thus, my arguments against list-substantivism serve a double function: they serve to defend the version of substantivism I favor – namely, particularist substantivism – *and* to undermine the motivation to offer a non-moral justification of morality.

I argue for my view by excluding all the alternatives: in a first step I

---

[12] I suppose that one might call this position "consequentialism." However, that would be misleading in two ways. First, the view I am talking about here maintains that it is *rational* to be moral and to accept certain moral norms because morality is a way of realizing certain non-moral goods. Consequentialism, however, is most commonly understood as a thesis about what makes an action *morally right*. One could easily hold the view I am talking about here without accepting a consequentialist analysis of moral rightness. Second, although consequentialism assumes that actions are right because of their consequences, not all consequentialists hold that it must be possible to identify those consequences non-morally.

exclude rationalism, in a second formalism, in a third list-substantivism, in a fourth I then use my argument against list-substantivism
to undermine the motivation for foundationalist substantivism.
What remains is my own position: *non-foundationalist particularist
substantivism*.

Fig. 2. Substantivisms

	list-substantivist	particularist substantivist
foundationalist	*foundationalist list-substantivism*	*foundationalist particularist substantivism*
non-foundationalist	*non-foundationalist list-substantivism*	*non-foundationalist particularist substantivism*

PART II

Against rationalism

6

Gauthier's contractarianism

In this part of the book, my aim is to argue that the rationalists' conclusions do not follow from their premises. In this chapter, I outline Gauthier's position, and in the next I criticize it. I shall argue that Gauthier's utility maximization conception of rationality is too thin to demonstrate the rationality of his method for justifying moral principles. I then lay out Habermas' views in chapter 8 and argue against them in chapter 9. The expository chapters 6 and 8 are necessary background for the comparative argument in favor of the substantive approach to be presented in Part III. However, those readers who are only interested in this argument could skip the critical chapters 7 and 9.

I THE MORAL ALTERNATIVES PROBLEM

In the first chapter, I distinguished between the *basic choice problem* and the *moral alternatives problem*. In this section, I shall further elaborate on these problems as they pertain to the sense of justice. Since my criticism of Gauthier will be confined to his solution of the moral alternatives problem, I shall also explain the importance of solving this problem. I start by discussing how Gauthier understands the sense of justice.[1]

According to Gauthier, justice concerns the distribution of the benefits of human interaction. Justice requires that the benefits be so distributed that each receive her due.[2] A person who possesses a sense of justice is disposed neither to seek nor to accept more than her due and neither to participate nor to acquiesce in any arrangement that

---

[1] I will not discuss all aspects of Gauthier's account. Since I am primarily interested in his *justification* of the sense of justice, I will say no more about the sense of justice than is needed to explain his justification.

[2] Gauthier 1993a, 189.

would deprive anybody (including herself) of her due.[3] She does not value justice merely instrumentally: "she views just social arrangements as morally valuable because they afford every person, and not merely herself, his due of the fruits of social cooperation."[4] In this way she values persons as ends in themselves: to value justice is to value persons as ends in themselves.[5]

As far as the sense of justice is concerned, the basic choice problem amounts to the following issue: is it rational to have a sense of justice *at all*? In other words: is it rational for a person to be disposed to seek or accept no more than her due? Now even though it is rational to have *a* sense of justice, it still needs to be asked *what* sense of justice it is rational to have. This is the moral alternatives problem.

In Gauthier's view, it is not only important to solve the basic choice problem. Assuming that it is rational to have *a* sense of justice, it is important that people also have a way of settling *what* sense of justice it is rational for them to have. Otherwise they can be exploited by others. Everybody who has a sense of justice will seek her due, but people may differ as to what they think is due them.[6] Now a person's idea of what is her due share may keep her from taking advantage of the opportunities that cooperation with others would afford her. This idea may thus subject her to being exploited by others, even to such a great extent that she will be worse off than she would have been without any sense of justice. And even if she is not worse off than she would have been without a sense of justice, she might be worse off than if she had a different sense of justice; and in that case she might also be exploited by others. Gauthier, speaking as a contractarian, gives expression to this worry in the following passage: "[T]he contractarian sees sociability [embodied, for example, in a sense of justice] as enriching human life; for him, it becomes a source of exploitation if it induces persons to acquiesce in institutions and practices that but for their fellow-feelings would be costly to them. Feminist thought has surely made this, perhaps the core form of human exploitation, clear to us."[7]

According to Gauthier, a person cannot just rely on her moral intuitions to decide whether she is being exploited. Moreover, a person's moral intuitions *invite* exploitation: unless it can be settled

---

[3] Gauthier 1993a, 193.   [4] Gauthier 1993a, 197–198.
[5] Gauthier 1993a, 198.   [6] Gauthier 1993a, 205.
[7] Gauthier 1986, 11.

without appeal to moral intuitions what sense of justice to have, the sense of justice – despite its potential value – remains a dangerous instrument that may create more problems than it solves. A person's sense of justice may be a piece of false consciousness in that it gives the person reasons to act contrary to her own interests and to accept relationships with other people that are coercive and exploitative.[8] The worry here is not that some people may take advantage of the person's sense of justice while they themselves only pretend to be loyal to this sense of justice. The worry concerns the particular sense of justice itself: even if all are faithful to *this particular* sense of justice, this person may nevertheless be exploited. In order to alleviate these concerns about false consciousness, coercion, and exploitation, Gauthier offers a non-moral justification of a certain principle of justice. I disagree with him that moral intuitions may not play any role in settling what sense of justice to have (see 11.3). However, I think that he has demonstrated that it is important to show how it can be rationally settled *what* sense of justice to have: that it is important to solve the moral alternatives problem.

2 THE SOLUTION OF THE MORAL ALTERNATIVES PROBLEM

Gauthier offers a rationalistic solution of both the basic choice problem and the moral alternatives problem: he argues that it is of necessary instrumental value both to have some sense of justice or other and to have one specific sense of justice. However, it is only in dealing with the moral alternatives problem that Gauthier's idea of morals by agreement comes into play.[9] Since it is necessary to grasp Gauthier's notion of rationality as utility maximization in order to understand his idea of morals by agreement, I will start by examining the first notion.

Gauthier identifies practical rationality with the maximization of utility, where utility is understood as a "measure of outcomes

---

[8] Gauthier 1988b, 385–389; Gauthier 1991a, 28–29.

[9] It is only in writings more recent than *Morals by Agreement* that Gauthier has argued that what I call "the basic choice problem" can be solved independently of his idea of morals by agreement; the most important papers are here Gauthier 1991b, Gauthier 1993a and Gauthier 1996. In Gunnarsson 1995b (27–31), I discuss how his recent solution of the basic choice problem differs from his contractarian solution of the moral alternatives problem.

representing relations of preference."[10] In fact, utility is *nothing but* a measure: to say that one outcome has a higher utility than another means nothing but that the agent prefers the former to the latter.[11] Thus, according to Gauthier's account of rationality, in a choice situation the rational actor chooses the action with the outcome most preferred among the relevant outcomes.[12] However, the rational agent does not aim to maximize the satisfaction of just any preferences but rather her *considered* preferences. We must thus turn to Gauthier's notion of considered preferences.

The preference I verbally express in a choice situation or reveal in my choice may be based on inexperience. I am an inexperienced Icelander and I find myself in a Chinese restaurant expressing a preference for a hot and spicy dish and revealing it in my choice. Halfway through the meal, I realize that my preference is for a milder dish. My misguided choice was simply based on inexperience. My choice may also go astray if I fail to reflect. Despite my experience with spicy food, I may – without reflecting on it – accept a friend's proposal to order some spicy items. On reflection, I realize that I would prefer something milder. My order of the hot entrée merely revealed a tentative preference, which I then revised.[13] Gauthier takes preferences to be *considered*, if they are stable under experience and reflection and, in addition, none of them is a verbally expressed preference in conflict with a preference revealed in my choices (or vice versa).[14] My preference would fail to meet the additional requirement, if, for example, I express a preference for reading Kant to reading Nietzsche and constantly find myself reading Nietzsche while Kant gathers dust on the shelves.[15]

According to Gauthier, "[o]ne chooses rationally in endeavouring to maximize the fulfilment of those preferences that one holds in a considered way in the choice situation."[16] This does not mean that the agent's choice is irrational if it is not based on her considered

---

[10] Gauthier 1986, 23. In order to define utility as such a measure, the agent's preferences must be coherent. For example, it is not possible to define utility for an agent who prefers A to B, B to C, and C to A. I shall leave the conditions on coherent preferences aside (Gauthier 1986, 23, 38–46).

[11] For my present purposes, I can ignore choice under uncertainty and the notion of *expected* utility (Gauthier 1986, 43–44).

[12] Gauthier 1986, 22–23.   [13] Gauthier 1986, 29–31.

[14] Gauthier 1986, 32–33.   [15] Gauthier 1986, 27–28.

[16] Gauthier 1986, 32.

preferences; for example, there may be no time for reflection or it may be too costly. Nevertheless, the rationality of choice is measured against considered preferences: in order to be rational, the choice must be based on the best estimate of one's considered preferences that one could make in the circumstances (without making it too costly).[17]

Gauthier identifies *value* with utility as the measure of considered preference. What is valuable to me depends on what my considered preferences are. This means that value is both *relative* and *subjective*. A state of affairs does not as such have any value: it has value only relative to an individual. To say that one state of affairs has more value than another for individual x just means that x prefers the first to the second. States of affairs do not have value in any other way than this. Value is therefore relative (states of affairs only have value relative to individuals) and subjective (it depends on individual preference).[18]

Since value depends in this way on individual preferences, it does not provide a standard for evaluating preferences. The only rational requirement with respect to preferences is that they be considered.[19] Thus, neither value nor rationality put any restrictions on the *content* of a person's preferences. What the contents of one's considered preferences are simply depends on what one happens to prefer after having considered the matter. And value and rationality put no restrictions on how one should consider the matter. It is rational for a person to maximize the fulfillment of her considered preferences, no matter what their content.[20]

The concept of rationality as utility maximization plays a central role in Gauthier's idea of morals by agreement. He embraces the

[17] Gauthier 1986, 31. It is important to notice that, according to Gauthier, rationality is maximization of the fulfillment of the preferences *held in a choice situation*. Anna spends most of her twenties reading philosophy and staring into a computer screen. Later on in life, she comes to regret having strained her eyes rather than committing her energy to political activities. In her twenties, her preferences were neither inexperienced nor unreflective: reading philosophy and reflecting on what she was doing did not change her preference. Even if she does later on in life consider her earlier preference to be inferior to her current preference, this in no way shows her earlier choice to have been irrational. The fact that she now considers her earlier preference to be inferior simply means that her current considered preference is different from her earlier considered preference (Gauthier 1986, 31–32, 36–37).

[18] Gauthier 1986, 24–25, 46–55.

[19] Remember that I am ignoring the requirement that the preferences be coherent.

[20] Gauthier 1986, 25–26.

familiar contractarian idea that principles of interaction are justified if
and only if they would be agreed upon in a certain hypothetical
situation. According to Gauthier's theory, people in the hypothetical
situation are utility maximizers, and it is rational for each of them to
accept the agreement where rationality is understood as utility maximization.[21] Since the agreement involved is made in a *hypothetical*
situation, the contractarian must answer the question why we – who,
after all, are not in this hypothetical situation – should accept the
agreement. In other words: how is the hypothetical contract justified
to us? In this case as well, Gauthier offers a utility maximization
justification.[22] He writes: "Our theory must generate, strictly as
rational principles for choice, and so without introducing prior moral
assumptions, constraints on the pursuit of individual interest or
advantage that, being impartial, satisfy the traditional understanding
of morality."[23] The principles justified are identified as moral by
being shown to be impartial. The justification of those principles,
however – both the justification given to us *and* the justification
given to the people in the hypothetical situation – is supposed to be
given in terms of rationality alone, and is thus not based on any moral
assumptions.

By thus characterizing the aim of his theory, Gauthier means to
distinguish his ambitions from those of Rawls.[24] The contrast with
Rawls is, indeed, very instructive. Rawls distinguishes the point of
view of the hypothetical situation – that is, the original position –
from the point of view of you and me. In the latter case, the
construction of the hypothetical situation and its role in the theory of
justice are justified to actual people, to you and me. It is a reflective
equilibrium justification which is meant to show that a particular
conception of justice is reasonable (rather than just rational) for us.[25]
As such, the justification will draw on moral sensibilities insofar as

21 Gauthier 1986, 6–9.
22 However, "[t]he conclusion of the contractarian argument is not that rational
persons, whatever their actual circumstances, must comply with the constraints of
morality. No argument could show that morality is rational in that sense" (Gauthier
1991b, 330). Nevertheless, the rationale that Gauthier offers to people in actual circumstances is a utility maximization rationale.
23 Gauthier 1986, 6.
24 Gauthier 1986, 4–6. Here he also distinguishes his aim from the aim of Harsanyi
1982.
25 Rawls 1993, 28. For my purposes, I can ignore the third point of view he mentions,
that of citizens in a well-ordered society.

these are relevant to the subject of justice. In contrast, the merely rational (rather than reasonable) parties in the hypothetical situation do not draw on any moral sensibilities in concluding that it is rational to choose a certain principle of justice.[26] As I understand Gauthier's theory, the justification to actual people and the justification to the parties in the hypothetical situation cannot be distinguished in this way: in both cases, the hypothetically agreed-upon principles are to be given a utility maximization justification relying on no moral premises (this is what makes Gauthier's theory rationalistic).

This difference in approach affects how Rawls and Gauthier construct the hypothetical situation. The parties to Rawls' original position are situated behind a veil of ignorance; they do not have knowledge of their own specific capacities or ideals, or of who they are going to be in the society for which they are choosing principles of interaction. This veil of ignorance is imposed to ensure the fairness of the hypothetical situation.[27] This is crucial, since the principles chosen have to be justified to you and me, and we are concerned with fairness. The people in Gauthier's hypothetical situation lie behind no such veil of ignorance. Even though we – you and I – do in fact accept some moral principles, Gauthier's justification is addressed to us as utility maximizers. The point of the justification is precisely to give moral principles a utility maximization rationale. The point of the hypothetical situation is not to rule out knowledge of morally irrelevant factors, but to offer a position from which we can ask whether there is a utility maximization rationale for certain moral principles. Consequently, in asking what we would agree upon in a hypothetical situation, we are not inquiring what we would agree upon cloaked in a veil of ignorance, but rather what we (knowing who we are) would agree upon as utility maximizers in a pre-moral situation (and not reasoning in terms of moral principles).[28]

As already explained, Gauthier thinks that any considered preference is just as rational as any other considered preference. Now, a particular sense of justice can give rise to a considered preference for certain distributive patterns. It seems that Gauthier cannot say that this preference is any more or any less rational than a considered

---

[26] Rawls 1993, 11, 48–54, 72–81. Since the justification given to you and me explicitly draws on moral conceptions, I do not consider Rawls to be a rationalist.
[27] Rawls 1971, 12–13.
[28] Gauthier 1986, 4–6, 9.

preference for another distributive pattern. Still, Gauthier wants to be faithful to the intuition that a sense of justice and other normative dispositions may "fail to be rationally sustainable . . . because possessing them and attending to their deliverances is contrary to the fullest realization of their possessor's overall concerns."[29] There is a problem about accounting for this intuition while insisting that considered preferences are, as such, beyond rational criticism. In the lives of many people, moral dispositions play an important role and are bound to deliver many considered preferences. Assuming that these dispositions are important to a person, it is unlikely that an *instrumental* investigation into how best to satisfy the person's given preferences (many of which will be moral) will reveal the moral dispositions to be rationally unsustainable. Even in cases where such an instrumental investigation fails to reveal this, however, we may want to say that some of the person's moral dispositions are not rationally sustainable. As I understand him, Gauthier himself wants to be able to say this. He wants to say that such moral dispositions may be pieces of false consciousness and may subject the person to exploitation.[30] Since he wants to say this *and* wants to understand practical rationality instrumentally, he must find a way of showing a person's moral dispositions to be *instrumentally* irrational *without* taking the person's particular preferences as *given*. This he wants to accomplish by showing that a sense of justice is of *necessary* instrumental value; in other words, that it is of instrumental value *whatever* the person's particular aims and concerns are.[31]

Within a contractarian framework, the idea of showing that a particular sense of justice is of necessary instrumental value requires that it be shown that the initial agreement is rational for each party, *whatever* her preferences.[32] In order to explain this idea further, the following three comments must be made:

(1) The fact that the initial agreement is to be made in a pre-moral situation suggests that it is to be rational for each party, whatever her

---

[29] Gauthier 1993a, 203.   [30] Gauthier 1991a, 28–29.
[31] Gauthier 1993a, 198–199.
[32] In other words, the rationale for the agreement may make "no reference to the content of anyone's preferences" (Gauthier 1991a, 23). Here Gauthier is actually talking about a rationale that belongs to the solution to the basic choice problem. It becomes clear in this article, however, that he also takes this – subject to some qualifications (which I will subsequently discuss) – to be a solution to the moral alternatives problem.

non-moral preferences. In a pre-moral situation, people have, by definition, no views as to what is right or wrong and thus no moral preferences. This is, indeed, how Gauthier understands his approach in *Morals by Agreement*. However, in a recent article, "Value, Reasons, and the Sense of Justice," he makes a different claim:

> Now I do not want to reject a distinction between moral and nonmoral concerns, although I do not suppose that there is a neat and exhaustive division between the exclusively moral and the exclusively nonmoral. But in thinking of persons as naturally possessing a sense of justice, I am embracing a quite different starting point from that in my book [i.e., *Morals by Agreement*]. Moral dispositions are as natural to human beings as nonmoral ones, so that in considering real persons we cannot distinguish a nonmoral base and a moral superstructure. And so in claiming that a sense of justice is necessarily of instrumental value to persons, I am not saying that it is of instrumental value simply to realize nonmoral ends. Rather my claim is that the concerns expressed in our sense of justice are integrally related to our capacity to realize, under normal conditions, any set of aims that could be adequate to a human life.[33]

Even with this different starting point, the aim can still be to give a non-moral justification of morality. Although a sense of justice is not shown to be of instrumental value to realize exclusively non-moral goals, it is to be shown to be of instrumental value. And it is to be shown to be of *necessary* instrumental value: although it is of instrumental value to realize moral ends, among others, no assumption is made as to what those moral ends might be. It is supposed to be crucial to the justification that no such assumption be made. In this sense, the justification is non-moral. It seems that this different starting point is more appropriate, given that Gauthier also wants to address the justification to people who have moral ends and not only to people in a pre-moral situation. Those people want to know that a sense of justice is instrumental not merely to realizing their non-moral ends, whatever those are, but to realizing their moral *and* non-moral ends, whatever those are.

In whichever sense the starting point is supposed to be non-moral, in both cases the justification is supposed to be *formal*, in that no

---

[33] Gauthier 1993a, 201.

appeal is made to the contents of people's preferences. Since my subsequent claim – that Gauthier fails to justify a unique principle of interaction to utility maximizers in the actual world – depends on the formality of the justification, my criticism is applicable no matter in which of the two senses his starting point is non-moral.

(2) In *Morals by Agreement*, Gauthier assumed that the parties to the initial agreement were not only utility maximizers but also "non-tuists," i.e. devoid of interest in the interests of those with whom they interact.[34] This special motivational assumption was criticized by several commentators: is there any reason to think that it is in general rational for persons with tuistic preferences to accept principles agreed upon by persons with non-tuistic preferences? Also, since for Gauthier no set of considered preferences is, as such, more rational than another, he cannot assume non-tuistic preference in order to evaluate the validity of tuistic preferences: he cannot show tuistic preferences to be exploitative by evaluating them from the standpoint of an agreement made by non-tuists any more than he can show non-tuistic preferences to be exploitative by evaluating them from the standpoint of an agreement made by tuists.[35]

If Gauthier's project is to be interpreted along the lines I just sketched in comment (1), then that interpretation must surely include a provision to the following effect: that the goal of the project is not simply to show that a sense of justice is instrumental to realizing non-tuistic ends, but to show that it is instrumental to realizing the agent's ends, whatever those ends are (non-tuistic or tuistic, non-moral or moral, etc.). Since my criticism of Gauthier's contractarian justification will be directed at its formality rather than at the restriction that he actually makes on the contents of the preferences of the agents in the initial position, it will be valid even if Gauthier could restate his contractarian argument without assuming that the initial situation is a pre-moral situation occupied by non-tuists.

(3) Whereas the two previous comments concern cases where *Morals by Agreement* may have been too restrictive in its assumptions

---

[34] Gauthier 1986, 87, 311. This goes beyond the assumption that the preferences of the parties are non-moral, since agents who have no concept of right and wrong might nevertheless take an interest in the interest of those with whom they interact.

[35] See Sumner 1987, Morris 1988, Thomas 1988, and Vallentyne 1991b. For Gauthier's reply to Morris 1988 and Thomas 1988, see Gauthier 1988a.

about the motives of the people in the initial situation, this one concerns a case where the book was not restrictive enough:

> My aim in *Morals by Agreement* was to defend the rationality of morality, and so the incorporation of moral considerations among an agent's reasons for acting, whatever her concerns might happen to be. In effect I sought to impose no material restrictions on the contents of her life-plans. But this is unsound. Consider an agent whose life-plan is focused on the destruction of his fellows, who lives to kill. He has no interest in interactions that reflect mutual agreement and advantage, though he might find his victims more easily were he to simulate such interest. But of course others have no interest in interacting with him at all; knowing his life-plan, they would want to exclude him from their midst. And the impossibility of reaching agreement with him on mutually advantageous terms of interaction, and so of making him party to a social contract, gives them a principled basis for such an exclusion.
>
> I must therefore amend my aim. My defence of the rationality of morality must be limited to those persons whose overarching life-plans make them welcome participants in society. Such persons are potential parties to an agreement that would determine mutually advantageous terms of interaction.[36]

The amendment seems not to present a fundamental change in Gauthier's project. He has limited the group of people to whom his contractarian justifications are addressed. However, he may not have excluded a great number of people. Moreover, for the group he addresses, his aim is still to show that it is rational for each person in this group, whatever her preferences (given that they are consistent with her membership in the group), to accept a specific principle of interaction.

As already indicated, the story told in *Morals by Agreement* may be problematic in that it assumes that the parties to the original agreement have non-moral and non-tuistic preferences: this raises the question of how to justify the content of the initial agreement to people in the current situation – people who may have moral and tuistic preferences. I am willing to assume that *these* differences between the initial and the current situation – differences pertaining to the issues of whether the preferences are moral and tuistic – do

---

[36] Gauthier 1993b, 188–189.

not present a difficulty for Gauthier's justification, which (in its revised form) is supposed to be acceptable *whatever* people's preferences may happen to be. However, if a hypothetical rather than an actual contract is to be the justification of moral principles, then there must be *some* difference between the initial and the current situation. In other words, in accepting the initial agreement, people in the current situation would have to make certain abstractions from their situation.

Since Gauthier wants to give a utility maximization rationale for a certain moral principle not only to people in the initial situation but also to people in the current situation, the abstractions that people in the current position are required to make must be given a utility maximization rationale. In other words, the *rationality* of making the agreement in Gauthier's initial situation, rather than in some other initial situation, must be demonstrated to each person in the current situation. In the absence of such a utility maximization rationale, Gauthier's characterization of the initial situation lacks the necessary justification and must be suspected to be based on a moral premise (Gauthier himself insists that the initial situation is fair).

Gauthier's initial position is an initial *bargaining* position, and it has to be determined what the bargaining parties are allowed to bring to the bargaining table. Gauthier rejects the view that the parties are allowed to bring the benefits of their natural interaction to the bargaining table.[37] Rather, the contract is to be made by people whose natural interaction is constrained by a proviso that "prohibits worsening the situation of another person, except to avoid worsening one's own through interaction with that person."[38] Why though should rational utility maximizers accept this proviso? Gauthier argues that "it is rational for utility-maximizers to accept the proviso as constraining their *natural* interaction and their individual endowments, insofar as they *anticipate beneficial social interaction* with their fellows."[39] As the italicized phrases make clear, this argument is addressed to people who are in a state of nature and anticipate benefiting from social interaction. Thus, I will not discuss this

---

[37] Gauthier 1986, 193–199. This view is defended in Buchanan 1975.
[38] Gauthier 1986, 205. This is the so-called "Lockean Proviso." Gauthier's proviso is a refinement of Nozick's refinement in Nozick 1974 (175–179) of Locke's proviso; see Gauthier 1993b, 182.
[39] Gauthier 1986, 193 (emphasis added).

argument. What is needed is an argument addressed to people already engaged in social interaction, which gives them a utility maximization rationale for accepting the principles that would be agreed upon in the initial situation as characterized by Gauthier.[40] Gauthier has offered such an argument and I shall present it in the next section.

3 GAUTHIER'S INITIAL SITUATION

Is it rational for utility maximizers in the current situation to accept principles that would be agreed on in the initial position? Obviously, some people would be worse off if current principles were abandoned in favor of hypothetically-agreed-upon principles. Gauthier responds to this problem by considering how rational utility maximizers, who recognize the rationality of constraining the direct pursuit of their interests, would reflect upon their own situation, if this situation did not satisfy the principles rationally agreed upon in the initial situation.[41] These agents recognize that they benefit more from the currently generally accepted constraints than they would benefit from a situation in which no constraints were accepted. Gauthier says that they are bound to ask themselves whether they would not benefit more from some other constraining practices than they do from the present practices. One alternative which will be considered will be the one that would be the result of a bargain taking place in the current situation. People who expect to benefit from renegotiations will have some incentive to demand a change in current practices, and the demands of these people will tend to make the existing order unstable. The alternative practice would be more stable, because it is what people would rationally agree upon were they to bargain in the existing situation.[42]

Gauthier argues that this is not the end of the story:

The reflective capacity of rational agents leads them from the given to

---

[40] This is not the same problem as the issue of whether persons who have a good reason to make a contract also have a good reason to comply with it. Even if a person *would* have had a good reason to make a contract and *would* have had a good reason to comply with it *if* she *were* in a certain situation, she may not have a good reason to make and comply with such a contract, given that she is not in that situation.

[41] This answer was first developed as a response to Buchanan 1988, Fishkin 1988 and Harman 1988 in Gauthier 1988a. In my summary, I leave out some aspects of the original answer and present it essentially as it appears in Gauthier 1991a.

[42] Gauthier 1991a, 26–27; cf. Gauthier 1988a, 179–180.

the agreed, from the existing practices and principles requiring constraint to those that would receive each person's assent. The same reflective capacity, I claim, leads from those practices that would be agreed to, in existing social circumstances, to those that would receive ex ante agreement, premoral and presocial. As the status quo proves unstable when it comes into conflict with what would be agreed to, so what would be agreed to proves unstable when it comes into conflict with what would have been agreed to in an appropriate presocial context. For as existing practices must seem arbitrary insofar as they do not correspond to what a rational person would agree to, so what such a person would agree to in existing circumstances must seem arbitrary in relation to what she would accept in a presocial condition.[43]

The reason why a rational agreement reached in the existing circumstances seems arbitrary is that it will be influenced by these circumstances, which are themselves arbitrary. The awareness of the arbitrariness of rational agreement made in the present circumstances undermines the stability of the agreed-upon practice. The practices which would receive ex ante agreement will prove more stable because this agreement is seen as less arbitrary.[44]

The agents in the existing circumstances understand the value of practices constraining their direct maximization of utility. They understand the value of complying with such practices and therefore the value of stable compliance. This, in turn, should lead them to favor the practices that would receive ex ante agreement, since they are the most stable ones.[45]

How are we to understand Gauthier's argument? He himself writes the following:

What is the practical import of this argument? It would be absurd to claim that mere acquaintance with it, or even acceptance of it, will lead to the replacement of existing moral practices by those that would secure presocial agreement. It would be irrational for anyone to give up the benefits of the existing moral order simply because he comes to realize that it affords him more than he could expect from pure rational agreement with his fellows. And it would be irrational for anyone to accept a long-term utility loss by refusing to comply with the existing

---

[43] Gauthier 1991a, 27; cf. Gauthier 1988a, 184–185.
[44] Gauthier 1991a, 27–28; cf. Gauthier 1988a, 184–185.
[45] Gauthier 1991a, 29.

moral order, simply because she comes to realize that such compliance affords her less than she could expect from pure rational agreement. Nevertheless, these realizations do transform, or perhaps bring to the surface, the character of the relationships between persons that are maintained by the existing constraints, so that some of these relationships come to be recognized as coercive. These realizations constitute the elimination of false consciousness, and they result from a process of rational reflection that brings persons into what, in my theory, is the parallel of Jürgen Habermas's ideal speech situation. [Footnote omitted.] Without an argument to defend themselves in open dialogue with their fellows, those who are more than equally advantaged can hope to maintain their privileged position only if they can coerce their fellows into accepting it. And this, of course, may be possible. But coercion is not agreement, and it lacks any inherent stability.[46]

Here, Gauthier rules out the interpretation that in his argument he is trying to show that for each and every person in the current situation it is rational to accept the principles that would be agreed upon in the initial situation.[47] In this passage, he speaks of both stability and coercion, and it seems to me that we get two different interpretations of his argument, depending on which notion is emphasized. In my view, the argument cannot serve to justify the initial contract to people in the current situation if stability is taken to be its point. People in the current situation might accept Gauthier's argument and nevertheless quite reasonably believe that the present practices will remain stable *in their life-time*. Thus, unless they care about what happens after they are dead – remember that Gauthier's argument was not supposed to appeal to the contents of preferences – a concern with stability does not seem to give them a good reason to accept the initial contract. Gauthier's argument is much more interesting if it is interpreted in the light of the role that the notions of coercion and false consciousness play in it. This is how I will interpret it.

According to this interpretation, the initial agreement is the only agreement that meets two conditions: (1) it is rational for each utility maximizer to accept it *and* (2) none of the utility maximizers who make the agreement has in any way been coerced to accept it. The

[46] Gauthier 1991a, 28–29.   [47] See also Gauthier 1991b, 330.

initial agreement is to be shown to be non-coercive by an appeal to a notion of repeated negotiations which start in the present circumstances (as opposed to the initial position). In each of the negotiations, the parties enter into a bargain that forms the basis of an agreement concerning the principles which are to govern their interaction. Nobody is permitted to use coercion to maintain the status quo or to prevent renewed negotiations. In the end, the utility maximizers will reach an agreement of which none can ask for a renegotiation without violating one of the two conditions. This agreement is the uniquely non-coercive agreement of rational utility maximizers, and it is supposed to be identical with the one which would be made in the initial situation. This account of the non-coerciveness of the agreement is at the same time an account of why rational utility maximizers in the present circumstances should care about the initial hypothetical agreement. They should care if they want not only to maximize their utility but rather to maximize their utility without (overtly or covertly) coercing any of those with whom they interact into benefiting less than they would in the absence of any coercion.

Gauthier's argument, on this interpretation, has a moral premise in the sense that it simply assumes that utility maximizers in the present situation care about not coercing others.[48] In the present context, however, I am willing to assume that this is not a serious difficulty. Remember that we are here concerned with the moral alternatives problem rather than the basic choice problem. If the basic choice problem has been solved, we know that we have a good reason to have *a* sense of justice. This may include knowing that we have a good reason not to coerce and exploit or take advantage of others.[49]

The moral alternatives problem is that we do not thereby know *which* sense of justice it is rational to have guide our actions. In other words, we do not know which sense of justice enables us to avoid coercing and taking advantage of others and being coerced and exploited by them. Gauthier wants to give us a non-moral test for finding this out in terms of utility maximization. More precisely, he wants to resolve the complex issue as to when a social system of

---

[48] The stability argument was supposed to show that utility maximizers have a good reason not to coerce, but I have already pointed out that this argument is problematic.

[49] If we were concerned with the basic choice problem, it would indeed be a serious difficulty for Gauthier if his argument were to have a moral premise.

distribution is coercive and exploitative by employing the idea of repeated negotiations among utility maximizers, where it is not permitted to use coercion to maintain the status quo.

For this to work, it must be possible to give an uncontroversial account of what "use of coercion to maintain the status quo" means. Since Gauthier wants to employ this account to give a non-moral test for settling the issue of what makes a social system coercive and exploitative, his account of "use of coercion to maintain the status quo" may not draw on any interpretation of what makes a social system of distribution coercive. Otherwise, Gauthier's test will be circular. In addition, the account may of course not draw on any moral intuitions. In my criticism of Gauthier's argument in the next chapter, I will not question that there is such an uncontroversial account of "use of coercion to maintain the status quo" available to him, but will rather argue that this account, together with a notion of utility maximization, fails to determine uniquely when the renego tiations are to come to an end and thus what system of distribution is to count as coercive and exploitative.

The people in the current situation want to know whether they suffer from false consciousness and consequently participate in coer- cive and exploitative social arrangements. On the face of it, Gauthier's renegotiation argument seems to provide a plausible way of meeting their concerns. These people are worried that by accepting certain moral principles they have become victims of false consciousness and that moral intuitions will not help solve the problem, because they are part of the problem rather than its solution. Apart from relying on an uncontroversial idea about coercion, Gauthier's argument is not supposed to rely on any substantive – and thus potentially dubious – intuitions: the argument is addressed to us as utility maximizers. We are being addressed simply as utility maximizers and not as utility maximizers who also have certain specific moral or non-moral preferences. This gives us a basically non-moral way of testing whether somebody, in accepting certain moral principles, has sub- jected herself to exploitation. She has subjected herself to exploitation if her utility is lower than it would have been under an agreement into which nobody is coerced. Since *nobody* is being coerced into the agreement at the end of the renegotiations, she is not being coerced into that agreement and thus is not being exploited. Of course, she might be receiving less than she would have if somebody else were being exploited, but that is beside the point, given that we are concerned with ensuring that *nobody* is exploited.

Does the renegotiation argument really justify to people in the current situation the principles that would be agreed upon in Gauthier's initial position? I believe that it does not. To do so, it would have to be the case that the last renegotiations take place in a situation identical to Gauthier's initial position. However, I will argue in the next chapter that the renegotiation argument cannot determine the situation in which the last renegotiations are to take place. I will argue this by describing another initial situation and arguing that no utility maximization rationale can be given for not letting the last renegotiations take place in this alternative initial situation, rather than in Gauthier's. If that is so, however, then the renegotiation argument also fails to give us a test for false consciousness, exploitation and coercion, since the agreement made in the different initial situation will count different principles as exploitative.

7

From here to pre-social agreement

If people were to bargain about the distribution of benefits in the current situation, some people would have better bargaining positions than others. What about Gauthier's initial situation? Do some people in that situation have a better bargaining position than others? The answer is "yes." Gauthier's Lockean proviso, which defines the rights that people have in the initial situation, allows you to make yourself better off than another person *prior to making the social contract* assuming that you "[d]o not make yourself better off than you would have been in someone else's absence, by making that person worse off than he would have been in your absence."[1] Thus, the naturally better endowed[2] are permitted to enhance their bargaining positions as long as they do not thereby violate this proviso.[3] Now the question is whether the situation in which the last renegotiations take place is also a situation in which the naturally better endowed have a better bargaining position. If not, then Gauthier's renegotiation argument fails to justify the initial agreement to people in the present situation.

The renegotiation argument is addressed to utility maximizers in the current situation who also want no one to be coerced. One of these utility maximizers – call her "the pure utility maximizer" – may argue that the repeated negotiations would not lead to Gauthier's initial situation. According to her, Gauthier gives the naturally better endowed something for free that should itself be subjected to utility maximization considerations. Thus, the repeated negotiations will

---

[1] Gauthier 1993b, 182.
[2] "Each person's basic endowment is what he can make use of simply in virtue of his presence in a situation, and what no one else can make use of in his absence. It thus comprises his physical and mental capacities" (Gauthier 1986, 100).
[3] Gauthier 1986, 208–210.

71

not lead to Gauthier's initial situation, since in this situation the naturally better endowed do in effect coerce the worse endowed to make an agreement that is unacceptable to the latter as utility maximizers who want that nobody be coerced. Rather, the negotiations should be taken one step further, to a situation in which people – as pure utility maximizers who get nothing (including their natural capacities) for free – bargain about what use to make of people's basic endowments; in this way, the better endowed would not have a bargaining advantage.

It might appear that the pure utility maximizer is offering – in a Rawlsian spirit – a moral argument to the effect that the distribution of natural endowments should be considered a common asset.[4] While she may indeed, however, be said to urge that the distribution of natural endowments should be considered a common asset, she does not support her suggestion by a moral argument. On the contrary: she stresses that we must engage in the renegotiations from the current position *qua* utility maximizers. No other fact about us except that we are utility maximizers should be given independent weight. If we want to relieve suffering in distant parts of the world or want income not to be distributed too unevenly, this is not true of us as utility maximizers. These considerations should therefore not be given any independent weight in the renegotiations. Similarly, it is not true of a person *qua* utility maximizer that she is naturally better endowed than another person. Therefore, the fact that one person is naturally better endowed than another person should be given no independent weight. There is no other way of ensuring that *nobody* is being exploited. If considerations external to utility maximization are allowed to enter the scene, we run the risk that someone is being exploited. If the distribution of natural endowments is not considered a common asset, then some people have something for free that is no part of their being utility maximizers. It is true that these people would not have *done* anything to take advantage of others; they *are* simply naturally better endowed. However, they have something the holding of which has not been justified by utility maximization, and this gives them an advantage over their fellows.

According to the test proposed by the pure utility maximizer, every advantage which has not been justified by considerations of

---

[4] Rawls 1971, 101–102.

utility maximization amounts to exploitation. This does not mean
that this advantage will be subjected to utilitarian considerations. In
the initial bargaining situation the parties all have certain preferences
and bargain on the basis of those preferences. However, in bargaining
with others, no one is permitted to make use of her natural capacities
to get a better deal, and it is to be determined by the agreement what
use is going to be made of people's natural capacities.[5] Nothing more
is meant when it is said that the distribution of natural endowments is
to be considered a common asset.

The point of introducing the pure utility maximizer's understanding of the repeated negotiations is not to argue that she – as opposed
to Gauthier – is right. They both offer a utility maximization rationale
to people in the current situation. What I want to argue is that
considerations of utility maximization fail to settle the issue as to
which position – the pure utility maximizer's or Gauthier's – the
people in the current situation should accept; my argument is meant
to show that Gauthier has therefore failed to give a non-moral
justification of his view to people in the current situation.[6] This also
means that he has failed to provide a non-moral solution to the moral
alternatives problem. I will argue for this conclusion by considering
(in §§2–6) attempts to defeat the proposal of the pure utility
maximizer on non-moral grounds and by showing that they all fail.
The response to these failures should not be that the pure utility
maximizer can be seen to be right on non-moral grounds, but rather
that the issue between the two positions cannot be settled on non-
moral grounds.

2 THE NORMATIVITY OBJECTION

Since the pure utility maximizer wants to treat the distribution of
natural endowments as a common asset, Gauthier might argue that
there is no way to unpack the notion of a common asset without
appealing to some normative considerations. It is a brute, non-

[5] The pure utility maximizer's initial situation differs from Rawls' original position in
two important ways: (1) the parties in the pure utility maximizer's initial situation are
not prevented from using their capacities to get a better deal by a veil of ignorance,
but rather are simply required not to do so; (2) these parties have knowledge of and
are motivated by their own individual preferences.
[6] The ban on use of coercion to maintain the status quo also will not settle the issue
(unless it is given a richer sense than Gauthier is entitled to give it).

normative fact that I can do certain things that you cannot do and vice versa. It is also a brute, non-normative fact that contributions to a cooperative enterprise differ from person to person. He might argue that his theory shows how agents of whom these two non-normative facts are true could rationally agree to introduce certain normative structures into their interaction. Therefore, there is a sense in which his theory shows how it can be rational to introduce a normative structure where there was none before. He might then argue that if the parties to the agreement are to consider the distribution of natural endowments as a common asset they have to think in terms of normative structures from the very beginning. There is no way to make sense of the notion of a common asset, except by saying that in the bargaining process no one *should* use their natural capacities as a bargaining advantage.[7]

I grant Gauthier that the two facts he mentions are brute, non-normative facts. The question is what their relevance is. These facts are compatible with various distributions. This means that they are compatible with various different starting points of an agreement to cooperate (initial bargaining positions). It is noteworthy that Gauthier argues against any position that allows the parties to bring the fruits of prior predatory/defensive activity to the bargaining table and take them away as part of the overall outcome:

> [C]learly an individual would be irrational if she were to dispose herself to comply, voluntarily, with an agreement reached in this way. Someone disposed to comply with agreements that left untouched the fruits of predation would simply invite others to engage in predatory and coercive activities as a prelude to bargaining. She would permit the successful predators to reap where they have ceased to sow, to continue to profit from the effects of natural predation after entering into agreements freeing them from the need to invest further predatory effort. Co-operative compliance is not compliant victimization. We do not deny that, as long as her costs in resisting actual predation exceed any benefits such resistance would bring her, the victim rationally must acquiesce. But if predatory activity is banned, then she no longer has reason to behave in a way that would maintain its effects.[8]

---

[7] In this paragraph I have attempted to summarize an argument that Gauthier proposed in conversation.

[8] Gauthier 1986, 195; Gauthier is arguing against the position defended in Buchanan 1975.

The point of Gauthier's Lockean proviso is precisely to restrict the ways in which the parties are allowed to make use of the fact that they can do things that others cannot do and will be able to contribute more to the cooperative scheme than others in order to better their own bargaining position. Gauthier's argument against the proposal of the pure utility maximizer can therefore not be that her suggestion imposes normative restrictions on the initial bargaining position. Gauthier does that himself.

It might be argued that the pure utility maximizer's reasons for imposing normative restrictions on the initial situation are misguided. People are naturally different and therefore some can acquire more than others. According to Gauthier, we take it from there and ask what initial position rational utility maximizers should accept "in so far as they anticipate beneficial social interaction with their fellows."[9] We never question their natural holdings, however, except insofar as these affect the rationality of the agreement to cooperate. The pure utility maximizer's mistake is to think that there is something wrong with the natural holdings as such.

This argument is simply based on a misunderstanding of the pure utility maximizer's position. She would not ask for a justification of distributions in the State of Nature if there were no prospect of a beneficial social interaction. However, she insists that nothing should make a difference in social distribution without being subjected to utility maximization considerations, and to them alone; and therefore that nobody may appeal to their natural capacities to get a better deal for herself. The pure utility maximizer agrees that the concept of exploitation makes no sense in the State of Nature except insofar as the parties anticipate beneficial social interaction. However, given that utility maximization is the only rationale for entering society, it should also be the only criterion for distribution in society. Therefore, the parties should get nothing for free that would give them a better bargaining position. If natural endowments were permitted to give people bargaining leverage, then some people would be getting something for free that gives them a better bargaining position.

9 Gauthier 1986, 193.

3 THE TAKING ADVANTAGE OBJECTION

If natural endowments are permitted to provide bargaining leverage in an initial bargaining position, then the outcome for the worse endowed will be worse than if natural endowments were not allowed to be used in this way. Now it may be argued that if the pure utility maximizer's argument is only based on the fact that, in another situation, the worse endowed would have gotten a better deal, then her argument lacks an essential element which is present in Gauthier's argument.[10] After all, a claim analogous to the one about the worse endowed can be made about the better endowed: if natural endowments cannot be used to get a better deal, the better endowed are guaranteed to get a smaller share than if natural capacities could be used as a bargaining leverage.[11] In his argument, Gauthier does not rely only on this fact. In addition, so one may argue, he shows that his initial position is non-coercive and that, in this position, none of the agents has taken advantage of any other.[12] If the pure utility maximizer fails to demonstrate this for her initial position, then her argument must be rejected in favor of Gauthier's.

In response to this line of reasoning, it must be pointed out that the pure utility maximizer has indeed argued that her version of the initial position is non-coercive and that in it nobody has taken advantage of anybody else. The pure utility maximizer argued that the social contract should be thought of as an agreement of *pure* utility maximizers. Thus, in the initial situation none of them should get for free something that is not part of being a utility maximizer – including the benefits of superior natural endowments. In that situation, precisely granting someone something that does not belong to her simply as a utility maximizer would make the situation coercive and would allow some utility maximizers to take advantage of others.

It must be concluded that both Gauthier (with his Lockean

---

[10] Cf. the criticism of Gauthier's proviso in Danielson 1988 and Gauthier's answer in Gauthier 1988b, 411.

[11] It should be noted that in criticizing the pure utility maximizer it is not enough to point out that the worse endowed are (in the case of an agreement made in Gauthier's initial position) at least better off than if no agreement to cooperate had been reached. This is true, but it is also true that people who (according to Gauthier, irrationally) agree to a bargain that allows fruits of a predatory activity to be brought to the bargaining table are better off than if no agreement had been made.

[12] Gauthier 1986, 193–205.

proviso[13]) and the pure utility maximizer offer accounts of coercion and what it is to take advantage of others. In other words, we have the following argumentative standoff: according to the pure utility maximizer, it is irrational for the worse endowed to accept an agreement made in Gauthier's initial position. The reason why it is irrational is not only that they would get a better deal in another initial position, but also that in Gauthier's initial position they have been taken advantage of. According to Gauthier, it is irrational for the better endowed to accept an agreement made in the pure utility maximizer's initial position. The reason why it is irrational is not only that they would get a better deal in another initial position, but also that in the pure utility maximizer's initial position they have been taken advantage of.

My aim is not to decide which of these accounts is correct. The question here is whether the issue can be decided on non-moral grounds. In *Morals by Agreement*, Gauthier offers arguments for his construal of the initial situation by arguing both that it is fair or impartial[14] and that it is rational for people in the State of Nature to accept it as the situation within which to make a contract, insofar as they expect benefits from social interaction.[15] However, neither of these arguments satisfactorily answers the present question, since the first one gives a moral reason and the second one is not addressed to people in the *current* situation. In the search for such a non-moral rationale for Gauthier's account, I now turn to his discussion of the notion of agency.

4 THE AGENCY OBJECTION

Gauthier does not address his theory to *pure* utility maximizers. In other words, his addressees are not individuals who are defined only by their utility function (the function that converts outcomes into individual utilities). Rather, his theory is addressed to persons where "each person may be defined by his utility function and his factor endowment. These fix his preferences and capacities."[16] Thus, his theory is from the very start addressed to persons *as* individuals with certain preferences and certain capacities. This, he believes, is of crucial importance:

[13] Gauthier 1986, 200–205.   [14] Gauthier 1986, 208–223, 245–261.
[15] Gauthier 1986, 223–232.   [16] Gauthier 1986, 86.

Each human being is an actor with certain preferences and certain physical and mental capacities which, in the absence of her fellows, she naturally directs to the fulfilment of her preferences. This provides a basis, in no way arbitrary, from which we may examine and assess interaction, introducing such conceptions as bettering and worsening. A principle that abstracted from this basis would not relate to human beings as actors. A principle that did not take this basis as normatively fundamental would not relate impartially to human beings as actors.[17]

In the pure utility maximizer's initial situation the parties all have certain preferences, and they bargain on the basis of those preferences. Each of them aims to maximize her utility. However, even though each of them has knowledge of her own capacities, she does not try to reach an agreement that would be favorable to a person with those particular capacities.[18] For example, if she is one of the better endowed, she will not draw on this fact in order to get a better deal. In the bargaining situation, she will only draw on her preferences. How people's capacities are to be used to satisfy people's preferences is supposed to be an outcome of the agreement. In this sense, the parties in the pure utility maximizer's initial situation *abstract* from the fact that they have certain capacities, but is that really a problem, in the way that Gauthier suggests?

The pure utility maximizer will argue that it is not a problem. The parties to the initial situation are *actors*. They have certain preferences and aim to act so as to maximize the satisfaction of those preferences. And they have knowledge of their own capacities and know how to act so as to satisfy their preferences. However, according to the pure utility maximizer, the parties in the initial situation must not get any advantage from the fact that they happen to have certain natural endowments, precisely in order to avoid making the social agreement on an *arbitrary* basis. Having certain natural endowments is not part of the individual *qua* utility maximizer, and letting the parties get an advantage from their capacities would thus be arbitrary (and partial) from the standpoint of utility maximization. Thus, the pure utility maximizer's proposal relates to human beings as actors: it relates to them as utility maximizers capable of acting on their preferences but

---

[17] Gauthier 1986, 221.
[18] Of course, she will be indirectly influenced by her capacities. She is more likely to have a preference for horse riding if she is actually capable of riding a horse.

choosing not to take advantage of their natural endowments in the initial agreement.

The pure utility maximizer has answered Gauthier's criticism by insisting that justifications to people in the current situation should be addressed to them *qua* utility maximizers. The burden of proof is on Gauthier to give a non-moral rationale for addressing them to people, not *qua* utility maximizers, but *qua* utility maximizers who have certain natural capacities.

In response, Gauthier might argue that it does not make sense to speak of a *pure* utility maximizer, since the idea of a utility maximizer can only be understood as part of a richer notion of an agent. We come to have preferences among states of affairs when we see ourselves as capable of producing results in the world. In other words, we come to have preferences in the first place – and thus get to be utility maximizers – only as agents capable of realizing states of affairs. By addressing people *qua* utility maximizers rather than as full-blown agents, one is thus artificially severing the notion of utility maximization from the only context in which it makes sense. Consequently, Gauthier might conclude, even though it is *possible* to abstract from the fact that we have particular capacities, to do so is to distort grossly our own sense of agency.[19]

A similar argument against the pure utility maximizer's proposal could also be made in terms of the concept of identification. In this case, the argument would be that by asking the people in the current position to accept the agreement made in her initial situation, the pure utility maximizer is requiring people to identify with constructed parties who have nothing to do with people as they understand themselves in the current situation. This comes out in the pure utility maximizer's answer to the better endowed when they claim that they are being taken advantage of in her proposal. The answer is that *qua pure utility maximizers* they are not being taken advantage of. The trouble, however, is that the pure utility maximizers making the initial agreement are such barren entities that no one in the current situation can identify with such a "person." Therefore, it is a mistake to think that it is rational for people in the current position to accept the pure utility maximizer's hypothetical agreement.[20]

The issue is whether people in the current situation should be

---

[19] Again, I am interpreting a suggestion made by Gauthier in conversation.
[20] Cf. Gauthier 1986, 250–254, even though the topic there is Archimedean choice.

addressed *qua* pure utility maximizers or *qua* utility maximizers who have certain natural endowments. The argument just given against the former proposal is that it distorts our sense of agency and that it asks us to identify with something that we cannot identify with. It was argued that we form preferences as agents capable of realizing states of affairs, and thus the notion of a utility maximizer should not be severed from the notion of a full-blown agent.

The first clue to the proper response to this argument comes from the fact that the issue is how to address people in the current situation. Now, people in the current situation (or most of them) are moral agents. As already discussed (in 2.1), Gauthier believes that, for moral agents, morality is an independent source of reasons that can conflict with straightforward utility maximization. This means that Gauthier himself – in addressing the people in the current situation as utility maximizers with certain natural endowments – is asking people in the current situation to perform significant abstractions. He is asking them not to reason as moral agents, and this is asking them – for the purpose of the question whether they should accept the agreement made in the initial position – to change the very way in which they reason as practical agents. It seems to me that this shows that the arguments just considered fail to offer a rationale for Gauthier's proposal as opposed to the pure utility maximizer's proposal.

Consider first the claim that by addressing people in the current situation as pure utility maximizers, the pure utility maximizer distorts our sense of agency. The problem is that if this is a good argument against the pure utility maximizer's proposal, it is also a good argument against Gauthier's: by performing the abstractions that Gauthier requests, people distort their sense of themselves as *moral* agents. Of course, Gauthier thinks that there is a good reason to distort this sense of agency by making the abstractions that he asks for, but the pure utility maximizer also believes that there is a good reason to make the abstractions that she requests, even if they involve "distortions." What remains is that the mere fact that there is a "distortion of a sense of agency" cannot be used to settle the issue between Gauthier and the pure utility maximizer.

The same sort of reply can be given against the argument offered in terms of identification: if the argument works against the pure utility maximizer, it also works against Gauthier. People in the current position accept various moral ideals, and some of them regard living according to these ideals as constitutive of their own identity. In their view, betraying these moral ideals would amount to betraying themselves. Thus, the suggestion that in accepting these moral ideals they may be making themselves subject to exploitation will sound strange to them. How can something that is constitutive of their identity, something that is part of *themselves*, make *them* susceptible to exploitation? In asking them to accept an agreement made in Gauthier's initial bargaining position, one would not be asking them to accept an agreement they themselves would have made under other conditions, but rather an agreement made by some other people. A person like that would not consider this to be an agreement that she herself would have made, since whoever does not accept certain moral ideals is not the same person as she is. The pure utility maximizer is simply asking people in the current position to make one more abstraction than Gauthier asks them to do. However, this does not mean that the additional abstraction she asks them to make is harder for them to make than the one that Gauthier has already requested. Some people may consider their ideals as essential to their identity but their talents as merely accidental to it. For these people it will be easier to make the additional abstraction than to make the abstractions that Gauthier has already asked them for.

5 THE MANNA FROM HEAVEN OBJECTION

Gauthier might argue that the pure utility maximizer has a dubious conception of the goods to be distributed. In Gauthier's picture, the initial agreement is an agreement of producers in the sense that people who are capable of producing – and at least some of whom have already used their capacities to produce goods – make an agreement on how to distribute the goods produced in society. Since the goods to be distributed are the fruits of these people's labor,[21] since these goods are there in the first place only as a result of people's productive efforts, each party may use her own capacities as leverage in the initial bargain. However, if – as the pure utility maximizer suggests – the parties to the agreement are not permitted to use their specific capacities as leverage, then the agreement is not conceived of as a contract of producers about the fruits of their labor, but rather as

---

[21] Of course, this is not to be understood as a Marxist labor theory of value; Gauthier 1986, 110–112.

an agreement on how to distribute manna from heaven. The goods to be distributed in society, however, are not manna from heaven.[22]

It is not true, however, that the pure utility maximizer conceives of the goods to be distributed as manna. Her proposal is addressed to people in the current situation, and she thinks of all of her addressees as contributors to the production of goods in social interaction.[23] The important issue is how to distribute the goods produced by the addressees. According to the pure utility maximizer, the fact that some may contribute more in virtue of their better natural endowments does not, in itself, entitle them to a greater share or a better bargaining position. It is possible that the better endowed will be granted more in the social contract, but in order to avoid exploitation (by the now-familiar argument of the pure utility maximizer), they should not have a more advantageous bargaining position: if they are granted more, this should be done on the basis of utility maximization considerations.

6 THE SEPARATENESS OF PERSONS OBJECTION

Perhaps the most direct response in Gauthier's written work to the difficulty posed by the argument of the pure utility maximizer can be found in the following passage:

> At the outset of these reflections I referred to Weale's thesis [in Weale 1993] that "any adequate theory of justice will have to strike a justifiable balance between the principle of separateness of persons on the one hand and the ideal of a social union on the other." The *principle* of separateness is not the simple *fact* of separateness. How should we understand it? I suggest that the principle rests on the capacity each person has for a normative motivation, determining herself to act on what she takes to be reasons. Allan Gibbard (1990, pp. 56–7) suggests that "peculiar to human beings" is a "psychological faculty" that we might call "the *normative control system*." Gibbard suggests this system makes possible "both complex coordination among individuals and complex individual plans"; think of these as the roles of *intrapersonal*

---

[22] This is an interpretation of an argument offered by Gauthier in conversation. Cf. Nozick 1974, 149–150, 198.

[23] This raises the question of whether she addresses people who are arguably not contributors, such as the seriously disabled. This issue can be ignored, since the same question comes up in Gauthier's theory.

integration and *interpersonal coordination*. I interpret the former as leading to the idea of the individual as a normative unit, and the latter then as concerning the relations among these units. If this is indeed a correct interpretation of normative motivation, then it supports my emphasis on the normative separateness or independence of persons. [Footnote omitted.] This account affords no rationale for the *interpersonal integration* of persons into a single normative unit, and no basis for treating the natural differences of persons as arbitrary contingencies to be "corrected" in a "well-ordered society." I shall expand on my idea of a social union presently, but I want to insist that its primary role is to enable each individual to improve on her natural condition by effectively coordinating the exercise of her basic endowments with those of her fellows.[24]

According to Gauthier, the normative control system makes intrapersonal integration and interpersonal coordination possible. However, this idea of a normative control system "offers no rationale for the *interpersonal integration* of persons into a single normative unit." But given intrapersonally integrated individuals, there is a rationale for interpersonal coordination, since those individuals can benefit from coordination. Thus, assuming that the pure utility maximizer is demanding interpersonal integration, it would seem that Gauthier's argument presents her with a serious difficulty.

To answer his argument, it is important to remember that the question of rationale should be asked from the current situation. Gauthier's initial situation is composed of intrapersonally integrated individuals and it is presumably true that in that situation there is only a rationale for interpersonal coordination. However, the very question I have been asking is whether there is a rationale for people in the current situation to accept a contract made in that initial situation. And it seems to me that if this is the question being asked, then the idea of a normative control system offers no more of a rationale for the interpersonal coordination of already intrapersonally integrated individuals than it does for interpersonal integration.

The persons in the current situation are faced with the important choice of whether to accept the agreement in Gauthier's initial situation (which I am assuming requires the interpersonal coordination of already intrapersonally integrated individuals) or the pure

[24] Gauthier 1993b, 181.

utility maximizer's initial situation (which I am assuming requires what Gauthier calls "interpersonal integration"). Given that this is the choice that people face in the current situation, the question that they must ask is not whether the idea of a normative control system offers a rationale for interpersonal integration, but whether it offers a rationale for the interpersonal coordination of already intrapersonally integrated individuals *rather than* for interpersonal integration. And it seems to me that the answer to the latter question is surely "no." Pretty clearly, a person's normative control system not only makes possible intrapersonal integration and interpersonal coordination but also interpersonal integration. In fact, many people in the current situation will accept normative control systems that are designed to achieve interpersonal integration. Thus, I conclude that the idea of a normative control system gives no rationale one way or the other when the issue is a choice between interpersonal coordination of already intrapersonally integrated individuals, on the one hand, and interpersonal integration, on the other.

It might be argued that since the pure utility maximizer makes interpersonal integration a matter of justice rather than something which already intrapersonally integrated individuals may voluntarily choose (say, in the form of friendship), she lacks the rationale for her account that Gauthier has for his. All intrapersonally integrated individuals have a rationale for interpersonal coordination (since it brings them benefits), but only some have a rationale for interpersonal integration. Thus, interpersonal integration should be a matter of voluntary choice rather than a matter of justice.[25]

The answer to this last argument can be given in the form of a dilemma which reflects the structure of the line of reasoning I have been pursuing against Gauthier in this chapter. Gauthier must here be giving either a moral reason ("interpersonal integration violates individual integrity") or a utility maximization rationale against interpersonal integration. In the former case, he will fail to prove his case on non-moral grounds. In the latter case, he will simply be disputing that which the pure utility maximizer has been arguing for – namely, that there is a utility maximization rationale for inter-personal integration: she thinks that not only some, but all, people

---

[25] Again, I have tried to reconstruct an argument given by Gauthier in conversation.

(*qua* utility maximizers) in the current situation have a utility maximization rationale for interpersonal integration.[26]

I have now discussed several attempts to provide a utility maximization rationale for deciding the issue between Gauthier and the pure utility maximizer. Having argued that they are all a failure, I conclude that Gauthier has not succeeded in giving a non-moral justification of his construal of the initial situation. I therefore come to the conclusion that Gauthier has failed to give a non-moral solution to the moral alternatives problem.

Although I have only shown that Gauthier's rationalism is a failure, it is tempting to draw some further lessons from my argument. First, since we failed to settle the issue between the two different contractarian proposals on non-moral grounds, perhaps the issue should, after all, be settled on moral grounds. All contractarian ideas of a hypothetical situation require people in the current situation to abstract from their social and moral identities. The argument of this chapter suggests that the justification of these abstractions should itself be moral.[27] Second, it is tempting to conclude not only that Gauthier has failed to give a utility maximization rationale of his initial situation as he would construe it, but also that it is *in principle* not possible to give a utility maximization rationale of it. This then suggests that the utility maximization notion of rationality is simply not rich enough to deliver any substantive moral results. It is also tempting to generalize yet further and to conclude that no subjectivistic notions are rich enough to yield such results. Accordingly, although unable to argue for this here, I want to suggest that all subjectivistic rationalisms will face the same kind of problems as Gauthier's. In the next two chapters, I shall examine whether Habermas' inter-subjectivist rationalism fares any better.

[26] Remember that I have simply assumed that the pure utility maximizer's proposal amounts to that which Gauthier calls "interpersonal integration."
[27] As I mentioned earlier, this is how Rawls' reflective equilibrium justifications of a conception of justice should be understood.

8

Habermas' discourse ethics

In this and the following chapter, I shall discuss Habermas' moral theory. However, since my aim is only to argue that his rationalistic argument for certain moral principles is invalid, I deliberately leave out many aspects of his theory. In fact, I intend to explain no more and no less of Habermas' so-called "discourse-ethics" than is needed to present his rationalistic argument and my criticism of it. Bluntly put, I think that one of Habermas' central arguments for his discourse ethics is rationalistic, though his discourse ethical approach itself is not. Consequently, my argument will not be directed at his discourse ethics as such but only at this rationalistic argument. In this chapter I present his discourse ethics and his rationalistic argument, and in chapter 9 my criticism of the latter.

I THE BASIC IDEAS

Since *discourse* is one of Habermas' central concepts, I need to start by saying a few words about it. According to Habermas, if a practice is to count as discourse, then the participants in the practice must make certain *pragmatic presuppositions* (see 2.2): they must unavoidably presuppose that their interaction is (to a sufficient extent) regulated by certain conditions. We need to distinguish between two Habermasian ways of speaking about the presuppositions of discourse as *unavoidable*.

(1) In order for their interaction to count as discourse, each participant in it must presuppose that the discursive situation fulfills certain conditions (e.g., that all have a right to equal participation) to a sufficient extent. Even if these presuppositions are not completely fulfilled (e.g., if people do not in fact have equal rights to participate), the participants must proceed as if they are sufficiently fulfilled in order for the interaction to count as discourse. In this sense, the

making of these presuppositions by the participants *makes* this kind of practice (discourse) *possible*.[1] Other kinds of practice differ from discourse in that the participants are not conceptually required to make these presuppositions. For example, therapeutic talks are not a form of discourse, properly speaking. They are a well-defined form of communication, in which it would be inappropriate for the participants to make the presuppositions conceptually required for discourse.[2]

(2) There is another way in which the presuppositions of discourse (or better, of *rational* discourse) are unavoidable. The conditions that the participants must suppose to be sufficiently fulfilled if the practice is to count as discourse might, in fact, not be sufficiently fulfilled for the discourse to count as *rational* discourse. Thus, a practice might fail to count as *rational* discourse – not (as in the case of therapeutic talk) because the participants are not conceptually required to make certain presuppositions, but rather because the presuppositions that the participants make and are conceptually required to make are not in fact fulfilled.[3] Here we have another sense in which the presuppositions can count as unavoidable: no practice which does not actually sufficiently fulfill the conditions in question counts as a *rational* discourse.[4]

With the notion of rational discourse at hand, we can now turn to the centerpiece of Habermas' discourse ethics: the *discourse principle* (D). In his *Faktizität und Geltung*, Habermas formulates this principle in the following way: "Exactly those norms of action are valid which could meet with the consent of all the possibly affected parties as

---

[1] Habermas 1991f, 132–133, 160–162 [31, 54–57].

[2] Habermas 1987a, 42–43, 69–71 [20–21, 41–42]. I do not think this distinction between therapeutic talks and discourse is undermined by Habermas' recent widening of the application of the word "discourse" so as to allow talk of ethical discourses where "clinical knowledge" is of importance. It will nevertheless be possible to distinguish between different kinds of "discourses" in terms of the different presuppositions the participants are conceptually required to make (Habermas 1991e, 108–115 [8–14]; 1994, 197–201 [159–162]).

[3] Cf. Habermas 1994, 138–139 [107–108]; 1984b, 160–161; 1988d, 98–99 [88–89].

[4] Since Habermas does not now want to understand the presuppositions as representing ideals which could be more or less well realized, it could be argued that he does not count the presuppositions as unavoidable in this sense (Habermas 1994, 391–392 [322–323]). I leave this issue aside. For arguments to the effect that Habermas cannot fully avoid treating the presuppositions as such ideals, see Rehg 1994, 65, and Tietz 1993, 338–339.

participants in rational discourses."[5] This principle holds both for moral norms and for legal norms (*Rechtsnormen*). It specifies a generic sense of normative validity in which both moral and legal norms are valid. If either a moral or a legal norm fulfills the requirement of D, then it has been given an *impartial* justification.[6] Even though moral and legal norms fall under the same generic category of validity, they are in the final analysis not valid in the same sense (moral norms are "right" or "just" whereas legal norms are "legitimate"). Moral and legal norms are not justified in the same way, since they are not required to be accepted in exactly the same discourses.[7]

According to Habermas, moral commands are categorical imperatives. The sense in which one *should* carry out a moral command is not that doing so would be good for me as an individual or good for my community. A moral norm is only valid if everyone can will that this norm be followed by everyone in similar circumstances. "Everyone" does not just mean everyone in my community, but rather each subject capable of action and communication. Moral norms are justified in moral discourses and moral discourses are open to all such subjects. The aim of moral discourses is to agree on a norm for the regulation of interaction which expresses a universalizable interest.[8]

Given that this is the aim of moral discourses, each participant is required to consider a candidate norm from the point of view of each other participant. They are not just to do this imaginatively, but rather to convince each other that this norm is acceptable from the standpoint of each and every subject capable of action and communication. This requirement for how to proceed in moral discourses amounts to a rule of argumentation for these discourses. Habermas calls this rule the "*moral principle*" (or the "*principle of universalization*" ["U"]):[9]

---

5 Habermas 1994, 138 [107]. Unless I mention that a direct quote from Habermas is a modified or an unchanged version of a published English translation, the translation is mine. However, even if mine, I have sometimes borrowed phrases from the existing translations.

6 Habermas 1994, 138–143 [107–111]. For a discussion of the problems relating to understanding D as holding for both moral and legal norms in this way, see Kettner 1999.

7 Habermas 1994, 192–194 [155–157].

8 Habermas 1994, 194, 200 [156–157, 161–162]; 1991e, 107–108, 112–114 [7–8, 12–13]; 1991f, 168–170 [62–63].

9 Habermas 1987b, 141–147 [92–96]; 1988d, 75–77 [65–67]; 1991d, 60–62 [235–236]; 1994, 140–141, 282 [108–110, 230].

A norm is valid if and only if *all* the affected can *jointly* [*gemeinsam*] and freely [*zwanglos*] accept the consequences and side effects its general observance can be anticipated to have for the interests and value-orientations of *each* single one.[10]

In order to explain how Habermas understands this principle, it is best to start by making clear how it is *not* to be interpreted. The agreement that the parties who reason in terms of this principle aim to reach must be distinguished from three other kinds of agreements.

(1) With respect to the first kind of agreement, the agents interact *strategically* with each other in the following sense:[11] each of them is only concerned with getting an agreement that she herself has a good reason to accept, whether or not the other agents have a good reason to accept it. Thus, the ultimate aim of each agent is to influence the others in such a way that they will make an agreement that she herself has a good reason to accept: showing others that they do in fact – from their point of view   have a good reason to accept the agreement is viewed as merely one means among others that the agent can employ to get others to accept an agreement that is favorable to herself. Other means might be threats and deception.

(2) The second case is just like the first, except that the conditions under which the agreement is made have been somehow so designed that each party has a fair chance of promoting her own interests. Such an agreement might be called a fair compromise.[12]

(3) The third case differs from the other two in that there is a sense in which the parties do not interact strategically with each other. Instead, each party is concerned with reaching an agreement that all the others also have a good reason to accept. However, each is concerned with ensuring that each has a good reason to make the agreement from her *own point of view*. Thus, the parties may all have very different reasons for making the agreement. We might call this an agreement of "benevolent strategic reasoners." Since each of the parties is "benevolent," she wants all the others to get a good deal. Nevertheless, it is a matter of getting a deal: the agreement is guided only by the different individual goods, each of which is judged to be

[10] Habermas 1996, 60. Cf. Habermas 1988d, 75–76, [65]; 1988e, 131 [120]; 1991b, 12 [197]; 1991c, 32; 1991f, 134 [32].
[11] For Habermas' explication of strategic action, see Habermas 1987a, 129–132 [86–88]; 1984e, 571–579; 1988f, 64–75.
[12] Habermas 1994, 205–206 [166–167].

good from the standpoint of some individual. The interaction is not strategic, however, in the sense that each person is "benevolent": she tries to make sure that all the others also have a good reason to accept the agreement from their own point of view.

At first it might seem that these "benevolent strategic reasoners" fulfill the requirement that U is supposed to make, namely that each party take up the perspective of other parties and make sure that the conclusion is also acceptable from their point of view. Each party is benevolent and is thus willing to sacrifice some of her interest in order to ensure that the interests of others are better satisfied. This, however, is not how Habermas wants to understand U.[13] U is supposed to require that the conclusion of the discourse is accepted by all the participants for the same reason (rather than for different "agent-relative" reasons plus the common reason of benevolence) and for a reason that ceases to be a reason for the others if it ceases to be a reason for one of them. Since U is supposed to articulate what it means that a norm expresses a universalizable interest, it is the participants' common insight into a universalizable interest which is supposed to be their common reason for accepting the norm.[14]

According to Habermas, legal norms do not have the universal application that moral norms do. Law (*Recht*) serves as a medium of self-organization for communities in particular historical circumstances. Thus, the legitimacy of legal norms – as opposed to the rightness of moral norms – is dependent upon the goals of the members of those communities. A legitimate legal norm must be consistent with the outcome of moral discourses, but more than a moral discourse is needed for its legitimation. Legal norms also need to be filtered through other processes such as pragmatic discourses, ethical–political discourses, and fair negotiations. Contrary to moral discourses, these forums do not produce outcomes which all communicative subjects must accept.[15] In the following, I will discuss D only insofar as it concerns the justification of *moral* norms.

---

[13] I leave aside the issue of whether his *formulation* of U captures his intention.

[14] Habermas 1996, 60; 1988d, 75–78, 82–86 [65–68, 72–76]; 1973, 148–155 [107–112].

[15] Habermas 1994, 187–207, 221–226, 677 [151–168, 180–184, 459–460]. In moral discourses, what Habermas calls "pragmatic" and "ethical" reasons do have a role to play in the articulation of the "interests" and "value-orientations" (see the formulation of U) of the participants. However, in the course of the use of U in moral discourses, these reasons only serve as input to be turned into a common reason

Habermas emphasizes that D is to be interpreted as saying that substantive moral norms derive their justification from *real* and public discourses among the affected parties.[16] Thus, the role of discourse in Habermas' theory is different from the role of the original position in Rawls' theory. The construction of the original position allows the theorist to arrive at certain substantive conclusions, such as Rawls' difference principle. In contrast, D is not meant to give the theorist a tool to generate substantive moral rules.[17] Substantive moral norms are justified by being the conclusion of a real discourse of the affected parties, and it is not the job of the moral theorist to come up with a theoretical construction from which substantive norms can be derived.[18]

It follows that in order to justify a norm it is *not enough* to refer to the result of a *hypothetical* discourse: a norm has not been adequately justified unless a real discourse has been carried out.[19] And a real discourse is carried out by the *actual* individuals affected by the norm.[20] In this respect, Habermas' justificatory framework differs from both Rawls' and Gauthier's. The parties to Rawls' original position differ from the actual individuals of the society for which they are to choose the fundamental principles of interaction, e.g., in that they do not know their position in that society; they make their choice behind a veil of ignorance.[21] The agents in Gauthier's *ex ante* position have not been placed behind any veil of ignorance by the theorist, but their agreement is nevertheless a hypothetical one. It is the agreement actual individuals *would have* rationally made in the *ex ante* position (see 6.2).

acceptable to everybody (see Habermas 1996, 60). Thus, moral norms do not depend on pragmatic and ethical reasons in the same sense as legal norms do.

[16] Habermas 1988d, 76–78, 103–104 [66–68, 93–94]; 1988e, 133 [122]; 1991d, 60–62 [235–236]; 1991f, 156, 171 [51, 64]; 1996, 46–49. The subjunctive formulation of D obscures this feature of discourse ethics. I believe that the use of the subjunctive is an attempt to make clear that the fact that a norm has actually been agreed to in a real discourse does not guarantee its validity.

[17] Habermas 1988d, 76–77 [66–67]; 1988e, 133 [122].

[18] Habermas 1988d, 96 [85–86]; 1991f, 124–125 [24–25]; 1995, 117–119, 126–131.

[19] As I understand Habermas, it may not be appropriate in all circumstances to engage in an actual discourse about a moral norm, but the ultimate justification of it requires that such a discourse take place. See Habermas 1988d, 104 [94].

[20] Habermas 1991f, 163–164 [57–58].

[21] I do not mean to imply that acceptability in the original position is the ultimate justification of principles of justice for Rawls; see the discussion later in this section and 6.2.

Even though it is *necessary* for the justification of a norm to have been agreed to in real discourse, it is *not sufficient* that agreement has been reached in *some* real discourse among all the affected parties. First, the parties must reason in terms of U. Second, the agreement cannot be taken as definitive, if the real discourse in which the parties reason in terms of U fails to fulfill certain ideal conditions – if it falls short of a *rational* discourse.[22] The discourse required by D is conducted by actual individuals and it is not hypothetical, but these individuals and the conditions under which the real discourse takes place are subject to criticism from the standpoint of D if they do not adhere (in so far as this is reasonable in the given situation)[23] to the conditions of ideal discourse.

The point of these ideal conditions is to ensure that that there is no systematic distortion of the communication between the parties to the discourse,[24] and that the discourse stands under no other constraint than the force of the better argument.[25] Habermas explicates these ideas of "undistorted communication" and "the force of the better argument" in terms of the *formal* qualities of a speech situation.[26]

Since Habermas does not want to commit himself to an exhaustive specification of these formal conditions,[27] I let it suffice to mention the conditions which are of central importance for *moral* discourse (and for Habermas' up-argument for U):

(3.1) Every subject capable of speech and action may participate in discourses.

(3.2) a. Everyone may problematize any assertion.

b. Everyone may introduce any assertion into the discourse.

c. Everyone may express his attitudes, wishes, and needs.

(3.3) No speaker may be prevented by force existing inside or outside of the discourse from claiming his rights as laid down in (3.1) and (3.2).[28]

---

[22] Habermas 1984b, 160–161, 179.

[23] Cf. Habermas 1991f, 136–137 [34–35].

[24] Habermas 1984b, 177.

[25] Habermas 1984b, 161; 1987a, 47–48 [24–25].

[26] Habermas 1984b, 161, 177.

[27] Habermas 1987a, 47 [25]; 1988d, 98–99 [88].

[28] Habermas 1988d, 99 [89]. Habermas borrows these rules from Alexy 1978. Cf. Habermas' own previous analysis in Habermas 1984b, 177–178. The argument for U in Habermas 1996 relies on differently formulated rules. These will be introduced in my discussion of this argument in 9.2.

These rules of discourse must be distinguished from the moral norms which are to be justified in real discourses. D says that only those norms are valid which would be agreed to in real discourses, and the above-listed rules lay down some of the conditions under which the real discourses should take place. These rules must also be distinguished from U: these rules define the conditions under which the discourse is to take place, whereas U is a rule of argumentation in terms of which the parties are to reason.[29] Moral norms are valid if and only if they express a universalizable interest and U is supposed to explicate what it is to express such an interest. The point of insisting that norms be justified in real discourses is precisely that only in real discourses can it be tested whether something is a universalizable interest.[30] Thus, in order to be justified in taking a norm to be morally valid, we must not only have agreed to it in discourse fulfilling certain formal conditions but also have good reasons for thinking that the norm expresses a universalizable interest. Of course, these reasons are always open to a renewed discursive criticism.

In summary, if we are to be justified in taking a norm to be morally valid, three conditions must be fulfilled:

1. the norm has been agreed to in a real discourse.
2. this real discourse fulfills certain formal conditions to a sufficient extent.

[29] Habermas 1988d, 103–104 [93–94].
[30] Habermas 1988d, 75–78 [65–68]; 1984d, 532 [257]. This might suggest that the relation between discourses and moral validity is merely an *epistemic* one: moral validity is defined in terms of universalizable interests and discourses are merely the best means of discovering what interests are universalizable. Such a reading – as an interpretation of a strand in discourse ethics rather than of Habermas' official view – is developed in Davis 1994. Habermas would reject this epistemic account of the relation in favor of a *constitutive* one: just as validity is to be understood in terms of reasons for validity claims, universalizable interests are to be understood in terms of the reasons for taking something to be a universalizable interest, and in both cases the reasons must be understood discursively. I take it that this is why Habermas explicates the notion of universalizable interests via a rule for argumentation in discourse (see Habermas 1988d, 75–78 [65–68]; 1996, 54–55; 1998, 187–188, 194–198, 201–205). It seems to me that this also favors understanding universalizable interests not as preexisting interests which people happen to share, but as interests formed and transformed in discourse (see Benhabib 1986, 310–315; Habermas 1998, 203). For a discussion of Habermas' thesis that there is an immanent (as opposed to merely epistemic) relation between validity in general and discursive reasons, see Gunnarsson 1995b, 90–115, 258–269. (It should be noted here that these pages in Gunnarsson 1995b are based on Gunnarsson 1994, but include important revisions.)

3. the agreement on the norm was supported by good reasons for taking the norm to express a universalizable interest.

A distinction can be made between a weak version and a strong version of D, WD and SD.[31] D makes the validity of a norm dependent upon agreement in discourse. On the weak version of D, WD, it is *not excluded* that the agreement in question is an agreement which is only *indirectly* about the norm in question. In other words, it is not excluded that the affected parties would in rational discourse agree that norms affecting them should not be discussed directly. Rather than discussing the pros and cons of these norms directly, they could agree that the validity of these norms should be decided by the principle of utility, or they could agree that the validity of these norms should be decided in a Rawlsian original position, etc. On this account, the validity of, e.g., the principle of utility would derive from the fact that *it* would be *directly* agreed upon by the affected parties. WD can be formulated in the following way:

> Exactly those norms of action are valid which could be DIRECTLY OR INDIRECTLY agreed to by all the affected parties as participants in rational discourses. A norm of action has been indirectly agreed to if and only if it has been justified by a principle which could be directly agreed to.

One way of formulating WD would be that it requires that *principles of justification* be directly agreed upon and allows that *norms* (justified by the principles of justification) not be directly agreed upon. However, it requires that a norm be agreed upon in the sense that its justification must be derived from a principle which has been directly agreed upon.

WD could be a part of a "utilitarian" or a "Rawlsian" justificatory scheme. Thus, a utilitarian could answer the question "Why should one accept the principle of utility?" by saying that it is justified by WD. Similarly, a Rawlsian could respond to "Why should one accept the norms chosen in the original position?" by arguing that all

---

[31] I draw this distinction in Gunnarsson 1995a, which is based on a talk delivered at the 16th World Congress in Philosophy of Law and Social Philosophy in May 1993.

the parties affected by these norms would as participants in rational discourses agree that the norms are properly justified by a choice in an original position rather than by direct discussion of these norms by parties who know their own interests. In this Rawlsian justificatory scheme, rational discourse would be playing the role that is played in Rawls' own theory by the point of view of you and me.[32] The strong version of D, SD, requires that norms be discussed directly:

> Exactly those norms of action are valid which could be DIRECTLY agreed to by all the affected parties as participants in rational discourses.

SD excludes the possibility that the parties agree not to discuss every norm directly. Or more precisely, the parties may be allowed only for the sake of *convenience* not to discuss each norm directly, but the validity of all norms (including the ones not discussed directly) will nevertheless depend on whether it would be agreed upon in a direct discussion about it among the affected parties.

Just as WD can be combined with utilitarianism and Rawlsianism, it can also be combined with SD. SD would then be treated as a principle of justification which is itself justified by WD. In response to the question "Why should it be required that norms be directly discussed by the affected parties?" the answer would be that the affected parties, as participants in a rational discourse, would agree that this is the proper way of justifying norms.

A brief comparison with Rawls' theory is useful in this context. SD is a principle of justification which *competes* with the original position as a principle of justification. WD does not. This affects the way in which the call for real discourses must be interpreted in each case. In the case of SD, it means that the justification of substantive principles of justice requires direct discussion of those principles by people who know their own interests *rather than* support from the choice that would be made by parties in an original position.[33] The aim of the

---

[32] Rawls 1993, 28; see also my 6.2.

[33] This does not mean that SD itself – without the direct discussion called for by SD – does not have normative implications for the institutions of society. According to Habermas' *democracy principle* – where the democracy principle is D transformed into the form it needs to take if the norms in question are legal norms – only those laws are legitimate which can meet with the consent of all comrades in law (*Rechtsgenossen*) in a discursive legislative process. The talk of a discursive legislative process is to be taken seriously. The idea is *not* that the conclusion of a legislative process – which may or may not itself be discursive – is to be checked against the conclusion of some discourses which are themselves not part of the system of law. It is supposed to be a nor-

direct discussion is to find out which interests are universalizable: U seems to be designed as a rule of argumentation for SD-discourses, whereas the validity of SD and U may be in question in WD-discourses. In the case of WD, the justification given in real discourses does not compete with the employment of the original position as part of a justificatory scheme. Real discourses may rather serve to justify this employment and serve as a check upon the principles accepted in the original position and upon the construction of that position itself.

Since Habermas seems to take D to be in competition with the original position in this way, SD seems to be his intended understanding of D.[34] The distinction between SD and WD throws some light on Habermas' criticism of Rawls to the effect that the original position is a "monological" position that allows Rawls to act as an "expert" on justice.[35] In reply to this criticism, Rawls writes:

> Habermas sometimes says that the original position is monological and not dialogical; that is because all the parties have, in effect, the same reasons and so select the same principles. This is said to have the serious fault of leaving it to "the philosopher" as an expert and not to citizens of an ongoing society to determine the political conception of justice . . . The reply I make to his objection . . . is that it is you and me – and so all citizens over time, one by one and in association here and there – who judge the merits of the original position as a device of representation and the principles it yields. I deny that the original position is monological in a way that puts in doubt its soundness as a device of representation.[36]

Habermas' criticism of Rawls stems from Habermas' acceptance of SD, and Rawls responds, I venture to say, by pointing out the compatibility of his theory with acceptance of WD (assuming that the

mative consequence of D itself that the legislative processes themselves be discursive (Habermas 1994, 138–143, 153–155, 160–162 [107–111, 120–122, 126–128]). As I have argued in Gunnarsson 1995a, this is a plausible claim only for SD, and not for WD.

[34] Habermas 1991d, 54–62 [228–236]; 1995, 117–119, 126–131. It should be noted, however, that the distinction between SD and WD is mine, not Habermas'.
[35] Habermas 1988d, 76–77 [66]; cf. Habermas 1991d, 54–58 [228–231]; 1995, 117–119, 126–131.
[36] Rawls 1995, 140n.

topic and resources of WD are restricted to the political in Rawls' sense).[37]

Before discussing, in the remainder of this chapter, Habermas' rationalistic justification of U, I should stress that D and U themselves have no rationalistic implications. According to these principles, norms are to be supported in discourses by reasons which show that these norms express a universalizable interest. Obviously, one can accept that norms are to be justified in this way without assuming that the reasons offered in discourse for these norms, or D and U themselves, must be shown to be acceptable to a moral skeptic. My arguments against Habermas' rationalism are therefore in no way directed at the principles D and U.

3 THE AIM OF THE RATIONALISTIC ARGUMENT

Habermas presents his argument for U as an answer to a certain kind of skepticism. Before spelling out what kind of skepticism this is, a few remarks on what the argument is not supposed to accomplish are in order. First, Habermas notes that the argument is not supposed to, as it were, make weakness of the will impossible: nothing can guarantee that those who have an insight into what their duty is can actually be brought to (intend to) act on it.[38] Second, in addition to not being designed to add a special *motivational force* to moral insights, Habermas' argument for U is not meant to add any *moral binding force* to norms and imperatives. According to Habermas, one can explain the moral binding force of norms not in terms of the argument for U itself, but rather because these norms could have been agreed to in a discourse where U is the rule of discourse argumentation.[39] Thus, as I understand Habermas, he does not employ an up-argument to explicate the categorical force of morality.[40] Third, the argument for U is not supposed to open people's eyes to the moral perspective.

---

[37] See Rawls 1995, 139–142. Since reflective equilibrium is the test by which political conceptions are assessed from the point of view of you and me, perfect compatibility of WD with Rawls' theory would also require that assessment of reasons in a WD-discourse can be understood in the same way.

[38] Habermas 1991f, 135–137, 184 [33–35, 75].

[39] Habermas 1991f, 132–135, 187–188 [31–33, 78–79]; 1996, 62–63. However, it seems that according to Habermas it is a necessary condition of the tenability of such an explanation of moral binding force that U be shown to be universally valid (see the next passage quoted from Habermas).

[40] As I already mentioned in 2.2, in this he differs from Apel and Kuhlmann.

According to Habermas, philosophical arguments are not the best means to bring people to see things from a moral point of view. Fourth, this argument is not meant to diffuse the cynicism of those who – even though capable of seeing things from a moral perspective – do not see the point of leading a moral life. Doing that would require making claims about the ingredients of a meaningful life and no such claims are universally valid.[41]

What *is* the argument for U supposed to accomplish? Habermas writes:

> The demonstration that the moral point of view, as expressed by (U), is generally valid and does not merely express a culture-specific or class-specific evaluative orientation prevents us from succumbing to a relativism that robs moral commands of their meaning and moral obligations of their peculiar force. Hence moral theory is competent to clarify the moral point of view and justify its universality.[42]

The goal is to establish two non-trivial results: that questions of justice do admit of rational answers and how – that is, by means of which rule of argumentation or which moral principle – they can be answered.[43]

In the light of these remarks, the most natural interpretation of the aim of the argument for U is the following: the argument is supposed to demonstrate the universal validity of U. And if U has been shown to be universally valid, then it has thereby been shown that it does not just express intuitions specific to a certain culture (the problem of ethnocentricity[44]) and that (by using U) questions of justice can be resolved rationally. Since Habermas' concern does not seem to be the question whether it is rational to have *a* sense of justice, but rather the question whether it can be rationally settled *which* principle of justice to accept, I assume that he has here the moral alternatives problem rather than the basic choice problem in mind.

In the next chapter, I will argue that Habermas' argument can demonstrate *at most* the validity of WD. Given this interpretation of the aim of the argument for U, it seems that my argument, if successful, would show that Habermas does not reach his aim: since

41 Habermas 1991f, 184–185 [75–76].
42 Habermas 1991f, 185 [76; unchanged translation].
43 Habermas 1991f, 186 [76–77; modified translation].
44 Habermas 1988d, 86–89 [76–78]; 1991b, 12–13 [197–198]; 1996, 61.

the solution of the ethnocentricity problem and the moral alternatives problem seems to be dependent upon demonstrating the universal validity of U, and since U is a rule of argumentation for SD-discourses rather than WD-discourses (where its validity may be in question), doing no more than demonstrating the validity of WD would seem to leave the two problems unresolved.[45]

In arguing that U does not follow from Habermas' argument, I will be understanding the argument for U as a rationalistic argument. In other words, I will understand it as an argument which is supposed to address the skeptic on her own grounds and which is meant to show that, given the skeptic's aspirations, she must also accept U. Thus, my argument will be that, given these rationalistic restrictions on the interpretation of the premises of the argument for U, the conclusion does not follow. In the rest of this chapter, I will elaborate on the structure of this argument and argue that it is indeed intended as a rationalistic argument.

4 THE STRUCTURE AND STATUS OF THE ARGUMENT

Habermas' remarks about the skeptic to whom the argument for U is addressed strongly suggest that he understands it as a rationalistic argument. In the paper in which Habermas offers the first formulation of the argument for U, he refers to it as an up-argument.[46] He describes how up-arguments with a normative conclusion must be able to avoid the charge that this conclusion was simply built into the characterization of the practice which is supposed to have this

---

[45] Of course, I am not suggesting that these two problems cannot be overcome. The point of comparing rationalism and the substantive approach is precisely to show that the aspiration for rationalistic justifications in ethics is misguided. Once this has become clear, then the two problems will dissolve as philosophical problems, although in real life it will continue to be a worry whether we are in fact justified in taking up a certain position, or whether this simply reflects our prejudices (see 11.4). Here I am simply arguing that the argument for U falls short of solving these two problems.

[46] As already discussed in 2.2, the notion of an up-argument can be explained in terms of the concepts of *inescapable presuppositions* and a *performative self-contradiction*. For example, in asserting "I do not (here and now) exist" I *inescapably* make a presupposition whose propositional content can be expressed by "I do (here and now) exist" which in turn *contradicts* the propositional content of the first assertion. The contradiction is *performative* in the sense that it amounts to a contradiction between the presupposition of the first assertion as a performance or action (assertion in its performative sense) and the propositional content of the first assertion.

"conclusion" as a pragmatic presupposition. He seems to want to join Apel's response to this charge by offering an up-argument which does not uncover the presuppositions of *moral* argumentation, but of argumentation *as such*: "With this argumentative strategy he [Apel] reaches also the skeptic who is set on a meta-ethical treatment of moral-theoretic questions and consequently refuses to be drawn into *moral* argumentation."[47] This suggests that Habermas understands the argument for U as an argument which is supposed to meet the moral skeptic on her own ground in just the way required by rationalistic up-justifications (see 2.2): the moral skeptic aspires to be rational in the formal sense – she aspires to meet all the requirements of argumentation as such – and the up-argument is meant to show that she must thereby willy-nilly accept a certain moral principle.[48] Habermas writes:

> The role which the transcendental pragmatic argument can play there [in the justification of U] may now be so described that with its help it can be shown *how the principle of universalization, which functions as a rule of argumentation, is implied by the presuppositions of argumentation as such.* In order to meet this requirement it suffices to show the following: each one who accepts the universal and necessary presuppositions of argumentative speech, and who knows what it means to justify a norm of action, must implicitly assume the validity of the principle of universalization.[49]

The italicized phrase supports understanding the argument for U as a rationalistic argument in just the way I have described. However, the way in which he continues in this passage to elaborate on how this argument is to be carried out complicates the matter. He does not say that U is shown to be implicitly assumed by everyone who only

---

[47] Habermas 1988d, 95 [85; modified translation].
[48] Habermas' replies to the skeptic who refuses to engage in argumentation and the skeptic who declines to act communicatively at all are different and I will not discuss them in the text. These replies are themselves not strictly speaking rationalistic, since they do not seem to appeal only to the skeptic's ambition to be rational in the formal sense. In both cases, Habermas says that the only way open if one completely rejects argumentation and communicative action would be suicide or severe mental illness (Habermas 1988d, 109–112 [99–102]; cf. Habermas 1998, 207–208). Assuming that the unattractiveness of suicide and severe mental illness is to be explained purely non-morally, these replies might nevertheless be understood as having the rationalistic ambition of justifying morality on non-moral grounds.
[49] Habermas 1988d, 97 [86].

fulfills the condition that she accept the presuppositions of argumentative speech. Rather, it is supposed to be implicitly assumed by anybody who *both* (1) accepts the presuppositions of argumentative speech *and* (2) knows what it means to justify norms of action[50] (knows what it means to discuss hypothetically whether action norms should be put into force[51]). In fact, it seems that Habermas is *not* offering an *up-argument* for U at all. Rather, the argument for U has *two premises*, from which U follows, as Habermas puts it, by "material implication."[52] The first premise states the presuppositions of argumentation as such and is itself supported by an up-argument. The second premise states what is involved in justifying a norm.[53] This complicates the question of whether Habermas' argument is really a rationalistic argument. To answer the question, we must consider how he might want to justify the first two premises and the claim that U follows from them by material implication.

It is clear that the first premise is to be supported by a rationalistic up-argument. The argument is addressed to a moral skeptic who aspires to engage in rational argumentation, and it is meant to show her that, as a participant in such an argumentation, she must make certain pragmatic presuppositions, since the making of such presuppositions is what makes rational argumentation possible in the first place.[54] Since these presuppositions make argumentation possible in the first place, the moral skeptic has no alternative but to make them, insofar as she wants to engage in rational discourse. That there is no alternative to these as the conditions of rational discourse, however, need not mean that in the future there will be no alternative to them. A fundamental change in our form of life might change the conditions of rational discourse. As things stand, though, there is no alternative.[55]

---

[50] Habermas 1988d, 97 [86]; 1991f, 133–134 [31–32].
[51] Habermas 1988d, 103 [92]. See also Habermas 1996, 59–63; there Habermas offers a new formulation of his argument for U which is less explicitly rationalistic in its intentions. I discuss and criticize this version of the argument in 9.2.
[52] Habermas 1988d, 107 [97]. Ott 1996 (13–14) argues that Habermas is mistaken to speak here of a *material* implication.
[53] Habermas 1988d, 92–93, 97–103, 106–107 [82, 86–93, 97]; 1991f, 133 [32].
[54] Habermas 1988d, 95–102, 109 [84–92, 99]; 1991f, 132–133 [31–32].
[55] Habermas 1991f, 194–195 [83–84]; 1988d, 105–106 [95–96]. These remarks are supposed to anticipate a disagreement between Habermas, on the one hand, and Apel and Kuhlmann on the other hand, since the latter believe that there is not only no alternative to these conditions as things stand, but *absolutely* no alternative (see the Appendix).

It is less clear whether the justifications of the second premise and of the claim that U follows by material implication are rationalistic. Habermas distinguishes between (1) U, (2) the substantive norms which are the object of the practical discourse, (3) the normative content of the presuppositions of argumentation, and (4) D. The difference between U and the presuppositions of argumentation is that the former functions as a rule of argumentation *within discourse*, whereas the latter are (possibly counter-factual) presuppositions which people must make in order to make *discourse possible in the first place*.[56] This distinction opens up the possibility that U might not be "unavoidably presupposed" in the same sense as the presuppositions of argumentation. If it is not "unavoidably presupposed" in the same way, either the second premise must have a different status than the first, or the material implication must not transfer the "unavoidability" of the premises to the conclusion. Even if U does not have the same "unavoidability" as the presuppositions of argumentation, however, it is supposed to be universally valid.[57] And it seems that Habermas is very much concerned that the second premise be acceptable to the moral skeptic on her own grounds:

> The program of justification pursued by discourse ethics sets itself the task of deriving from suppositions of rationality of this kind [the presuppositions which make rational argumentation possible] a rule of argumentation [U] for discourses in which moral norms can be justified. In this way it is to be shown that moral questions can at all be rationally decided. Among the premises of such a "derivation," moreover, belong not only the suppositions of rational argumentation as such (expressed in the form of rules) but also a more detailed specification of what we intuitively appeal to when we wish to *justify* a moral action or an underlying moral norm. Knowing what "to justify" means in this context does not of itself prejudge the further question of whether moral justifications and justificatory discourses are at all possible. This further issue is to be resolved by specifying a rule of argumentation that can perform a role in practical discourses similar, for example, to that played by the principle of induction in empirical–theoretical discourses.
>
> Controversies concerning assertions make clear what justifications

56 Habermas 1988d, 101–104 [91–94]; 1991f, 132–133 [31]. Habermas emphasizes that U is a rule of argumentation, whereas he seems to believe that it is optional to present the presuppositions of argumentation in rule-form.
57 Habermas 1991b, 12–13 [197–198]; 1991f, 194–195 [83–84].

consist in and are generally supposed to accomplish. They resolve disputes [*Dissens*] about facts – disputes, that is, concerning the truth of the corresponding assertion – through arguments, and thereby lead to an argumentatively achieved consensus. Furthermore, we know from everyday life what disputes concerning the rightness of normative sentences involve. We have an intuitive mastery of the language game of norm-guided action in which agents adhere to or deviate from rules while possessing rights and duties that can clash with one another and lead to practical conflicts understood in normative terms. Thus, we also know that moral justifications resolve disputes concerning rights and duties, that is, concerning the rightness of the corresponding normative statements.[58]

It is important that the explication of the second premise – the explication of what it means to justify a norm – is supposed to be thin enough to not prejudge the answer to the question whether "moral questions can at all be rationally decided" and the question whether "moral justifications and justificatory discourses are at all possible." This explication is supposed to represent a weak sense of what it means to justify norms:[59] "The idea of the justification of norms may not be too strong and may not already introduce into the premises that which is to be concluded – namely, that justified norms must be able to meet with the consent of all those affected."[60] Precisely to avoid making the second premise too strong, Habermas changed the formulation of the second premise (in the second edition of the paper in which the first formulation of the argument for U is presented).[61]

This makes it plausible that Habermas' argument is addressed to a skeptic who is willing to accept a minimal characterization of what it *would* mean to justify norms, if it *were* possible to justify them.[62] Habermas' skeptic, however, questions whether these "justifications" are *real* justifications, *real* in the sense of rationally showing which moral position to adopt, and consequently, she questions whether

---

[58] Habermas 1991f, 133–134 [31–32; modified translation]; cf. Habermas 1996, 59–61.

[59] Habermas 1991f, 134 [32].

[60] Habermas 1991b, 13n [212 (endnote 7)]. Thus, the remark at the end of the long passage to the effect that moral justifications dissolve disputes over the correctness of normative statements is not supposed to say already that those norms are correct upon which all the affected could agree.

[61] Habermas 1991f, 134n [179 (endnote 17)]; Habermas 1991b, 13n [212 (endnote 7)].

[62] See Habermas 1996, 59.

one way of going beyond this minimal characterization to flesh out how norms are to be justified is more rational than another. Now if his argument is addressed to such a skeptic, it is safe to assume that Habermas is indeed offering a rationalistic argument: the skeptic aspires to respect all the rules that argumentation as such requires (first premise), and she aspires to have a clear sense of what a justification of norms would minimally amount to, if there were indeed any such justification, which she wants to remain skeptical about (second premise). And it is to be shown that to fulfill these aspirations, she must willy-nilly accept U.[63]

5 WEAK AND STRONG RATIONALISM

In order to clarify further what it means to say that Habermas' argument is rationalistic, it might help to consider the following possible response to his argument: "I do *not* doubt that U follows from the two premises. However, I find U morally counter-intuitive; it seems to me that other rules of argumentation capture better how we *should* reason about moral issues. Therefore, I conclude that one of the two premises must be rejected." Does the fact that Habermas' argument is rationalistic commit him to consider it *irrelevant* if the principle following from the two premises is morally counter-intuitive, and thus to assume that this response can *never* be a good response to the argument for U? I think that it does not.[64] We must distinguish between two positions, only one of which is part of rationalism as such:

Weak rationalism (WR): It is possible to justify a principle (a principle doubted by the moral skeptic) from premises which the moral skeptic herself endorses.

Strong rationalism (SR): If our moral intuitions conflict with a principle thus justified, this principle takes precedence.

---

[63] Habermas 1991f, 134 [32].

[64] I suppose that he is committed to rejecting it if this response involves a rejection of the *first* premise. Anybody who agrees to argue must presuppose the first premise. Thus, if U followed from the first premise alone, the person who finds U morally objectionable would simply have to alter her moral judgment: assuming that the first premise is indeed presupposed in all argumentation, it will also be presupposed in argumentation about the validity of U.

Gauthier's view is certainly strongly rationalistic.[65] However, only WR is part of rationalism as I have defined it. And if one assumes that the response under discussion here is *never* a good response, one must accept SR. What I have been arguing is that Habermas is committed to WR and wants to offer a rationalistic justification of U. It is less clear whether he is also committed to SR. WR certainly does not imply SR: even though a theorist believes WR and aspires to give a rationalistic justification, she may herself reject SR and allow moral intuitions to take precedence over the rationalistically justified principle.[66]

Even though Habermas may think that the kind of response under discussion here is sometimes a good response (given that he may not accept SR), nothing which is not acceptable to the moral skeptic may go into the construction of his rationalistic justification of U. And even though we may *arrive at* the formulation of U by bringing our intuitions – including moral intuitions – into reflective equilibrium, the *rationalistic justification* of U may not appeal to any intuitions doubted by the moral skeptic. In this way, the rationalistic justification of U is meant to demonstrate its universal validity:

> A discourse theory of ethics, for which I have just[67] presented a program of justification, is not a self-contained endeavor; it holds universalistic [*universalistisch*], and thus very strong theses, but claims for those theses a relatively weak status. Essentially, the justification consists of two steps. First, a principle of universalization (U) is introduced as a rule of argumentation for practical discourses; second, this rule is justified from the content of the pragmatic presuppositions of argumentation as such in connection with an explication of the sense of normative validity claims. The principle of universalization can be understood – on the model of Rawls' reflective equilibrium – as a reconstruction [*Rekonstruktion*] of those everyday intuitions underlying the impartial judging of moral conflicts of action. The second step, which is designed to show the universal [*allgemein*] validity of U, a validity which ranges beyond the perspective of a particular culture,

---

[65] Gauthier 1991a, 18–20.
[66] It should be noted that SR is indeed a plausible principle. In my argument (in 5.1) to the effect that McDowell does not succeed in undermining the motivation to give rationalistic justifications, I appealed, in effect, to SR.
[67] The reference is to Habermas 1988d.

relies on a transcendental-pragmatic demonstration of universal [*allge-mein*] and necessary presuppositions of argumentation.[68]

As I understand Habermas, the acceptability of the second premise in the argument for U is supposed to be independent of any particular interpretation of what it means to judge something from a moral point of view. What is at issue – the issue stated by the moral skeptic – is precisely whether it can be settled rationally which interpretation to adopt. And the universal validity of one particular interpretation – U – is to be shown by demonstrating that it follows from premises which even the moral skeptic can accept. The passage that I just quoted continues in the following way:

> But these arguments can no longer be burdened with the sense of an a priori transcendental deduction in the sense of Kant's critique of reason. They merely justify the fact that there is no recognizable alternative to "our" kind of argumentation. In this respect, discourse ethics, like other reconstructive sciences, relies merely on hypothetical reconstructions [*Nachkonstruktionen*] for which we must seek plausible confirmations – naturally, first on the level on which it competes with other moral theories. But, in addition, such a theory is open to, and indeed dependent upon [*angewiesen auf*], *indirect* confirmation by *other* theories consonant with it.[69]

It is important to note that "hypothetical reconstructions" do play a role in the argument for U. All that I have said is that these reconstructions must not draw on intuitions unacceptable to the moral skeptic. Habermas makes it clear that, for example, the up-justification of the first premise involves fallible hypothetical reconstructions.[70] This is perfectly compatible with assuming that the argument for U is rationalistic: rationalism does not demand infallibility but merely that the reconstructions not appeal to intuitions unacceptable to the moral skeptic.

Habermas' talk here about hypothetical reconstructions is related to his more general position that philosophy cannot play a founda-

---

[68] Habermas 1988e, 127 [116; modified translation].
[69] Habermas 1988e, 127 [116–117; modified translation]. He goes on to say that Kohlberg's developmental psychology would offer one such indirect confirmation. I have omitted all of Habermas' footnotes in both of these quotes.
[70] Habermas 1988d, 107 [97]; cf. Habermas 1991f, 194–195 [83–84]; 1988b, 14 [6]; 1984c, 380, 384 [21–22, 24–25].

tional role for the sciences. This does not mean that philosophy is relegated to a non-argumentative realm beyond science. Rather, philosophy may advance strong universalistic theses which are then supported by arguments from the (reconstructive) sciences and by philosophical arguments; there is a cooperation between philosophy and the (reconstructive) sciences.[71]

As I understand it, this cooperation is of two kinds. On the one hand, the reconstructions involved in a philosophical argument like the argument for U are themselves fallible empirical reconstructions.[72] On the other hand, these philosophical arguments are subject to indirect confirmation and disconfirmation from the sciences. The indirect confirmation that Habermas goes on to talk about after the passage that I just quoted is Kohlberg's developmental psychology. Just as premises of the argument for U are not to appeal to moral intuitions, they are not to appeal to the results of developmental psychology (which the moral skeptic might also question). However, just as the independence of the argument for U from moral intuitions is compatible with the rejection of SR, its independence from developmental psychology is also compatible with subjecting U to an indirect (dis)confirmation by developmental psychology. For example, Kohlberg's theory might undermine the psychological credibility of a moral theory. However, he does not believe that Kohlberg's theory can offer "independent evidence" for theories on the so-called post-conventional level: in order to describe the post-conventional level as the highest level, Kohlberg's theory must already assume the validity of a post-conventional moral theory and cannot directly argue for it. Philosophical ethics and developmental psychology can only give support to each other by being *in consonance*, by forming together a *coherent* theory.[73] And this holds not only for the relation between moral theory and developmental psychology: "The coherence theory of truth is certainly too weak to explain the concept of propositional truth; but it comes into its own at another

[71] Habermas 1988b, 20–24 [13–16].

[72] Despite the differences that Habermas sees between philosophy and the reconstructive sciences, on the one hand, and the nomological sciences, on the other hand, he takes them all to be empirical; see Habermas 1984c, 384–385 [24–25]; 1991f, 193–194 [83]. Habermas' view differs here from the views of Apel and Kuhlmann (see Appendix).

[73] Habermas 1988c, 47–49 [38–39]; 1988e, 128–130 [117–119]; 1984d, 534–535 [259].

level, the metatheoretical, where we put together the individual pieces of theory like a puzzle."[74] In other words, each sub-theory of a system of thought is to be tested by the measure of its coherence with the other sub-theories.

Of course, the fact that coherentism is valid on the "metatheoretical" level does not determine which theories are coherent. Even if such meta-theoretical coherentism is valid – a view according to which any part of a system of thought may, for the sake of coherence, in principle be subject to revision due to a change in another part of the system – it may be part of a particular coherent theory that the law of non-contradiction may not be given up just because of a change in moral intuitions: even though abandonment of the law of non-contradiction may not be excluded in principle by the coherentist meta-theory, a particular coherent theory may demand that in order even to consider discarding the law of non-contradiction, more must change than just a few moral intuitions. Thus, it seems that Habermas' acceptance of a coherence theory on the meta-theoretical level is perfectly compatible with acceptance of SR: he may believe that the *most coherent* theory demands that, in the case of a conflict between moral intuitions and a principle justified by premises acceptable to a moral skeptic, the latter must always take precedence. I conclude that Habermas' idea of the indirect (dis)confirmation of philosophical arguments by scientific considerations in virtue of coherence considerations – which should be applicable to his philosophical argument for U – is not only compatible with WR but also with SR. However, I have not argued that Habermas does in fact accept SR, and my interpretation that the argument for U is rationalistic does not depend on assuming that he does.

[74] Habermas 1984d, 506 [239; unchanged translation]. Cf. Habermas 1988e, 129–130 [118–119], and 1991f, 193 [82–83].

9

Discoursing about discourse

In this chapter, I argue that Habermas' argument for U, understood as a rationalistic argument, is a failure. I shall consider three formulations of the argument: Habermas' formulation in the second edition of "Diskursethik – Notizen zu einem Begründungsprogramm" (in §1), the formulation in Habermas' 1996 "Eine genealogische Betrachtung zum kognitiven Gehalt der Moral" (in §2), and the formulation proposed by William Rehg (in §3). I shall argue separately for each formulation that the argument fails.

I THE DISCOURSING UTILITARIAN

Habermas' first formulation of the argument for U is very sketchy. This is what he says:

> If each one who enters into argumentation must among other things make presuppositions whose content may be presented in the form of the discourse rules (3.1) to (3.3),[1] and if we further know what it means to hypothetically discuss [*erörtern*] whether action norms should be put into force, then each one who seriously makes the attempt to *discursively* redeem normative validity claims intuitively accepts procedural conditions that implicitly amount to acknowledging U. It follows, namely, from the aforementioned discourse rules that a controversial norm can meet with the consent of the discourse participants only if U holds, that is
>
> > if all can *freely* [*zwanglos*] accept the consequences and side effects the *general* observance of the controversial norm can be anticipated to have for the satisfaction of the interests of *each single one*.[2]

[1] For these rules, see 8.1.
[2] This formulation of U is slightly different from the formulation in Habermas 1996 which I quoted in 8.1.

But once it has been shown how the universalization principle can be justified via a transcendental pragmatic derivation from the presuppositions of argumentation, *discourse ethics itself* can be reduced to the economical principle D according to which

> only those norms may claim validity which meet (or could meet) with the consent of all the affected parties as participants in a practical discourse.[3]

In this passage, Habermas writes that "each one who seriously makes the attempt to *discursively* redeem normative validity claims" must accept something which amounts to acknowledging U and that "a controversial norm can meet with the *consent* of the *discourse participants* only if U holds."[4] Also, the skeptic to whom the argument is directed must share our view as to "what it means to hypothetically discuss whether action norms should be put into force." Given this talk of discourse and consent in what appear to be the assumptions of the argument for U, one might wonder what the relation of this argument is to SD: does the argument assume the validity of SD or not? I will consider both possibilities and argue that in both cases Habermas' argument, understood as a rationalistic argument, fails to solve the ethnocentricity problem and the moral alternatives problem.

SD is assumed

Recall that accepting SD as a principle of justification amounts to accepting it to the exclusion of other principles of justification, such as the principle of utility (see 8.2). Thus, if the argument for U assumes the validity of SD, it assumes the invalidity of other principles of justification. Clearly, however, SD is no less subject to the ethnocentricity problem and the moral alternatives problem than U is.[5] Therefore, as an answer to these problems, the argument for U is

---

[3] Habermas 1988d, 103 [92–93; modified translation].
[4] Italicisation of "consent" and "discourse participants" is mine.
[5] Habermas 1996 claims that the problem of ethnocentricity does not arise for D: "Because the practice of argumentation is universally spread and there is no alternative to it, it will be difficult to dispute the neutrality of the discourse principle. However, in the abduction of 'U', an ethnocentric preconception (and thus also a particular conception of the good) which is not shared by other cultures may have sneaked in" (61). Once we have distinguished between WD and SD, it should be clear that Habermas' claim is at most plausible for WD. As my subsequent arguments show, Habermas' ra-

a failure, unless Habermas has a separate argument meeting these problems for SD.

It could be argued that the argument for U assumes the validity of SD only *temporarily*. SD explicates what it means to give an impartial justification of norms of action. However, unless it can be shown that it is at all possible to settle practical questions impartially and rationally, SD would not be a reasonable justificatory principle. And it is precisely the purpose of the argument for U to show that moral questions can be settled rationally. Thus, the argument for U is neither an argument for SD nor does it *simply* assume it. It is meant to show that a necessary condition of the reasonableness of SD as a justificatory principle is fulfilled, namely that moral questions can be settled rationally.[6]

If this is right, then the argument for U is meant to demonstrate the validity of U as an SD-discourse rule against other possible discourse rules. However, in this form, the argument does *not* show that norms are to be justified by SD, rather than by the principle of utility. Thus, the same difficulty arises as before: the argument for U does not solve the ethnocentricity and moral alternatives problems as they pertain to SD.

SD is not assumed

The passage quoted above certainly suggests that SD is not supposed to be one of the premises of the argument for U, but rather a consequence of it.[7] Nevertheless, it seems clear that the argument is supposed to show that U must be accepted by *discourse participants*. Now, in this discourse where the discourse participants must presuppose U, does the issue of the validity of SD, as opposed to, say, the principle of utility arise? I will argue (1) that this issue is appropriately raised in this discourse, and (2) that, if it is raised, then the argument for U, as a rationalistic argument, fails.

(1) It might be argued that the discourse in question is a *practical*

tionalistic argument cannot get us from WD to SD or U. Thus, even if WD is not subject to the problem of ethnocentricity, this will not save Habermas' argument.
6 See Habermas 1994, 140 [108–109]; 1984b, 172–173; 1988d, 76 [66]; 1991f, 133, 186 [31–32, 76–77]; 1996, 59–60.
7 As will become clear in §2, in Habermas 1996, D is not understood as a consequence of U.

rather than a *philosophical* discourse. Practical discourses are called for in cases of conflict, e.g., when there is no longer consensus about norms. Practical discourses are directly about the cases and the norms in question and they are not philosophical discourses about justificatory principles for norms. In practical discourses, questions like "What is the appropriate way of justifying norms, SD or the principle of utility?" do not arise, since that would turn the discourse into philosophical discourse. The argument for U shows that anyone who seriously attempts to redeem discursively normative validity claims in practical discourse accepts U as a rule of argumentation for this discourse.

I do not wish to deny that it makes sense to characterize some discourses as philosophical rather than as practical. What I want to argue is that it is dubious to assume that the issue of the correct principle of justification – say, SD versus the principle of utility – is not appropriately raised in practical discourse. I present the following imaginary dialogue in support of my case:

Two persons lie in beds in a hospital. One of them is just waking up and notices the other one with surprise.
PATIENT: What are you doing here? You are my doctor!
DOCTOR: Yes, I know. But yesterday, as we were operating on you, we noticed that you had two healthy kidneys. Since I needed a kidney, another doctor took over the operation, and I now have your kidney. I hope you don't mind.
After initial reactions of disbelief and after having had the news confirmed by others, the patient continues the conversation. The interchange now turns into a discourse about the rightness of a norm.
PATIENT: You had no right to do that. Nobody has the right to remove another person's bodily organs without that person's permission.
DOCTOR: I disagree. Earlier you had two healthy kidneys and I had none. Now each of us has one. A person only needs one functioning kidney. Now we can both lead a normal life. I know that you are too egoistic ever to accept having a kidney removed, but you must agree that the situation is now fairer than before.
PATIENT: You have to see the matter also from my point of view, the point of view of the victim. By doing this without my

permission you have interfered with my right to have a final say over what is done to my body.

So far the discourse can be classified as an SD-discourse. The doctor and the patient are directly discussing the issue of whether one has the right to transplant someone's kidney without her permission. With the doctor's next contribution, the conversation takes a new turn. She makes a suggestion which – if it were accepted – would amount to a rejection of SD. The conversation moves up a level: it turns into a discussion of whether SD or some other principle of justification is the appropriate way of justifying norms.

DOCTOR: I see the matter from both points of view. I am just trying to be impartial. And I have reached the conclusion that the only way to be impartial is to let the decision rest on what produces more happiness, not on what we would agree to in discourse. If the rightness of a norm is to be decided in a discourse among those affected by the norm, there is no way the agreement is going to be impartial. We have to agree in advance (in discourse) that the rightness of a norm depends on its effect on happiness and not on the issue whether it would be agreed to in discourse.

PATIENT: I disagree. You are confusing impartiality with impersonality.[8] The rightness of a norm rests on direct agreement on the norm. This does not mean that in reaching agreement on the norm the participants do not consider how the norm affects the happiness of people. However, how happiness is to count in the decision-making has to be decided by the participants themselves.

With her last answer the patient has, in effect, let herself in on the changed terms of the discussion. She defends SD in a discussion which is no longer directly about the norm itself, but about how to decide on the rightness of norms.

I have tried to write the above dialogue so as to make the inclusion of the higher-level discussion seem inevitable. In order to defend her actions, the doctor must take up this meta-issue. The controversial point will simply not have been adequately discussed if the discourse stops short of a treatment of this issue.[9]

---

[8] The patient would do well to borrow here from Kettner 1992, 336–348.

[9] In saying that the discussion must move to a higher level, I am not assuming that it must *first* be settled on this level and this result must *then* be applied on the lower level. I am not even assuming that on the higher level the participants must be looking for a principle which is then to be *applied*. All I am saying is that to approach the issue, it is

113

(2) All I have tried to show so far is that the issue concerning principles of justification is properly raised in practical discourse. This does not yet exclude that it can be shown that the participants in such discourses must assume the validity of U and SD. Now I want to argue that, if it can be shown, it cannot be done by a rationalistic argument (an argument acceptable to the moral skeptic). First I will offer a short argument to the effect that a person may be a participant in practical discourse, accept Habermas' two premises, and nevertheless be a utilitarian while remaining rational in the way in which the moral skeptic aspires to be rational. Then I will argue that all attempts to refute my argument end up turning the argument for U into an argument which is not rationalistic.

Here is my short argument. The doctor in the imaginary dialogue may be an example of someone who participates in practical discourse, who accepts Habermas' two premises, and is nevertheless a utilitarian. I understand utilitarianism (or the principle of utility) to say that the ultimate criterion of the rightness of actions/norms is their effect on happiness (rather than whether people would agree upon them in discourse). Admittedly, this is not a precise account of utilitarianism, but this account suffices to contrast it with SD.

First, notice that the doctor's actions do not imply that she is acting strategically. If she is being honest in the dialogue, she does in fact aim to be guided by impartiality. In removing the patient's kidney, she is not acting strategically. On the contrary, she is guided by her concern for impartiality in its utilitarian interpretation: there is no reason for transplanting the kidney into the doctor rather than into someone else needing a kidney, other than that she is the only recipient available.

Second, given that the doctor's actions are not strategic, her dialogue with the patient is also consistent with assuming that she accepts Habermas' two premises. Judging from the dialogue, it is

appropriate that the participants move to a higher level where they address the fundamental concepts at work in their practice. It seems reasonable to assume, however, that to discuss these fundamental concepts properly, the people must also ask themselves what it would mean in practice to be guided by a certain – say, a utilitarian or a discourse-ethical – understanding of a concept and whether the results are acceptable. And if this is reasonable, it seems that the "lower-level" discussion should guide the "higher-level" discussion just as much as the other way around. In any case, I am not assuming that "higher-level" ("philosophical") issues must first be settled and these results then applied to "lower-level" ("practical") issues.

reasonable to assume that the doctor accepts both premises. She handles the dialogue in a way that indicates that she knows what it means to justify norms in Habermas' weak sense. She obviously knows that norms of action grant people certain rights; it was precisely such a right that she was acting on in removing the kidney. And she knows that the point of the practical dialogue is precisely to justify claims to rightness, such as the one she takes to justify her actions. Thus, she respects the second premise.

There is also no reason to think that she does not respect the first premise. The doctor fully respects the patient as a dialogue partner and there is no reason to think that she would not respect others as dialogue partners as well. They are permitted to introduce and criticize any claim they like and to express their wishes and needs. Of course, she removed the kidney without the patient's permission. However, since she is a utilitarian, her respect for them as dialogue partners does not include having to get their consent to particular norms, for example norms pertaining to the transplantation of organs. It is precisely the goal of the discourse, in which she respects them as discourse partners, to find out whether such consent is morally required or whether norms are to be justified in some other way, for example by the principle of utility.

The case of this utilitarian doctor refutes Habermas' argument for U as a rationalistic argument. The doctor participates in practical discourse and accepts the two premises, but she rejects U and SD. This does not mean that she is justified in rejecting them and in accepting the principle of utility. It just means that the fact that she is mistaken (if she is) is not implied by the two premises and the fact that she participates in practical discourse. In other words, U is not implied by premises which the moral skeptic accepts. The dispute between the doctor and the patient – between the utilitarian and the discourse ethicist – provides the moral skeptic with a perfect case in support of her skepticism.[10] The doctor and the patient are both

---

[10] It should be noted that it is not only the dispute between utilitarianism and discourse-ethics which the moral skeptic believes cannot be settled rationally. In my argument, instead of utilitarianism, I could have used any other approach to morality which does not in itself conflict with the possibility that this approach is to be given a discursive justification. For example, I could even have used the idea that those principles are just which would be agreed upon by strategic reasoners in an initial bargaining situation. If the justification of this approach itself is to be given in a discourse in which people interact communicatively rather than strategically, there is no conflict

rational in the sense that the moral skeptic aspires to be and the dispute between them cannot be settled on grounds which the skeptic endorses. From this the skeptic concludes – and so should the rationalist, given that she thinks that the skeptic must be refuted on the skeptic's own grounds – that the dispute cannot be settled rationally.

In presenting this short refutation of the argument for U, I have not been particularly concerned with a feature of up-justifications emphasized in 2.2. (Even though the argument for U is not, strictly speaking, an up-argument, I think that it is supposed to share this feature.) There I said that up-arguments against the moral skeptic differ from Gauthier's arguments in that Gauthier assumes that the skeptic has an adequate understanding of the *concept* of reason (but not of all its implications), whereas up-theorists think that the skeptic's understanding of the concept itself is inadequate. This means that the up-theorist cannot work with the skeptic's notion of rationality and demonstrate what follows from *it*. Rather, it must be shown that in aspiring to be rational in a certain way, the skeptic is aspiring to be rational in a sense whose meaning she does not fully understand.

It might seem that in my short argument I have not done justice to this feature of up-justifications. I have argued that one can accept the two premises and nevertheless remain a utilitarian. It might seem, however, that in this argument I have understood the two premises *as the moral skeptic understands them*, whereas the whole point of the up-argument is that the skeptic has an inadequate grasp of them. In other words, I have not done justice to the fact that the argument for U is supposed to reveal that the skeptic must implicitly assume something to be valid which cannot be validated in her own terms, since her grasp of how to show something to be valid is imperfect. The skeptic is only addressed on her own ground in the sense that she is supposed to assume this implicitly in her inspiration to be rational in a certain way.

In order for the argument for U to count as rationalistic, it must be possible to characterize the skeptic's aspirations to rationality in a way which is acceptable to the skeptic. As just explained, the fact that this characterization is acceptable to the skeptic does not mean that the skeptic has an adequate grasp of what it means to be rational in this

between it and the moral skeptic's commitment to argue about moral justification in discourse.

way. The point of the argument for U is precisely to show that she does not have an adequate grasp of it: if the argument for U is successful, one has uncovered commitments implicit in these aspirations which are not consistent with a rejection of U. In the following, I will argue that it is not possible *both* to characterize the skeptic's aspirations in a way which she accepts *and* to uncover a commitment to U in them. For any such characterization of the skeptic's aspirations, there will be another one which does not commit the skeptic to acceptance of U. And it will not be possible to judge the first characterization to be better without relying on reasons which already incorporate the supposedly uncovered elements. This does not mean that such an argument for U is unsuccessful. It just means that it is not successful as a rationalistic argument. To make my case, I will consider some arguments meant to show that the utilitarian does not respect the moral skeptic's aspirations. For each of these arguments, I will try to show that there exists another characterization of the skeptic's aspirations which is compatible with utilitarianism and that the former characterization cannot be shown to be better without relying on considerations disputed by the skeptic.

The moral skeptic aspires to respect others as dialogue participants. It may be argued that utilitarianism is, in the final analysis, not compatible with such respect. Even though the utilitarian is willing to justify the principle of utility to others in dialogue, the principle of utility itself shows that she does not conceive of people first and foremost as creatures to whom norms need to be justified, but rather as creatures whose happiness needs to be somehow taken into account. In other words, the utilitarian does not interact with others as creatures to whom you owe a justification which they cannot reasonably reject.[11] The kidney transplantation case is a clear example of the utilitarian attitude towards people.

We must distinguish between someone who is simply a utilitarian and someone who is a utilitarian and is willing to justify the principle of utility in discourse. There is a clear sense in which the latter does respect others as dialogue partners. She is willing to examine critically and undogmatically the validity of the principle of utility in discourse. The argument under discussion here is that there is a limit to her respect for others as dialogue partners, a limit which means that she

---

[11] Cf. Scanlon 1982; Scanlon 1998, 151–158, 213–218, 229–241.

does not respect others in a way in which she must be implicitly committed to respecting them, given her aspiration to respect others as dialogue partners. The claim is that it is only in the light of this further implicit commitment that we can really understand what it means to respect people as dialogue partners.

It seems to me that there is certainly a sense in which the utilitarian does not respect others as dialogue partners. And if we adopt the discourse-ethical understanding of what such respect amounts to and interpret the minimal respect which the moral skeptic aspires to have as a respect of this kind, then, unless they give up skepticism and utilitarianism, the moral skeptic and the utilitarian cannot respect people at all as dialogue partners. The trouble is that there is also a clear sense in which the utilitarian *does* respect others as dialogue partners, and it seems open to the skeptic to say that this is all the respect for others as dialogue partners that she, as a moral skeptic, aspires to have. It seems that in order to argue that the skeptic does not respect others as dialogue partners, one must already assume a rich notion of respect which, from the point of view of the skeptic, there is no good reason to accept.

As I shall argue in 12.3, I do not think that this is a problem as such. However, it means that the argument for U fails as a rationalistic argument. If this argument is to succeed as a rationalistic argument, it must be possible to characterize the aspirations of the skeptic in a way that is acceptable to her as a moral skeptic and use the characterization to compel assent to U. And I have just argued that this is not possible, at least if the aspirations concern respect for others as dialogue partners. To argue that the skeptic must assume U if she is to respect others as dialogue partners, one must characterize the skeptic's aspirations in terms of a kind of respect which the skeptic herself – in favor of another notion of respect – denies that she aspires to have.

The first objection to the supposition that utilitarianism is compatible with participation in practical discourse and with the two premises focused on the fact that the skeptic participates in dialogue and accepts the *first* premise. It could also be argued, however, that utilitarianism is not compatible with the *second* premise. According to the second premise, moral justifications resolve disputes about duties and rights. Of course, the doctor thinks that she has the right to have the kidney removed. However, it is well known that utilitarianism cannot really account for individual moral rights (as the example of the transplantation clearly demonstrates). Thus, since utilitarianism makes a mockery of the very concept of moral rights, the utilitarian cannot really be said to be engaged in a practical discourse where justifications involving disputes about *rights* are at stake.

The answer to this objection is the same as to the first: even though it may be a good objection against utilitarianism, it does not show the incompatibility of utilitarianism with the argument for U understood as a rationalistic argument. The moral skeptic has a minimalistic interpretation of the second premise, according to which moral justification does indeed resolve disputes about duties and rights. However, the minimalistic interpretation does not prejudge the matter in favor of a "Kantian" understanding of duties and rights. After all, as my argument in chapter 8 shows, Habermas wants the "Kantian interpretation" of the moral point of view to be the conclusion of the argument for U, not a premise of it. Thus, according to the minimalistic interpretation, moral justifications resolve disputes about rights and duties by justifying norms or principles which then determine what rights and duties we have. This is compatible with assuming that what rights and duties we have will be determined by the principle of utility.

Of course, if we have a discourse-ethical understanding of what it means to have rights and duties, then we will not take the utilitarian to be giving moral justifications resolving disputes about rights and duties. As in the case of respect for the dialogue partners, however, the moral skeptic has a clear and minimalistic understanding of the second premise, and from her point of view – as opposed to a point of view already informed by a discourse-ethical or at least a "Kantian" interpretation of rights – there are no good reasons to give it a richer reading. Thus, just as in the case of respect for the dialogue partners, the argument for U does not work unless the aspirations of the moral skeptic are characterized in a way that she would not accept. Thus, the argument for U fails as a rationalistic argument. The argument can *at most* show that the moral skeptic must accept WD.[12]

<hr/>

[12] It should be noted that since Benhabib's understanding of how to justify D – that is, SD – is not rationalistic, the arguments I have offered here do not apply to her discourse-ethical program. (She also wants to leave U out of discourse ethics.) See Benhabib 1989 and Benhabib 1990.

2 HABERMAS' SECOND FORMULATION

I now turn to a more recent and detailed formulation of the argument for U given by Habermas. This argument is less clearly intended as a rationalistic argument. Nevertheless, as in the first formulation, it is meant to solve the problem of ethnocentricity, and it seems to have the same two premises. This second formulation of the argument is interesting not only because it is a little more detailed, but also because it makes clear that the argument is bound to fail for the reasons mentioned in the last section.

Here U is introduced as an "operationalization" of D and as a principle which is "inspired through 'D', but at first no more than as an abductively obtained proposal."[13] Habermas then goes on to give an argument for U similar to the one I just discussed. This is how his presentation begins:

> We may assume that the practice of consultation and justification which we call argumentation exists in all societies and cultures (if not necessarily in an institutionalized form, then at least as an informal practice), and that no other way of solving problems is equivalent to this one. Because the practice of argumentation is universally spread and there is no alternative to it, it will be difficult to dispute the neutrality of the discourse principle. However, in the abduction of "U," an ethnocentric preconception (and thus also a particular conception of the good) which is not shared by other cultures may have sneaked in. The suspicion that the operationalization of an understanding of morality provided by "U" is ethnocentrically biased can be eliminated if this explanation of the moral point of view can be made "immanently" plausible: if its plausibility emerges from the knowledge of what one is doing by getting at all involved in the practice of argumentation. The discourse ethical justification at stake here is thus the following: the fundamental principle "U" can be obtained from the content implicit in the general presuppositions of argumentation in conjunction with the idea expressed in "D" of what the justification of norms means at all.[14]

13 Habermas 1996, 60; cf. Habermas 1998, 202–203.
14 Habermas 1996, 60–61. Habermas refers here to Ott 1996. My translation of the last sentence is based on the assumption that Habermas is here formulating the two premises in the argument for U discussed in the last section and that this sentence is supposed to say more or less the same as the following sentence: "Diesen Umstand hebe ich mit der Formulierung hervor, daß sich 'U' aus dem normativen Gehalt von

Here Habermas seems to be saying that he wants to justify the "abduction" of U from D by showing that U can be "obtained" from two elements which correspond to the two premises discussed in the last section: (1) "the content implicit in the general presuppositions of argumentation" and (2) "the idea expressed in 'D' of what the justification of norms means at all." Although this formulation of the second element does not make it clear that it, like the second premise, should be understood weakly, it seems that Habermas wants the second element to be so understood. After all, only two pages later he stresses that "'U' can be made plausible by reliance on the normative content of the presuppositions of argumentation *in conjunction with a* (weak, i.e. non-prejudiced) *concept of the justification of norms.*"[15]

Habermas says in the long passage just quoted that the problem of ethnocentricity arises for U, but not for D. This claim is at most plausible for WD. Since SD is a principle which competes with many other fundamentally different principles of justification, the problem of ethnocentricity is just as serious for it as it is for U. As we shall see, the distinction between SD and WD will make the failure of Habermas' argument obvious. Immediately after this passage, Habermas continues:

> Intuitively this is easy to see (while an attempt to give a formal justification would require an elaborate discussion of the sense and feasibility of "transcendental arguments"[16]). I content myself with the phenomenological comment that people undertake to engage in argumentation with the intention to convince each other of the correctness [*Berechtigung*] of the claims to validity which they make for their statements and are prepared to defend against opponents. The practice of argumentation establishes a cooperative competition for better arguments in which the orientation toward mutual understanding [mutual understanding = *Verständigung*] unites the participants from the very beginning. The assumption that the competition can lead to "rationally acceptable," i.e. "convincing [*überzeugenden*]," results is based on the

---

Argumentationsvoraussetzungen *in Verbindung mit einem* (schwachen, also nicht-präjudizierenden) *Begriff von Normenbegründung* plausibel machen läßt" (Habermas 1996, 63).

[15] Habermas 1996, 63.

[16] Habermas refers here to Niquet 1991 and Niquet, *Nichthintergehbarkeit und Diskurs*, Habilitation (Manuscript), Frankfurt-am-Main, 1995.

persuasive power [*Überzeugungskraft*] of the arguments. What counts as a good or bad argument can admittedly itself be put up for discussion. The rational acceptability of a statement therefore in the end rests on reasons in conjunction with certain features of the process of argumentation itself. I mention only the four most important ones: (a) no one who could make a relevant contribution may be excluded from participation; (b) everyone is given the same chance to make a contribution; (c) the participants must mean what they say; (d) the communication must be free of outer and inner forces in such a way that the participants are only motivated by the persuasive power of the better reasons when they take a yes or no position on a criticizable validity claim. Now if each person who gets involved in argumentation must make at least these pragmatic presuppositions, then the following holds: (a) because of the public aspect [*Öffentlichkeit*] and the inclusion of all the affected parties and (b) because of the communicatively equal rights of the participants, in practical discourses only those reasons can count which take the interests and value-orientations of each one equally into account; and because of the absence of (c) deception and (d) force, in practical discourses only reasons for consenting to a controversial norm can decide the matter. Finally, given that each one reciprocally assumes that each one is oriented toward mutual understanding, this "free" acceptance can only take place "jointly."[17]

For our purposes, the details of the first few sentences can be ignored. What matters is that Habermas arrives at the conclusion that, in argumentation, the rational acceptability of statements is based on the reasons offered in the argumentation and on "certain features of the process of argumentation itself." After enumerating a few of those features, Habermas then goes on to show how U can be obtained. From (a) and (b), Habermas obtains the conclusion that "in practical discourses only those reasons can count which take the interests and value-orientations of each one equally into account." The problem is that it is not clear whether by "practical discourses" he means SD-discourses (discourses which aim for *direct* agreement on norms) or WD-discourses (discourses in which the justification of this aim itself may be at issue). If he means the former, then he is simply taking SD as a justificatory principle for granted. In that case, he will not have solved the problem of ethnocentricity, since SD is just as ethnocen-

<hr />

[17] Habermas 1996, 61–62.

trically suspect as U. If he means the latter, then neither SD nor U as a rule of argumentation for SD-discourses has been made plausible. After all, in a discourse in which the issue is whether to accept SD or the principle of utility as a justificatory principle, the utilitarian will argue that her principle articulates the correct way of taking "the interests and value-orientations of each one equally into account." As I said in the last section, the utilitarian may not be right about this, but she cannot be shown to be wrong on purely rationalistic premises.

From (c) and (d), Habermas arrives at the conclusion that "in practical discourses only reasons for consenting to a controversial norm can decide the matter." Here a similar problem arises. If he means SD-discourses, then the problem of ethnocentricity has not been solved. If he means WD-discourses, then U as a rule of argumentation for SD-discourses has not been made one bit more plausible. After all, the utilitarian can accept that in WD-discourses the matter is to be decided by *reasons* for consenting to a *principle of justification*.

I can now summarize the argument I have given in this and the last section against Habermas' argument. My argument can be presented in the form of a dilemma: either Habermas assumes SD or he does not. If he does, then the problem of ethnocentricity has not been resolved. If he does not, then his argument fails to establish either SD or U. Even if he manages to show that the participants in argumentation must assume the validity of WD, he fails to show that a moral skeptic who participates in WD-discourse and accepts Habermas' two premises must therefore also accept SD or U.[18]

3 REHG'S FORMULATION

I want to conclude by saying a few words about William Rehg's reconstruction of Habermas' argument (in its first formulation). I will not go into any details, since I only want to indicate why I think that it faces the difficulties I just mentioned.

My objection to Habermas' argument relies crucially on the claim that – contrary to what is presupposed by SD – practical discourse

---

[18] For arguments to the effect that Apel's and Kuhlmann's transcendental pragmatic arguments for discourse ethics suffer from the same difficulties as those of Habermas, see Gunnarsson 1995b, 148–153.

need not aim for direct consent of the participants to norms, but may include as a topic the legitimacy of principles of justification which would exclude direct agreement on norms as an element in the justification of those norms. Rehg's detailed reconstruction of Habermas' argument for U does not undermine this claim and thus, it seems to me, does not succeed in resolving the difficulties I have raised. One of three premises in Rehg's reconstruction of the argument – the other two being Rehg's renderings of Habermas' two premises – is the assumption that "a pluralistic group decides to resolve their conflicts of interest cooperatively by reaching argued agreement (as rational conviction) on a norm."[19] He notes that in this premise "we already find something looking quite close to (D)"[20] and says that it is beyond the scope of his study to determine whether Habermas succeeds in supporting this premise.[21] If Rehg has SD in mind here, his admission that this premise needs further support would amount to admitting that the problem of ethnocentricity has not been resolved. However, if he has WD in mind, I think that the arguments of the last two sections show that U does not follow from the premises.

Rehg actually goes on to consider elements in Habermas' justification of the premise in which "we already find something looking quite close to (D)." In this further discussion, Rehg does not undermine the claim on which my objection to Habermas is based. My claim is that there are two kinds of discourses (SD-discourse and WD-discourse) and that the skeptic may consistently choose to engage only in WD-discourse. In his discussion of Habermas' justification of the premise under discussion, Rehg does not argue explicitly that the skeptic cannot consistently opt for only one kind of discourse, but rather that she cannot consistently completely abandon discourse in favor of some other form of interaction.[22]

Rehg wants to make plausible "that in today's world rational actors cannot *in general* forego the good of cooperation in contexts marked by conflict potentials."[23] In order to make this plausible, Rehg considers two alternatives to U and wants to argue against the claim that "a rational actor may dispense with (U) *generally* in favor of the alternative principle."[24] These two principles are "That action/norm

[19] Rehg 1994, 66.   [20] Rehg 1994, 67; cf. Rehg 1991, 36–38.
[21] Rehg 1994, 69.   [22] See Rehg 1994, 134–172.
[23] Rehg 1994, 161.   [24] Rehg 1994, 162.

is right by which one furthers one's own self-interest (or happiness, or good)" and "That action/norm is right by which one follows/ enforces the dictates of the group's worldview."[25] I leave aside whether Rehg's arguments against these two principles are convincing. What I want to point out is that both of these principles amount to giving up discourse in favor of something else, in one case in favor of strategic interaction and in the other case in favor of a dogmatic attitude (this is what Rehg's argument turns on).[26] The person who accepts the principle of utility and is willing to argue about it does not do that. She is neither dogmatic nor does she interact strategically with others.[27] She is willing to justify the principle of utility in discourse.[28] However, since she accepts the principle of utility she does not think that the justification of moral norms calls for *SD-discourse*. Thus, since Rehg's arguments do not address the possibility of distinguishing between these two kinds of discourse, they do not undermine my thesis that Habermas has not offered a good rationalistic argument in favor of either U or SD. Habermas' argument is *at most* a good rationalistic argument for WD.[29]

[25] Rehg 1994, 162.   [26] Rehg 1994, 162–167.

[27] Precisely for these reasons my argument has a certain advantage over the argument in Leist 1989 where he argues that a person – he gives an example of people who kidnap a scientist and an example of a racist – can accept Habermas' two premises and still deny U without a contradiction. It is much clearer for my utilitarian than it is for Leist's candidates that she is indeed willing to engage in a discourse with anyone about the validity of her view and to respect them as equal dialogue partners.

[28] The argument in Wingert 1993 (esp. pp. 259–263, 281–294) for the "epistemic" superiority of what he calls "the morality of twofold respect" suffers from a defect similar to the one in Rehg's argument: Wingert fails to consider the more interesting alternatives to his own approach. Even if the morality of twofold respect is epistemically superior to a religious or a traditional morality, it is by no means clear that it is epistemically superior to an alternative which endorses WD while rejecting the morality of twofold respect (as the utilitarianism which I have in mind does); cf. Gunnarsson 1997b, 128–130.

[29] The same holds of the argument for D offered in Ott 1996, 42–43: it can at most establish WD. Like Rehg, Ott does not distinguish between SD and WD and considers strategic reasoning as an alternative to argumentation about norms, but fails to consider a utilitarian or a moral skeptic who participates in WD-discourse. Since Ott's argument for U has D as a premise, it also suffers from these difficulties.

PART III

For the substantive approach

10

Self-understanding and self-assessment

It is time to get back to the main topic of the book: to show that morality does *not need* a rationalistic justification *even if* there is a successful justification of this kind available. Thus, whereas I argued in Part II that Gauthier's and Habermas' conclusions do not follow from their premises, I am in this part willing to assume that they do. Here my aim is to argue that the supposition that morality needs a rationalistic justification distorts our view of morality and rationality. I shall proceed by considering the problem of the rationality of morality and by arguing that the substantive approach's solution to this problem should be favored over the solution offered by rationalism.[1]

The problem of rationality arises both in the context of self-assessment and in evaluating others (see chapter 1). Depending on the context, the emphasis gets placed on one or another issue. In the context of self-assessment or self-evaluation, the focus is on such questions as whether a person who guides her life by moral reasons may thereby be losing sight of her real interests. Even if rationalism or the substantive approach were to solve the problem as it comes up in self-assessment, there would still remain the issues of whether and how we can justify the use of morality to evaluate others. This problem becomes particularly pressing when moral norms accepted in one culture are employed as standards to criticize another culture.

I start by considering the topic of self-assessment and then move on to the question of evaluating others in the last two chapters of this part of the book. In the discussion of self-assessment, I shall focus on the comparison with *subjectivist* rationalism, whereas with respect to the evaluation of others I shall compare the substantive approach with *inter-subjectivist* rationalism. I have chosen to divide the comparison in this way for the following reasons: the case of self-assessment is

---

[1] The problem of the categorical force will be discussed in 11.5.

fundamental for Gauthier. For him, the important question is whether morality is advantageous to each individual. Thus, if it can be shown that his approach is misguided for the case of self-assessment, then by his own standards it must also be misguided for the criticism of others. It is natural to consider inter-subjectivist rationalism in the context of the criticism of others rather than in the context of self-assessment. Inter-subjectivist rationalism does not focus upon the issue of how to determine which (if any) moral concepts it is good for a person to use in her self-assessment. Rather, the focus is on the question of whether certain moral principles are universally valid. Thus, it makes sense to discuss inter-subjectivist rationalism when the question is how to justify criticism of others.

I THE PROBLEM OF FALSE SELF-ASSESSMENT

The reasons which a person takes herself to have are not always *good* reasons. The problem of false self-assessment is the problem of how to determine whether the reasons that a person takes herself to have are good reasons.[2] In this sense, the problem of the rationality of morality is just the one specific version of the problem of false self-assessment in which the person takes herself to have *moral* reasons and the question is whether these reasons give her good reasons for action. In another sense, the problem of the rationality of morality is more general, since it concerns not only self-assessment but also the justification of moral criticism of others. In this chapter and the next, I shall argue that the substantive approach's answer to the problem of false self-assessment should be favored over the answer offered by subjectivist rationalism.

As already discussed in chapters 6–7, Gauthier offers the following simple test for determining whether someone suffers from false self-assessment in accepting a particular sense of justice: are the reasons which the person takes herself to have reasons that she as a utility maximizer would rationally accept "whatever her preferences"? If

[2] The fact that the phrase "false self-assessment" is used to describe the state of the person who is thus mistaken about the reasons she has should not be taken to mean that this person must have engaged in a process of assessing her reasons. I should also mention that what I mean here by "false self-assessment" is the same as what some people mean when they speak of "false consciousness" (this is how Gauthier sometimes uses the latter phrase; see 6.1).

"no," then her self-assessment is false; if "yes," then it is not. If the argument in chapter 7 is correct, there is no principle which it would be rational for all utility maximizers to accept "whatever their preferences." However, here I am interested in *another* question: *if* there were such a principle, ought it to be the standard by which we determine whether we suffer from false self-assessment? It would seem that it ought to be. Gauthier's test is plainly *very attractive*: in determining whether accepting reasons with a certain content would subject us to false self-assessment, this test *by-passes* all appeals to controversial substantive considerations. It simply asks what we as utility maximizers would rationally accept "whatever our preferences."

I think that despite its obvious attractiveness, Gauthier's test should be rejected. I shall argue that any test which entirely by-passes the appeal to substantive reasons is not a good test for false self-assessment. As such, my argument is not only directed at Gauthier's rationalism, but at subjectivist rationalism as such.[3] In fact, my argument will be even more general, since I shall argue that subjectivism itself should be rejected.

2 ASSESSIVE AND NON-ASSESSIVE SELF-UNDERSTANDING

According to subjectivism, the rationality of an agent's actions is relative to her subjective motivational set, and there are no non-relative rational constraints on the contents of this set (see 3.1). According to Gauthier's version of subjectivism, rationality requires no more and no less of the agent than that she maximize the fulfillment of her considered preferences no matter what their content (see 6.2). Subjectivism generally, which includes Gauthier's specific version, is a theory of *rational* or *normative* evaluation: it is meant to specify the ways in which the acts or intentions of an agent can be rationally criticized or supported.

Subjectivism is most commonly criticized by arguing *directly* that it offers the wrong view of rational evaluation. In saying that the criticism is direct, I mean that the critics make rational evaluation their topic of inquiry. Having made it their topic, they then argue

---

[3] Accordingly, in the ensuing discussion, difficulties relating to Gauthier's appeal to the initial situation play no role.

that rational evaluation can never (or at least not generally) be understood subjectivistically.[4] In contrast, my first argument against subjectivism will be *indirect*. Instead of making rational evaluation my
direct topic of inquiry, I shall make self-understanding my subject-
matter. I shall then argue that there is a kind of self-understanding
which *presupposes* that there are other forms of rational evaluation
than those licensed by subjectivism.

My argument will turn on showing that a certain kind of self-
understanding presupposes *substantive strong evaluation* and I begin by
distinguishing between *weak* and *strong* evaluation.[5] This distinction
may best be explained by an example. There are two fundamentally
different ways of approaching the question of whether one should eat
pork. On the one hand, a person may consider it to be a matter of
weak evaluation. In that case, the only relevant question is whether
eating pork would satisfy the person's own desires. Thus, to settle the
matter, the person only has to determine the *strength* of her desires: if
an estimation of this strength shows that pork eating would best satisfy
her desires, then weak evaluation would recommend pork consump-
tion for her. On the other hand, a person may approach the issue as
something to be settled by strong evaluation. In that case, the criterion
she uses is not whether eating pork would satisfy her desires. She uses
some other criteria, perhaps substantive criteria. Thus, she might hold
against eating pork that pigs are holy or filthy or that the raising and
killing of animals is brutal, or she might say in favor of eating pork
that to do so is manly or healthy. This means that a person's strong
evaluations may recommend eating pork to her (perhaps because it is
healthy), even if none of her desires would be satisfied by eating pork.
Alternatively, her strong evaluations may recommend abstinence
from pork (perhaps because pigs are filthy animals), even if eating
pork would be the best way of satisfying her desires.

Turning now to self-understanding, it might be thought that self-
understanding and self-assessment are conceptually independent of
each other in the following sense: a person first reaches an understanding of herself (for example, by determining whether she actually

[4] Many philosophers have offered such arguments. I mention only a few recent ones:
Quinn 1993; Smith 1994, ch. 5; McDowell 1995a; Korsgaard 1996, Lecture 3;
Scanlon 1998, 41–55, 363–373.
[5] In making this distinction, I follow Charles Taylor; cf. Taylor 1985b, 18–27; 1989, 4
and 19–24.

desires to eat some pork) before she assesses herself (for example, by deciding whether the objects of her desires are holy, filthy or nutritious). I do not mean to deny that one kind of self-understanding is independent of self-assessment in this way. However, I want to argue that there is a species of self-understanding which is not conceptually independent of self-assessment in this way.

Consider a person who *identifies* with being a religious person – she takes this to be part of her *identity*. What does it take to identify with being a religious person? It seems to me that, in one common sense of identification, it requires that the person *evaluates positively* being a religious person: if the person did not evaluate this positively, being a religious person would not be something she could identify with. The self-understanding of a person who understands herself as identifying with being a religious person must now be interpreted accordingly: it is clear that it cannot be interpreted as a discovery of a given element in the person's psychological make-up. The person does not simply understand herself as happening to be a certain way. Rather, a presupposition of her being able to understand herself in this way is that she take herself to evaluate positively being religious.[6]

We may now distinguish between two kinds of self-understanding. On the one hand, there is *non-assessive* self-understanding. In such a case, in coming to understand something about herself – say, that she has a certain desire – a person is not assessing herself. On the other hand, there is self-understanding which presupposes self-assessment. In this case, by answering the question "Who am I?" by saying that she is religious, a person means, in part, that she *takes it* that she *should* be a religious person.[7] This "should-element" – this assessive dimension to a person's self-understanding – is missing in non-assessive self-understanding. For example, in answering the question "Who am I?" a person may answer by saying that she is a person who likes to play practical jokes on others. In doing so, she may not be evaluating whether this is a liking that she should have, but may merely be noting what she likes to do. Self-understanding which *presupposes* self-assessment also differs from *self-assessment*, since even though a

---

[6] I am not saying that *all* cases of identity or all cases of identifying oneself as a religious person must be interpreted in this way. I am only saying that there are *some* cases which are best interpreted in this way.

[7] I say "takes it that" rather than "judges that" in order to leave it open whether taking this stand is a matter of making a judgment. See Helm 1996 for an argument to the effect that judgments and emotions can be two separate sources of identification.

person's self-understanding may be correct, the presupposed self-assessment may be incorrect.

Self-understanding which presupposes self-assessment may be further divided into classes depending on what kind of assessment is at stake. I am interested in the division between cases in which the assessment amounts to substantive strong evaluation and cases in which it does not. Let me start with a case of the latter kind.

It seems to me that even Gauthier could allow that there are cases of self-understanding which presuppose self-assessment. However, since he takes rational assessment to be relative to given preferences, he would have to interpret such cases of self-understanding with the help of the following two-layer model of the self:[8] the self has a *core* and this core can be exhaustively understood in the mode of non-assessive self-understanding. It is the fulfillment of the preferences in this core which is to be maximized.[9] Now it may be that the agent comes to adopt other attitudes because doing so serves to maximize the utility of the core. These new attitudes can then be said to form *outer layers* of the self. The crucial point is that Gauthier's utility maximization test assumes that the agent's self-understanding with respect to the new attitudes must either *amount to* non-assessive self-understanding or be *based on* it: either these attitudes are directly the object of the agent's non-assessive self-understanding or she comes to take it that she has them on the basis of their utility maximization relation with elements in the self's core – elements which are all directly objects of non-assessive self-understanding. In the latter case, the agent would have arrived at self-understanding which presupposes self-assessment via utility maximization.

Let me now turn to the case of self-understanding which pre-supposes *substantive strong evaluation*. Examples of persons who identify with being religious or atheistic may serve to illustrate this case. The

---

[8] I am not saying that Gauthier's theory *forces* him to admit that there are such cases of self-understanding. I am only saying that he *could* allow that there are such cases and *if* he did, *then* he would have to think of them in the way I spell out in the text.

[9] It seems to me that Gauthier's utility maximization conception conceives of rational assessment as a matter of weak evaluation. Of course, it might be argued that there is an element of strong evaluation in Gauthier's conception. Since he thinks of the demand to maximize as a rational requirement, it does not depend on the strength of somebody's desire whether she should maximize utility. That she should is a requirement of reason. Nevertheless, it is the strength of the agent's desires and not their content which determines what it is rational for her to do. For this reason it is appropriate to say that for Gauthier rational assessment is a matter of weak evaluation.

religious person does not understand her religious attitudes as outer layers of the self standing in an instrumental relation to elements in the core. Rather, she supports and articulates her religious attitudes by means of such strong evaluations as the following: these attitudes express the appropriate humility with respect to man's place in nature; they express the proper respect for the sacredness of the creation.[10] Likewise the person who identifies with atheism. Her atheistic attitudes may be based on substantive evaluations such as these: these attitudes express a scientific and unmystical view of human existence and a rejection of any subordination of natural impulses to "spiritual" authorities. It is essential to a person's understanding of herself as religious or atheistic that she identifies with these attitudes on the basis of such strong evaluations rather than because holding them would help her satisfy desires in the self's core: if she did not accept some such substantive strong evaluations, then she could not understand herself as identifying with religious or atheistic attitudes.[11]

Self-understanding which presupposes substantive strong evaluation in this way I call *"assessive self-understanding."*[12] In coming to

[10] It could be argued that these are not evaluations which *support* the religious attitude, but rather evaluations which *constitute* it. For example, isn't the concept of *sacredness* obviously a religious concept which cannot be used to support a religious attitude without begging the question? In order to make my point here, I do not need to insist that such evaluations can *support* the religious attitude. What is crucial is that a person cannot understand herself as identifying with a religious attitude without also endorsing some such evaluations. Nevertheless, it is an interesting question whether such substantive evaluations could give support to a religious attitude. In chapter 11, I shall discuss how one substantive concept related to another one can be used to support the employment of the latter one. In order to prevent misunderstanding, however, I should stress that the examples of substantive evaluations I have given here are of course not meant to be sufficient to show that somebody should have a religious attitude. If all that somebody can say in support of a religious attitude is that this attitude expresses the proper respect for the sacredness of the creation, many questions need to be answered before this can count as a good justification. For example, one would have to give some justification for the employment of such concepts as *sacredness* and *the creation*.

[11] If the strong evaluations at stake here could be interpreted as a matter of second-order desires, then the self-understanding of a person who comes to understand herself on the basis of such an evaluation would be based on a non-assessive understanding. For a discussion of this possibility, see §4.

[12] As I shall argue in §3, subjectivism cannot allow that there is any assessive self-understanding. Thus, the subjectivist must interpret the examples I have given differently than I have done. In order to prove my case, I would have to show that my interpretation of these cases is superior to the one which the subjectivist must give. I think that my interpretation of these examples is indeed the most plausible. If that is so, then I will have offered an interpretation of *self-understanding* which delivers an argu-

reach assessive self-understanding, a person is coming to understand a dimension of herself which does not fit into either slot in the two-layer picture of the self: according to the two-layer model, all self-understanding either *is* an understanding of the self's core or is *based on* it. In the case of assessive self-understanding, however, a person comes to understand who she is by engaging in self-assessment *without basing this assessment on a prior understanding of herself or aspects of herself.*

This amounts to a new interpretation of the relationship between the questions "Who am I?" and "Who should I aspire to be?" In trying to reach assessive self-understanding, the person must treat the second question as logically prior to the first. Her answer to the first questions depends on how she answers the second one: she cannot understand herself to be a certain way without positively evaluating being that way (this distinguishes assessive self-understanding from non-assessive self-understanding). And the correctness of the answer to the second question is not relative to who she is: the correctness of the relevant strong evaluation is not relative to her psychological constitution (this distinguishes assessive self-understanding from an understanding of the self's outer layers which presupposes a utility maximization evaluation).[13]

In order to prevent misunderstanding, it must be emphasized that there is a sense in which the assessment presupposed in assessive self-understanding may be based on prior self-understanding. Of course, in answering the question "Who should I aspire to be?" the person may take account of her abilities, psychological strengths and weaknesses, etc. In other words, in forming a judgment based on strong evaluation, the person may take her own psychological constitution into account. However, since the judgment is based on strong evaluation, the correctness of the evaluation itself is not relative to the

ment against the subjectivist account of rational *self-assessment* (see the answer to the second objection in §4).

[13] It should by now be apparent that this section is deeply influenced by Taylor's writings (esp. Taylor 1985b; 1985c; 1989, Part I). By drawing the distinction between non-assessive and assessive self-understanding, I take myself to be merely clarifying a strand in Taylor's thinking. This distinction serves to make clear that, when Taylor speaks of basic re-evaluations in which the agent attempts to articulate her "deepest unstructured sense of what is important" (Taylor 1985b, 41), this should not be construed as an attempt to articulate non-assessively something which is important to her, but as an attempt to arrive at an understanding of what is important to her via an assessment of what is worthy of being taken to be important (I am also indebted here in different ways to both Velleman 1989 and Anderson 1993).

person's psychological constitution. If the judgment were based on utility maximization evaluation, then the evaluation would be relative to the person's psychological constitution, since it would simply depend on what the person's considered preferences happen to be.

It seems, then, that Gauthier's utility maximization account must falsely assume that there is no assessive self-understanding. In the next section, I shall deliver further support for this claim and argue that the same holds for other types of subjectivism. Before doing so, I should emphasize that I have only specified a *necessary* condition of being a certain kind of person, where being this kind of person is the object of assessive self-understanding: a person is a person of kind X (e.g., an atheist) only if she takes it that she should be a person of kind X on the basis of substantive strong evaluation. It is certainly not a sufficient condition.[14] A person who takes it that she *should be* an atheist and takes it that she *is* an atheist may not actually be atheistic. In other words, her assessive self-understanding may be false.[15] To illustrate this, I mention two kinds of false assessive self-understanding. In both cases, the person in question does indeed take it that she *should be* atheistic and take it that she *is* an atheist, but in fact she is *not*.

(1) If the person does indeed take it that she should be an atheist, then leading an atheistic life is indeed an ideal of the person in question. However, the person may be weak-willed and constantly act contrary to what her ideal would require. In that case, we might say that she is not an atheist even though she has an atheistic ideal.

(2) This case differs from (1) in that the person may not be weak-willed. To make clear what kind of a case this is, it is best to assume that those who correctly criticize the person's assessive self-under-standing are not at odds with her about her self-assessment: both sides agree that she should be an atheist. The question is whether she is one. What does it take to be an atheist? How does an atheist judge

---

14 I have said that a person may take it that she should *be* a certain kind of person and that she may *identify* with an attitude. However, I have not explained what the difference is between taking it that one should *be* a certain kind of person rather than just taking it that one should *have* a certain kind of attitude, and between identifying with an attitude and just taking it that one has it (assessively). I have just been concerned with spelling out one *necessary* condition of being a certain kind of person, where being this kind of person is the object of assessive self-understanding: one must take it that one should be that kind of person on the basis of a substantive strong evaluation.

15 If it is indeed the case that the person should not be an atheist, then her *self-assessment* would be false.

specific issues? In answering these questions, her critics are trying to understand a certain way of engaging in strong evaluation – the atheistic way. In other words, to answer the questions, the critics must themselves assess these issues from the atheistic point of view. Answering these questions, however – at least for the issues on which the person in question takes a stand – is also the only way of determining whether the person is right to think that she is an atheist. For example, if the critics of the person's assessive self-understanding argue that the person's stand on ecological issues seems to be guided by the idea that nature must be *respected*, they might argue that the person in question is not thoroughly atheistic, since to treat nature as something to be respected is to treat it as a rational being and to treat nature in that way amounts to a quasi-religious attitude.[16] In this case, the critics would have to conclude that the person's assessive self-understanding is false.

3 SELF–UNDERSTANDING AND SUBJECTIVISM

In this section, I shall argue that Gauthier's subjectivism and all other versions of subjectivism should be rejected because they do not allow there to be any assessive self-understanding.

According to Gauthier, to determine whether an agent who identifies with an attitude is guilty of false self-assessment, the attitude must be subjected to a utility maximization test: is it utility maximizing to have the attitude in question? Gauthier must assume that attitudes which people treat as objects of assessive self-understanding have to be tested in the same way. To apply this test, however, Gauthier cannot treat the attitude to be assessed as an object of assessive self-understanding. He has to interpret the "assessment" which the agent who treats the attitude as an object of assessive self-understanding engages in as something which does not serve to assess the attitude. If this "assessment" were allowed to count as assessment of the attitude, then the utility maximization test could not function in the way that Gauthier intends. The test is to be applied to a *given* considered set of preferences and amounts to the question whether

---

[16] If the person agrees that some of her particular attitudes are quasi-religious in this way and also thinks that she should have these attitudes, then she must either somehow reconcile this with her general commitment to being an atheist or revise her view that she should be an atheist.

the maximization of the satisfaction of the preferences has been achieved. *Prior to* the application of this test, one must have arrived at a correct understanding of what the agent's preferences are. However, this understanding must be entirely *non-assessive*. Otherwise the assessment presupposed in assessive self-understanding could come into conflict with the utility maximization test, and then the test could not be treated as the only way of evaluating attitudes.

This shows that when Gauthier applies the utility maximization test to determine whether something is rational *relative to given preferences*, he cannot allow that there is any assessive self-understanding. Now, Gauthier also uses this test to show that it is rational for each utility maximizer to accept a particular sense of justice, *whatever* the utility maximizer's preferences may happen to be (see 6.2). It can easily be shown that also in this application of the test he cannot allow that there is any assessive self-understanding.

Consider an agent who, on the basis of a substantive strong evaluation, accepts a particular sense of justice which differs from the one favored by Gauthier. This agent's sense of justice then gives rise to certain preferences. Could Gauthier possibly show that this agent should accept Gauthier's favored sense of justice *whatever* the agent's preferences? He could only do so by treating the agent's realization that she accepts a certain sense of justice as a matter of non-assessive self-understanding. If the agent's realization were treated as a matter of assessive self-understanding, then the substantive evaluation in question could come into conflict with Gauthier's utility maximization test. That is the same problem as we encountered in the application of the utility maximization test based on given preferences. In addition, in the case of such a conflict, it could no longer be said that Gauthier's favored sense of justice was acceptable *whatever* the agent's preferences. Since some of the agent's preferences are based on the alternative sense of justice, and these preferences are expressive of an evaluation in conflict with Gauthier's test, Gauthier's sense of justice is not acceptable as far as *these* preferences are concerned. Thus, it cannot be acceptable *whatever* the agent's preferences. In order to avoid these problems, Gauthier must assume that there is no assessive self-understanding.

This shows that in assessing some attitudes, Gauthier must treat these attitudes as something other than what they are. I have argued that it is only as something which the agent assesses positively on strongly evaluative grounds that some attitudes can count as expressing what an agent is. For the purpose of assessing those attitudes, Gauthier cannot treat them as attitudes with respect to which the agent achieves assessive understanding. The agent, however, treats them as precisely something with respect to which she can only achieve *assessive* self-understanding. Thus, Gauthier's utility maximization assessment can be said to *change the subject* in the literal sense that it is the *subject* or the *self* which it changes.[17] It falsely treats the self as something which has no dimensions which can be understood only in the mode of assessive self-understanding.[18]

It might be argued that I have overlooked a way in which Gauthier can acknowledge assessive self-understanding. After all, according to Gauthier, to have a sense of justice is to value justice intrinsically (see 6.1). Thus, even though Gauthier's justification is instrumental, the attitude justified amounts to valuing justice for its own sake. Now doesn't the person who understands herself to have this attitude precisely understand herself in the mode of assessive self-understanding? And, if that is so, why should the fact that Gauthier offers an instrumental justification of this attitude mean that he cannot acknowledge the existence of assessive self-understanding?[19]

It is of course true that Gauthier can allow that we do in fact treat

[17] Cf. Taylor's use of the phrase "changing the subject," which he acknowledges he is appropriating from Donald Davidson (1989, 57–58, 71–72).

[18] It should be clear that it would not help Gauthier to argue that he has already accounted for assessive self-understanding by his model of an understanding of what one's considered preferences are (see 6.2). On this model, reflection does not serve the purpose of answering the question whether it makes sense for the person to take up a certain attitude. It can only serve the purpose of preventing the agent from – hastily – misdescribing what her attitudes are. Of course, Gauthier can allow that a person has ideals in the sense that she has goals which she holds dearly. He must conceive, however, of the process of determining whether these goals are important to the agent as an attempt to reach non-assessive self-understanding. The question is not whether these goals are worthy of pursuit, but, rather, whether they are important to the agent. In attempts to reach assessive self-understanding, however, the question whether the goals are worthy of pursuit must be settled prior to deciding whether they are important to the agent. If the agent decides that they are not worthy of pursuit, then she must also conclude that they are not something she identifies with. (Of course, this does not exclude that she may be mistaken in her assessive self-understanding or that she has a strong desire to reach the goals.)

[19] This argument goes back to an objection made by Neera K. Badhwar to a talk I delivered at the 1997 Pacific Division Meeting of the American Philosophical Association. However, since I have revised my earlier text – including the account of assessive self-understanding – in order to respond to her objection, I cannot assume that she would make the objection in this form.

some attitudes as objects of assessive self-understanding. He must, however, assume that we are mistaken in doing so. Since he thinks that all assessment must be based on non-assessive self-understanding, he cannot count the "assessment" presupposed in assessive self-understanding as real assessment, as I already argued. For him, there are only two ways of understanding oneself as just. On the one hand, the agent can understand herself as just because of the instrumental relation of justice to the satisfaction of the preferences in the self's core. In that case, her self-understanding presupposes instrumental assessment, but it is based on non-assessive self-understanding. Thus, it does not qualify as assessive self-understanding as I have defined it. On the other hand, the agent may understand herself as valuing justice for its own sake. In that case, Gauthier cannot allow there to be any real assessment involved and must therefore count this as a case of non-assessive self-understanding. In his theory, there is simply no room for self-understanding which neither amounts to non-assessive self-understanding nor is based on it. Thus, there is no room for assessive self-understanding.

It should be noted that I have not argued that Gauthier offers the wrong approach to *justice*. As far as my argument goes, he may be right in arguing that the rational credentials of a sense of justice depend on its instrumental value. What I have been arguing is that there are *some* attitudes which agents treat as objects of assessive self-understanding and that Gauthier's model has no conceptual space for assessive self-understanding. I postpone the discussion of the possibility that justice is special in this way until 11.3.

Like Gauthier's theory, other subjectivistic theories have no conceptual space for assessive self-understanding. Subjectivism is the thesis that rational assessment is *relative* to the agent's subjective motivational set and that rationality sets *no non-relative* constraints on what must or may be included in such a set. The problem is that to maintain this relativity thesis, subjectivism must draw a sharp distinction between self-understanding and self-assessment. Self-understanding must be prior to self-assessment in the sense that correct self-understanding tells the agent what her subjective motivational set contains and correct self-assessment tells her – on this basis – what reasons she has.[20] This means that subjectivism has no conceptual

---

[20] This is true of Williams' view even though he thinks that the contents of the subjective motivational set are affected by deliberation and are thus not "statically given"

space for assessive self-understanding: it is definitive of assessive self-understanding that the assessment in question is not based on a prior self-understanding.[21] Thus, subjectivism must falsely pretend that there are no dimensions of the self which can only be understood in the mode of assessive self-understanding.

It could be argued that I have forgotten one option which is open to the subjectivist. After all, Williams says that a subjective motivational set may contain "dispositions of evaluation."[22] Thus, the subjectivist might interpret assessive self-understanding as follows: the person's dispositions of evaluation are *at work* when she reaches self-understanding on the basis of a substantive strong evaluation. This does not mean that these dispositions of evaluation are first the object of a non-assessive self-understanding and that the person's self-assessment is based on this prior non-assessive self-understanding. On the contrary, in cases of assessive self-understanding, the person's dispositions of evaluation are never the *object* of non-assessive self-understanding; they are merely *at work* when the person reaches assessive self-understanding on the basis of a strong evaluation.

In order to see why this subjectivist reply fails, let us recall that subjectivism maintains that there are no non-relative rational constraints on the content of a person's subjective motivational set. This means that as far as rationality is concerned, the person's dispositions

(Williams 1981, 105): some of what Williams thinks of as deliberation must be understood as a process aimed at arriving at a more complete non-assessive self-understanding and some of it must be interpreted as a process of self-assessment based on prior self-understanding (see the distinction between "theoretical" and "practical" deliberation as two versions of subjectivistically interpreted rational deliberation in 3.1).

[21] Subjectivism *can*, of course, accommodate cases of self-understanding which presuppose self-assessment in the following way: the presupposed self-assessment evaluates the agent's subjective motivational set according to how *coherent* it is. The conclusion of this evaluation may then be that something must be taken to belong to the set in order to render it more coherent. The understanding that this member belongs to the now more coherent set is therefore based on assessment, but it is nevertheless based on a prior non-assessive understanding of the contents of the previously less coherent subjective motivational set. This case fits the two-layer model of the self, but it differs from the earlier version of the model in that here the relation between the core and the outer layer is a coherence relation rather than an instrumental relation. Now, as already explained for Gauthier's theory, this will not help subjectivism because the objects of assessive self-understanding do not fit into either slot in this two-layer model.

[22] Williams 1981, 105.

of evaluation might have been completely different.[23] This also means that the person's self-assessment must depend on non-assessive self-understanding in the following way: what reasons the person has is relative to what her dispositions of evaluation happen to be, and what those dispositions happen to be is the object of non-assessive self-understanding.

Now this is not at all how things look from the perspective of the person trying to reach assessive self-understanding. In engaging in the relevant substantive strong evaluation, she does not suppose that she is merely relying on dispositions which are rationally optional.[24] Of course, in evaluating, she must draw on some evaluative standards. She supposes, however, that these are not standards that she merely happens to favor, or standards which are merely more or less rational relative to what other things happen to be in her subjective motivational set. Rather, she supposes that the support of these standards themselves is *substantive as opposed to subjective* and therefore also supposes that she has *external reasons* to employ these standards.[25] Thus, the evaluation presupposed in assessive self-understanding cannot be understood to be relative to elements in her subjective motivational set which may be made the objects of non-assessive self-understanding; the evaluation is not merely an attempt to draw out the consequences of something which she can exhaustively understand in the mode of non-assessive self-understanding.

4 OBJECTIONS

I have been arguing that subjectivism must falsely assume that there are no dimensions of the self which the agent can only understand in

---

[23] Or more precisely: the constraints on what dispositions of evaluation a person may or must rationally have are all relative to the rest of her subjective motivational set.

[24] As these remarks indicate, my arguments in this work are offered from the perspective of the agent engaged in rational evaluation. For a clarification and defense of this argumentative strategy, see 12.2.

[25] If she really supposes that she has irreducibly substantive reasons to employ these standards, then she must also suppose that she has external reasons to employ them (leaving aside the non-subjectivist internal reasons model mentioned in 3.1). However, it might be argued that she only supposes that she has external reasons, without thinking that they are substantive. For example, these reasons might rest on non-subjectivistically interpreted coherence considerations. I take up this issue in chapter 15, where I argue that substantive considerations cannot be eliminated in favor of non-subjectivistically interpreted formal considerations.

the mode of assessive self-understanding. In this section, I consider three objections to this argument.

1. I have said that to identify with being a certain way, a person must evaluate positively being that way. It might be suggested that this evaluation should be analyzed as a second-order desire about what first-order desires to have.[26] If that is so, then, contrary to what I have claimed, there would not really be anything like assessive self-understanding. After all, a second-order desire is just a desire. So, when a person comes to understand herself on the basis of an evaluation, her self-understanding would be based on non-assessive understanding of a second-order desire.

Since others have convincingly argued that evaluation cannot be understood in terms of second-order desires, I shall not say much about this objection.[27] It is essential to the objection that first-order and second-order desires are just desires. The problem is that if they are both really just desires, no basis has been given for identifying the agent's evaluations with second-order desires rather than with desires of a different order.

2. It could be argued that I have simply assumed what I wanted to prove. In my argument against subjectivism, I urged that assessive self-understanding presupposes a kind of evaluation which cannot be interpreted subjectivistically. This was especially clear in my argument against Williams. There I urged that the person aiming to reach assessive self-understanding must assume that the relevant evaluation relies on standards which cannot be interpreted subjectivistically. Now, given that this is so, it seems that my argument does not rest on an analysis of self-understanding but rather on an interpretation of rational evaluation for which I have given no argument. And it is this interpretation of rational evaluation which is the point of contention between subjectivists and their critics. Therefore, I would need an *argument* for the non-subjectivistic interpretation and that I have not delivered.

I answer by insisting that I have indeed offered such an argument. I first argued that there is a kind of self-understanding which presupposes substantive strong evaluation. I then argued that Gauthier and Williams cannot allow that there is such self-understanding because they cannot allow substantive strong evaluation to serve as real

[26] See Frankfurt 1988; Lewis 1989.
[27] See, e.g., Watson 1975; Smith 1994, 142–147; Quinn 1993, 238–240.

evaluation. Now, this argument relies on the assumption that substantive strong evaluation cannot be interpreted subjectivistically. In defense of this assumption, I have been urging that, in strongly evaluating substantively, the *agent herself assumes* that the evaluation is not to be interpreted subjectivistically. I do not want to deny that this defense relies on intuitions as to how agents actually engage in rational evaluation. However, in saying that the agent herself assumes that substantive strong evaluation is not to be interpreted subjectivistically, I have mainly been stressing that she assumes this in trying to reach a certain kind of *self-understanding* – namely, assessive self-understanding. Thus, my argument against subjectivism is meant to draw its main plausibility from the plausibility of this interpretation of self-understanding. The point of my argument has been to show that subjectivism does not merely give the wrong account of rational evaluation, but also of self-understanding.

3. I have argued that when agents engage in evaluation, they do in fact understand this evaluation non-subjectivistically. Now it could be objected that this only shows how people do *in fact* engage in evaluation. This leaves it open that they might be *mistaken* in engaging in non-subjectivistic evaluation. Thus, my arguments have not settled the *normative* question of whether we *should* ever engage in such evaluation.

It is true that my arguments have not settled this question. And it seems to me that this is the crucial question. After all, there are two serious worries about relying on substantive reasons rather than exclusively on subjective reasons, or more specifically, on subjectivist rationalistic reasons. These worries are at the same time arguments against the substantive approach as opposed to subjectivist rationalism.

(a) The first worry is, in effect, *the controversiality problem* raised in 5.1. According to the substantive approach, to determine whether a person's self-assessment is false, we must sometimes rely on substantive reasons. In other words, the question of whether the reasons that a person takes herself to have are good reasons must be answered in substantive evaluation, an evaluation where one candidate substantive reason is evaluated by appealing to other substantive reasons. The problem is that the substantive reasons used to evaluate the candidate reason are themselves essentially controversial: they cannot be shown to be good reasons by appeal to an uncontroversial criterion of rationality.

It could be argued that because of this essential controversiality we cannot solve the problem of false self-assessment by relying on substantive reason. On the contrary, it is substantive reasons which *create* the danger of false self-assessment: in taking something as a substantive reason, a person always runs the risk that she might be mistaken to take it thus. This then means, so the argument goes, that Gauthier's theory must be favored over the substantive approach. His theory offers a *solution* to the problem of false self-assessment. He relies on utility maximization as the only criterion of rationality and thus *by-passes* any appeal to *essentially controversial* substantive intuitions. By delivering a test which by-passes such intuitions, Gauthier enables the agent to determine whether the substantive reasons concerning justice which she relies upon subject her to false self-assessment. Therefore, it is not a problem that, for the purposes of assessment, Gauthier treats as a matter of non-assessive self-understanding that which the agent treats as a matter of assessive self-understanding. If, as this argument suggests, treating it in the way that Gauthier does is necessary to solve the problem of false self-assessment, then he is surely justified in thus treating it.

(b) The source of the second alleged problem is that in order to explain why a substantive reason is good we will have to refer to its content. At least for some substantive reasons, it cannot be exhaustively explained in terms of anything other than the content of the reason itself why this content plays a role in making the reason a good reason. Part of the answer to the question "What makes this be a good reason?" is "It has this content," and no appeal to something else will exhaustively explain what it is about this content – other than that it is the content it is – that allows it to contribute to the goodness of the reason. This gives rise to the worry that there will be no way to distinguish the good reasons from the bad reasons, since there will be no way to distinguish the "good contents" from the "bad contents." The worry is that it must be *arbitrarily* decided which are the "good contents." Let me thus call this worry "*the arbitrariness problem.*" If it cannot be resolved, it must be concluded that it is an illusion to think that substantive reasons have any critical potential at all.

If I am right that in our evaluative practices we do, in fact, assume that there are substantive reasons, then what the subjectivist rationalist is proposing here is that we should *revise* our practices. She is proposing that we revise our practices so as to let ourselves be guided only by subjectivistically acceptable reasons. And her argument is that we must revise them in order to avoid these two worries. I think that this is the real issue between the substantive approach and subjectivist rationalism: do we have a *good reason* to rely on substantive reasons rather than on subjectivist rationalistic reasons?

This would not be the real issue if it were *impossible* to revise our practices thus. However, I do think that it is possible (this I shall argue in chapter 12). Since it is possible, the crucial argument against subjectivist rationalism and in favor of the substantive approach is that we have a *good practical reason* not to revise our practices.[28] In the next section, I shall accordingly offer a practical argument for our practice of relying on substantive reasons.

The next section will deliver the *basic* practical argument. However, the advantages of the substantive approach over subjectivist rationalism will not unfold entirely until I say more about substantive reasons and why we should rely on them rather than on subjectivist rationalistic justifications in dealing with the problem of false self-assessment. This I shall do in the next chapter, where I also demonstrate the critical potential of the substantive approach. The final resolution of the controversiality problem and the arbitrariness problem is thus to be found in the next chapter.

5 A PRACTICAL ARGUMENT

In this section, I shall argue that we have a good practical reason for relying not only on subjective reasons but also on substantive reasons. Before actually offering the argument, I must make clear what it means to assume that there are substantive reasons and what it means to assume that there are only subjective reasons. As already mentioned in 3.1, to say that somebody has a *substantive* reason to do something means (1) that the person has an external reason to do it and (2) that the considerations which speak in favor of doing it are irreducibly substantive.

To see what it means to assume that there are only *subjective* reasons, let us recall what I said about Williams in 3.1. I argued that, though he thinks that it is indeterminate what counts as a rational

---

[28] That this is the crucial argument will be further defended in chapter 12, where I also discuss the status of the argument.

deliberative process, he must nevertheless assume that there is a difference between a change of mind as a result of rational deliberation and one as a result of conversion. I also said that, in subjectivistically understood rational deliberation, the agent cannot be responding to external reasons but must rather be drawing out the "rational implications" of her current subjective motivational set. This now has consequences for the ways in which somebody who accepts subjectivism – call her "the subjective evaluator" – must view revisions in her own attitudes, goals, actions, etc. Since conversions are by definition not supported by the subjective motivational set, and all rational evaluation is relative to the set, she cannot view conversions as changes for the better. Thus, she can count no revision of a person's attitudes, goals, actions, etc., which cannot be shown to be a rational implication of the person's current subjective motivational set as a *change for the better.*

To be more precise, it is only from the point of view of her *current* subjective motivational set that the subjective evaluator cannot count conversions as changes for the better. If we call the various subjective motivational sets which the agent consecutively acquires as a result of conversion "S1," "S2," "S3," etc., then the conversion from S1 to S2 cannot count as a change for the better *from the point of view of S1*, and the conversion from S2 to S3 cannot count as an improvement *from the point of view of S2*, etc. However, *relative to* subjective motivational sets *other than the current one*, conversions can count as changes for the better (or worse). For example, relative to the standards of evaluation which are part of S2, the conversion from S1 to S2 may count as progress (or regress), whereas the conversion from S3 to S4 may count as regress (or progress). Thus, the subjective evaluator *can* count a conversion from S1 to S2 as a change for the better, but only *relative to some S other than S1.*

The person who employs substantive reasons – call her "the substantive evaluator" – does *not* have to *relativize* thus the way in which changes can count as an improvement. Since she assumes that changes can be supported by external reasons, she can say that even the most radical revisions of her attitudes, desires and goals are *without qualification* a change for the better, assuming that the revisions are supported by external reasons.[29]

---

[29] Someone who accepts Blackburn's projectivistic expressivism cannot view changes in this way. Although Blackburn wants to allow that there is a certain sense in which

This difference shows that the substantive evaluator can view her life as having a certain purpose or meaning which the subjective evaluator's life lacks. The substantive evaluator can view the series of conversions she has gone through (and will go through) as part of a life developing for the better. The subjective evaluator cannot do this without first specifying the S from which this judgment is to be made. For example, relative to the S which she had when she was thirty years old her life may be a progress, relative to the S which she had when she was thirty-five it may be a regress, etc. However, as a subjective evaluator, she must admit that no one S is *as such* superior to any of the others. S1, say, can only count as superior to, say, S13, *relative to* some particular S. There is no way for her to privilege one S as *the* standpoint from which progress is to be judged. Thus, there is an important sense in which the subjective evaluator cannot think of her life as making progress. Her life consists of a series of standpoints, none of which can be privileged – not of points in a progressive development. Since the subjective evaluator cannot view her life as such a progressive development, her life cannot derive meaning from the possibility or realization of such progress.[30] The substantive evaluator, in contrast, can view her life as being meaningful for this reason. This is not to say that the subjective evaluator's life is meaningless. It lacks, however, a certain source of meaning which the substantive evaluator can draw upon.

It could be objected here that it is an old-fashioned and unmodern idea to suppose that life derives its meaning from the possibility of such a progressive development: such an idea presupposes that the individual must fit her goals to some pre-ordained objective pattern. According to this objection, the modern individual does not render her life meaningful by trying to match it with such a pattern, but rather by seeing *herself* as the source of meaning. What renders life meaningful for the individual is the adventure of choosing her own individually specific goals and values without any pre-ordained patterns. In short, only by seeing her own autonomy as the

there are reasons which are independent of the agent's actual motivational set, he clearly sees that his expressivism commits him to holding that an agent only has a reason to do something if doing it can be supported by something which is at least *implicit* in the agent's actual motivational set (Blackburn 1998, 264–266). Thus, the argument against subjectivism advanced in this section is equally applicable to Blackburn's position.

[30] For further discussion of this idea of progress, see 12.3 and 14.1–2.

source of life's meaning can the modern individual view her life as meaningful.[31]

Now – so the objection continues – it is not possible to view the individual's autonomy as the source of life's meaning if we suppose that the point of life is to make progress in the way that the substantive evaluator wants to make progress. What makes this idea of progress possible is precisely the assumption that a change in the individual's S1 may be progress even if this change is not supported by S1 or any S from the individual's future or past. Thus, so the argument goes, to see the individual's autonomy as the source of life's meaning, we must instead adopt the subjective evaluator's relative interpretation of progress.[32]

I have two answers to this argument. (1) First, the subjectivist herself cannot offer the argument in this form. The argument rests on a claim about what makes life meaningful and such a claim is evaluative. The subjectivist would thus have to interpret this claim according to the subjectivist account of evaluation. In other words, she would have to say that a person only has a good reason to accept this evaluation if something in this person's subjective motivational set speaks in favor of it. Therefore, the subjectivist could not claim that this evaluation concerning the meaning of life is rationally superior to any other evaluation. All she can say is that some people happen to share this evaluation, while others do not.

(2) Second, the notions of autonomy, adventure and individuality which are appealed to in the objection can all be understood as substantive ideals which are perfectly compatible with the substantive evaluator's idea of progress. In fact, a substantive evaluator may consider it a sign of progress if she manages in the course of her life to become more autonomous, more adventurous, and more of a distinctive individual. Of course, this is not what the objector had in mind in speaking of the individual as the autonomous source of meaning. It seems to me, however, that there is nothing desirable about these ideals which the substantive evaluator cannot reach. In

---

[31] I do *not* understand this objection as saying that the view that there are external reasons rests on questionable metaphysical assumptions. As already explained in chapter 4, I assume that McDowell has shown that there is nothing metaphysically weird about assuming that there are external reasons. Rather, I understand the objection as resting on an *evaluative* claim as to what makes life meaningful.

[32] Although he would certainly not endorse it himself, this objection was made by Jay Wallace.

striving to become more autonomous in the course of her life, she is precisely trying to make choices which are her own rather than choices recommended by society or her family. The fact that she hopes to be guided by external reasons does not mean that she must be looking for "pregiven patterns" in any objectionable sense. She is not trying to become like other people or some ideal type. Rather, she is trying to develop the fine distinctions which are necessary to find out what life *she* should lead, taking into account everything that is distinctive of her as an individual. Of course, I do not mean to suggest that every substantive evaluator should adopt autonomy as a substantive ideal, but this ideal is surely compatible with the substantive evaluator's understanding of progress.

In saying that the life of the substantive evaluator can be meaningful in a way that the subjective evaluator's cannot, I take myself to be offering a *practical reason* for relying on substantive reasons. It is a practical reason in the sense that it is based on the substantively evaluative reasoning I have offered. I have argued that one kind of life cannot be meaningful in a way that another kind of life can, and in doing so I have made a substantively evaluative judgment. This means that the reason I have offered for employing substantive reasons itself amounts to a substantive reason. Of course, this gives rise to the objection that my argument is circular, but I shall defer discussion of that objection to 12.3. Here I merely wanted to formulate the basic practical argument in favor of employing not only subjective reasons but also substantive reasons.

This basic argument naturally does not suffice to demonstrate this conclusion. Even if this is a good practical argument in favor of employing substantive reasons, there might be other practical arguments against employing such reasons. To establish the conclusion, such possible counter-arguments would also need to be considered. In this work, I cannot discuss all such possible practical arguments against the substantive approach. However, my practical arguments in favor of the substantive approach go beyond the basic practical argument just offered: in the next chapter, I shall elaborate on the advantages of using substantive reasons as opposed to only subjective or subjectivist rationalistic reasons. In later chapters, I shall then engage in practical deliberation to show that we should sometimes rely on substantive reasons, rather than only on inter-subjectivist rationalistic reasons or formal reasons.

11

The possibility of progress

In this chapter, I shall address the problem of arbitrariness and the problem of controversiality (see 10.4). In order to resolve these problems, I shall offer an account of substantive justifications which demonstrates the critical potential of the substantive approach. This account enables me to resolve the two problems and to show that to determine whether we suffer from false self-assessment, we should sometimes rely on substantive reasons rather than on subjectivist rationalistic reasons. In the third section, then, I shall discuss whether *justice* poses any special difficulties for the substantive approach to the problem of self-assessment. After concluding the discussion of self-assessment, I shall, in the last section, briefly talk about the problem of the categorical force of morality (see 2.1).

I SUBSTANTIVE CRITIQUE

Let us start by discussing *rudeness* as an example of a substantive concept often used to evaluate actions. *Rudeness* is a *thick evaluative concept* which means that it is *world-guided* (certain facts must obtain for it to be applied) and *attitude-guiding* (it offers reasons for actions and attitudes).[1] *Rudeness*, we may assume, guides our attitudes, at least in the following way: if we sincerely describe something as rude, we are thereby *criticizing* it. Thus, in one sense, it is not possible to ask for a justification of criticizing rude actions: to call the actions rude *is* already to criticize them. However, in another sense, it is possible. In saying that certain actions are rude, we are criticizing them. Are we, however, really justified in criticizing these actions?[2] If we are not,

---

[1] See Foot 1978b, 102–105; Williams 1985, 140–141; Anderson 1993, 98.

[2] My argument in this chapter does not rest on the assumption that by saying that an action is rude we are criticizing it. I have merely made this assumption here in order to make it clear that *even if we make it*, it is nevertheless possible to raise the question of

then – because of the criticism inherent in the concept of rudeness – we would have to stop using this concept.[3] The critic of the substantive approach thinks that it is not possible, with the help of substantive reasons, to settle whether we are justified in our criticism of people and their actions. I want to show that she is wrong, by showing that we can have good *substantive reasons* for criticizing actions which fall under such terms as "rude."

A rude action may at the same time also be, for example, insulting, impolite, cruel, insensitive, offensive, tactless, or belittling, demeaning, or humiliating for the affected person. This helps us to give an answer to the question why we should not perform rude actions. Sometimes we should not perform a rude action because it would be insulting. And sometimes when a rude action would not be insulting, we should not do it because it would be cruel or tactless, and so forth. In other words, rudeness involves an action-pattern which is objectionable because rude actions are often insulting, cruel, tactless, etc. Thus, we have a partial substantive justification for criticizing actions which fall under the term "rude": these actions are not only rude, but also often objectionable for other substantive reasons than that they are rude.

It is useful to compare this partial justification with another possible kind of justification. According to this alternative justification, there is *one* basic substantive reason for not being rude. For example, this reason might be that by being rude one shows disrespect for other people or that by being rude one harms them. More generally, the reason is that by performing a rude action, one also ϕs, where ϕ-ing is described in substantive terms. Assuming that we have a good reason not to ϕ, and that by being rude one ϕs, this is clearly a good justification for not being rude. The justification lays out one central point of not being rude: by being rude, one ϕs.

The partial justification I have described is just like this one, except that it does not give a *unified* reason for not being rude. What one does to others when one is rude cannot be subsumed under just one substantive concept as this alternative justification assumes. Rather, in

whether we are justified in criticizing actions which fall under the term "rude." The assumption that by saying that an action is rude we are criticizing does not settle the justificatory question: even if we are criticizing it, it might be that rudeness does not make actions worthy of criticism.
[3] Foot 1978b, 104.

order to understand what we do to others when we are rude, we must invoke various substantive concepts. Sometimes we are cruel, at other times we are merely insulting. Nevertheless, the partial justification I have offered is just as good as the unified justification: assuming that we have a good reason not to be cruel, insulting, etc., and that by being rude one is sometimes cruel, at other times insulting, etc., then we have on all of these occasions a good substantive reason not to be rude.

Now this cannot be a *complete* justification of the criticism of actions which fall under the term "rude." After all, rudeness is a different concept than impoliteness, cruelty, and the others. Thus, there will be cases in which a rude action is not criticizable for being insulting, cruel, or for any of the other substantive reasons. In those cases, the only point of criticism will be that the action is rude. In order to show that we are justified in using the concept *rudeness* rather than just the other substantive concepts, we must show that these cases are also worthy of criticism. Here nothing remains except to say that the actions are worthy of criticism because they are rude. Rudeness locates an aspect of these actions that makes them worthy of criticism not because these actions are cruel or insensitive but because they are rude. For this reason we need the concept of rudeness and not only the concepts of cruelty, tactlessness, etc., to criticize actions. We might say that this element in the justification of the use of rudeness concerns the "intrinsic appeal of the substantive concept itself."

Typically, a substantive concept can not only be supported but also be criticized by other substantive concepts. For example, one might argue that *rudeness* is a concept which is part of a bourgeois and hypocritical morality which stands in the way of honest and frank human relationships. Since the concept of rudeness cannot be separated from this objectionable bourgeois framework, it must be rejected. To answer this criticism, one must show either that rudeness is not thus connected with this moral framework, or that even if it is, there are nevertheless good substantive reasons for criticizing people for their rudeness.

Assuming that this discussion of the concept of rudeness can be applied to other substantive concepts, I conclude that a good substantive justification of the use of substantive concepts will rest on two different elements: (1) the *intrinsic appeal* of the substantive concept itself and (2) the *relationship* of the concept in question *to other substantive concepts.* In the latter case, one needs both to give positive support to the concept and to defend it against criticism based on other substantive concepts. I call the first element "the *intrinsic* element" and the second one "the *connective* element."

It is worth noticing that the question of what substantive reasons there are for and against using a substantive concept *at all* is bound to arise in many of the cases in which the initial question is merely how to *apply* the relevant concept to a situation. To see how this happens, consider the question of whether a woman who argues aggressively in a business context is to be called "rude."[4] Given that this is a business context, we may assume that a man who exhibited this behavior would not necessarily be taken to be rude. Since women, however, have not been as prevalent in this context, it may not be as clear whether a woman who behaved in this way should be called "rude" or not. This question cannot be treated as a purely factual or linguistic question as opposed to an evaluative one: we must ask whether the rudeness of the otherwise same behavior may or must vary depending on what gender exhibits the behavior, and asking this question is to ask for the deeper point of evaluating people according to rudeness. And we must ask whether it would be appropriate to discriminate thus between men and women in a business context. Having answered these questions, we will not only have decided whether we should call women who argue aggressively in a business context "rude," but also whether we should continue to use the concept *rudeness* at all. If we reach the conclusion that it is inappropriate to discriminate between men and women in a business context because doing so would be, for example, *unfair* to women, and the conclusion that evaluating people according to their rudeness demands such discrimination, then we would have a good substantive reason for ceasing to use the concept at all.[5] If, however, we conclude

---

[4] For this example and what I say about it in this paragraph I am indebted to Anderson 1993, 99–101. As Anderson says, she borrows the example from Judith Martin.

[5] The rejection of this concept as gender-biased may be usefully compared with the rejection of such concepts as *Boche* and *nigger*. The *circumstances of application* of "Boche" are that the person to whom it is applied is German whereas the *consequences of application* are that the person is cruel. Thus, if one objects to inferring cruelty from German nationality, one must refuse to use the term at all (see Brandom 1988, 270–280; and 1994, 116–132, for a discussion of the original treatment of this point in Dummett 1981, 453–455). Similarly, if the concept of rudeness were to be rejected for its gender bias, this would be because of the inferential link between being

that there is no gender bias inherent in rudeness, or that we can reform the concept so as to clear it of gender bias, then we may continue to use the concept.

At this point, it might be objected that my account of substantive critique does not meet the worry about the critical potential of the substantive approach which it was meant to answer. I have said that substantive justifications rest on two elements: the intrinsic and the connective element. Although my discussion was focused on *rudeness*, the same justification is supposed to apply to all other substantive concepts. This means that it holds for *each* substantive concept that a *part* of the justification of its use must be based on its intrinsic appeal. Thus, *no* substantive concepts can be *exhaustively* justified in terms of something other than the concept itself. If that is so, however, it seems that there is an ineliminable element of *arbitrariness* in the decision to use a substantive concept. For example, if the decision to use *rudeness* rests on the assumption that the rudeness of an action makes it worthy of criticism, how are we to decide rationally whether the rudeness of actions really speaks against them? More generally, if part of the decision to use a concept with a particular content will always be given in terms of the concept itself, how are we supposed to distinguish rationally the contents which speak for actions from the contents which speak against actions? Can this decision be anything but arbitrary?

Why should it be *arbitrary* to say that actions are worthy of criticism because they are rude? If *rudeness* were understood as a *mere projection* of our attitudes, it might be plausible to say that it is arbitrary. However, at this point in the dialectic, this is not an objection I am interested in. As already explained in chapter 4, I am interested in the possible difficulties that arise for a substantive approach which rejects such a projective account. As I also said there, I am assuming with McDowell that these difficulties are not of a metaphysical nature: there is nothing "metaphysically weird" about the supposition that there are substantive reasons.

What could the accusation of arbitrariness then be based on? The criticism seems to be that it is *arbitrary* to say that actions are worthy of criticism because they are rude and because they are X, whereas they are worthy of praise because they are Y (where "X" and "Y"

someone who argues aggressively and being a woman which may be built into the concept of rudeness.

stand for some substantive concepts). Now why should that be so? For example, if we substitute "friendly" for "Y," then the accusation of arbitrariness is no longer plausible. Surely it is *not arbitrary* to claim that the rudeness of an action would make it worthy of criticism, whereas the friendliness of an action would not. In fact, this is a highly plausible claim. Nevertheless, as I argued, it might be possible to give good reasons for ceasing to criticize actions for being rude. It seems to me that the defender of the accusation of arbitrariness faces here a dilemma: if she specifies what "X" and "Y" stand for, then the accusation of arbitrariness will be implausible. If she leaves "X" and "Y" unspecified, then it is unclear what the accusation of arbitrariness rests on.

I conclude that the accusation of arbitrariness is unfounded. However, the controversiality problem is still unresolved: although the fact that no substantive concept can be exhaustively justified in terms of other substantive concepts does not show that criticism based on substantive concepts is *arbitrary*, it seems to show that such criticism is *essentially controversial*. Since the use of no substantive concept can be exhaustively justified in terms of a secure external criterion, the use of each such concept must rest on something controversial. This I do not want to dispute. It does rest on something controversial.[6] However, I think that this is a price worth paying. As I shall argue, the controversiality of substantive concepts is a consequence of that which speaks in favor of employing substantive reasons. This controversiality is a consequence of an ideal of reason we should favor over the subjectivist rationalistic ideal. This will also amount to an argument to the effect that the substantive approach to the problem of false self-assessment is to be favored over the subjectivist rationalistic approach.

2 SUBSTANTIVE CRITIQUE AND SELF-ASSESSMENT

My argument here starts with the results of the practical argument offered in 10.5. There I maintained that we have a good practical reason to suppose that there are substantive reasons, because doing so gives our lives a meaning which subjectivism cannot give it. This supposition gives our lives meaning by enabling us to view changes in

[6] For the issue of whether substantive justifications are really more controversial than subjectivist rationalistic justifications, see the answer to the fourth objection in 13.3.

our attitudes, goals, actions, etc., as *progress* even if these changes cannot be supported by our subjective motivational set.

This was the practical reason for supposing that there are *not only subjective* reasons but also substantive reasons. Now a related reason can be given for supposing that there are *not only* external reasons based on *coherence* considerations but also on *substantive* considerations. If all external reasons were based on coherence considerations, then the explanation why a change is a change for the better would always be that the new state is more coherent than the old state. This, however, unnecessarily limits the kinds of change which can count as progress. If we allow substantive considerations to explain why something is a change for the better, then we have more various ways of counting something as an improvement. This amounts to a good practical reason for supposing that progress may be revealed by *substantive* reasons.[7]

Let us, therefore, assume that the life of the substantive evaluator is more meaningful than the life of the subjective evaluator. This provides the key to the resolution of the controversiality problem. If the use of substantive concepts does indeed contribute significantly to the meaning of life, then it is not a problem but a virtue that we cannot justify the use of one substantive concept exhaustively in terms of other concepts. Substantive concepts provide the agent with fine-grained ways of evaluating and describing the world. By means of such concepts, we are able to give expression to the fine differences in what we value.[8] And it seems that in a life where meaning is inseparably bound up with capturing the merits of ideals with the help of *substantive* reasons, it is part of the way things should be that we cannot exhaustively explain the merit of a particular ideal by referring to concepts that carve the world up differently than the

[7] I have not yet shown that it is not possible to squeeze enough out of an idea of coherence to account for whatever substantive reasons are supposed to account for. This possibility will be considered in chapter 15.

[8] According to the McDowellian view accepted in 4.2, concepts for which truth can be earned from within cannot be analyzed projectivistically. I accordingly assume here that these fine-grained ways of evaluating cannot be replaced by a naturalistic description of the world combined with an attitude towards the features thus described. Blackburn thinks that normative criticism is only possible if we are able to split the evaluation up into a naturalistic description and an attitude towards the relevant features (Blackburn 1998, 101–102). This chapter is meant to show precisely how normative criticism is possible on the basis of evaluations which cannot be thus split up.

substantive concept in question. Now if controversiality is a consequence of the fact that the use of substantive concepts cannot be exhaustively justified in this way, then controversiality is simply a price we have to pay for something which contributes importantly to the meaning of life.

It could be objected here that the practical argument in 10.5 cannot possibly help to show that the substantive approach is superior to *subjectivist rationalism*. According to the practical argument, the subjective evaluator cannot count changes which are not supported by her subjective motivational set as progress. Now there is a certain sense in which subjectivist rationalism could count such changes as progress. After all, subjectivist rationalism aims to show that it would be progress for an agent to accept certain principles, since it would be utility maximizing to accept them *whatever the agent's preferences*. This means that the acceptance of these principles could count as progress even if the elements which *happen to be* in the subjective motivational set speak against the principles.

I do not want to dispute that subjectivist rationalism can allow that there is a certain kind of progress which there could not be if all reasons were directly relative to the agent's subjective motivational set. However, as I argued, we have a good practical reason to suppose that progress may be revealed by substantive reasons. And I just explained how the multifarious substantive concepts express the subtle and rich ways in which something can count as progress. Thus, to be able to grasp and express the sense of progress which gives meaning to their lives, people must avail themselves of substantive concepts. Subjectivist rationalism cannot allow progress to be expressed in this way. Even if the use of substantive concepts could be rationalistically justified, the explanation why something counts as progress must be a utility maximization explanation. In other words, it must *by-pass* the substantive concepts. By thus by-passing substantive concepts, subjectivist rationalism eradicates the very differences which people use to express why something counts as a change for the better. Since the substantive approach makes these differences visible again, it must be preferred to subjectivist rationalism.

We now also have a good reason to accept the substantive approach to the problem of false self-assessment. Naturally, in relying on substantive reasons, we may fall prey to false self-assessment. We would, however, be misguided to think that the proper way to avoid false self-assessment is to rely on formal justifications of the kind offered by subjectivist rationalism. To try to by-pass substantive reasons would be to regress to a life which is less meaningful than a life in which we rely on substantive reasons. In the more meaningful life, the very issue of what reasons one really has – and, thus, whether one is subject to false self-assessment – must sometimes be settled by substantive reasons. Thus, it must also be concluded that – contrary to what was suggested when the controversiality problem was reintroduced in 10.4 – Gauthier cannot justify treating matters of assessive self-understanding as if they were matters of non-assessive self-understanding by arguing that doing so is necessary to deal with the problem of false self-assessment.

3 IS JUSTICE SPECIAL?

Questions like "Who am I?," "Who should I aspire to be?" and "What would make my life meaningful?" have played a central role in the argument for the substantive approach. Now it might be argued that there is a sense in which the issue of justice does not arise until these questions have already been answered. The answers to these questions tell each person who she is and what her personal ideals should be. The personal ideals of different people, however, may come into conflict in the context of interaction. And the point of a theory of justice is to determine how those conflicts are to be resolved.

Assuming that this is a central point of a theory of justice, Gauthier might argue that thus far I have shown at most that his approach is not correct for *all* cases. He might admit that as far as the question of which personal ideals to adopt is concerned, his theory does not provide the appropriate method of determining whether a particular answer to this question subjects the person at hand to false self-assessment. However, he might argue that his theory is superior to the substantive approach with respect to the issue of justice.[9] I see no reason to think that justice is special in this way, and to make this plausible, I want to discuss and answer two objections to the substantive approach.

According to the first objection, the substantive approach makes it

---

[9] As already pointed out, the principles which Gauthier means to justify in *Morals by Agreement* are principles of *justice*.

impossible to perceive some cases of exploitation. It is common that a person's views about justice become part of her personal ideals. For example, given a certain view about proper gender roles, a wife who works full-time may make taking care of the household a personal ideal of hers. This opens the door to her being exploited. The objection is that the substantive approach may make such cases of exploitation invisible. Precisely in accordance with the substantive approach's invitation to view not only personal ideals but also the terms of interaction as something to be settled by substantive reasons, the wife relies on substantive considerations in adopting her views about gender roles. It is reliance on these substantive reasons that subjects her to exploitation. Looking at the matter through the lens of the substantive approach, however, may make it impossible to see this as a case of exploitation. Since it was on the basis of substantive reasons that the wife adopted the personal ideal in question, the substantive approach cannot perceive the situation as one in which the wife is being taken advantage of, unless there are other and stronger substantive reasons she has for criticizing the situation: *given* her personal ideal, it seems that she is not being taken advantage of.

The problem with this objection is that it makes some unwarranted assumptions about the example it employs. It may be that the wife is relying on substantive considerations in adopting her views about gender relations, but it does not follow that these are *good* substantive reasons. Thus, the example simply does not show that the substantive approach makes certain cases of exploitation invisible to us. Given the arguments in §§1–2, there are good reasons to think that substantive reasons can and should be used critically to determine whether a person is subject to false self-assessment. The first objection provides no special reason for thinking that substantive reasons cannot be employed equally critically when the false self-assessment concerns justice.

The second objection rests on the accusation that the substantive approach draws no fundamental distinction between the question of whether I suffer from false self-assessment in letting an intuition about *justice* guide my life and the question of whether I suffer from false self-assessment in letting an intuition about *who I should be* guide it. The objection is then that, in failing to do so, the substantive approach is guilty of fusing two very different issues: the issue of *justice* and the issue of people's *self-definitions*. The substantive

161

approach treats the issue of justice as if settling it were a matter of completing people's self-definitions, rather than a matter of settling how the interactions between antecedently defined selves should be regulated.

The first response to this objection must be that the substantive approach itself does not take a position on the question of whether the issue of self-definition and the issue of justice should be fused. It is itself a substantive question whether we should take a "liberal" position which insists on separating the two issues or a "communitarian" position which fuses them.[10] Thus, the second objection is in this form not an objection to the substantive approach, but rather to views which take a position on issues about which the substantive approach is neutral.

The insistence that the substantive approach is neutral on this issue does not fully meet the second objection. This objection could be reformulated as follows: the *argument* for the substantive approach was that we need to rely on substantive reasons in order to give expression to a certain progress which can give *meaning* to our lives. Since the *support* for the substantive approach does in this way come from cases which concern the meaningful life, it is entirely unsupported to suppose that the substantive approach is also the right approach to justice.

If we accept this argument for the substantive approach, then we cannot plausibly deny that substantive reasons are relevant to questions of justice: if the agent must employ substantive reasons to articulate what makes her life go better, then these reasons are also relevant to the issue of how she should interact with others. However, in order to answer the second objection, more needs to be shown than simply that substantive reasons are *relevant to* questions of justice. The second objection does not doubt that substantive reasons are relevant to questions of justice; it only doubts that it has been shown that substantive intuitions *about justice* should be allowed to play any role in a theory of justice.

In order to support the second objection further, the following revised version of Gauthier's theory might be proposed: this version differs from the version discussed in earlier sections, since it allows

---

[10] Similarly, it is a substantive question whether we should abstract from those substantive concepts which concern the *good* life (as opposed to the *right* or *just* life) when we address questions of justice. For further discussion, see 14.3.

direct appeal to substantive reasons to play a role in answering questions such as "Who am I?" and "Who should I be?" This modification is meant to enable the theory to get around the criticisms offered in the last two sections and in the last chapter. The revised version of Gauthier's theory is then supposed to avoid fusing these questions and questions of justice by demonstrating that we should accept certain principles of justice "whatever our preferences." The preferences in question need not be limited to something which is the object of non-assessive self-understanding (as was the case in Gauthier's theory as understood thus far), but may themselves be based on substantive reasons, assuming that the scope of these reasons extends no further than answering questions like "Who should I be?" (rather than questions of justice). However, since the preferences in question may be based on substantive reasons, the claim that we should accept certain principles "whatever our preferences" must be modified so as to mean the following: whatever our preferences *within the group of preferences not based on intuitions about justice*. In this way, this theory allows substantive reasons to play a certain role (by allowing them to help answer the question "Who should I be?"), but it does not allow substantive intuitions about justice to count as substantive reasons for or against certain principles of interaction.[11]

The correct answer to the second objection is that my arguments for the substantive approach have undermined any motivation for keeping the issues of justice and the meaningful life apart in the way that *Gauthier* does. If we have good reasons to employ substantive reasons in some cases, why should we not draw on them directly in the case of justice? If the only motivation for Gauthier's theory is that we have to keep these issues apart, then we might as well accept another liberal theory like Rawls' which keeps these issues apart while drawing on substantive intuitions about justice. Of course, this does not show that we should indeed draw on substantive intuitions about justice. I take the first steps towards showing this in chapter 13, where I point out the attractions of the substantive approach when it comes to the evaluation of others.[12]

---

[11] I have here attempted to elaborate on suggestions made by Gauthier in conversation.

[12] It might be objected that substantive reasons should not be employed directly to approach the issue of justice because the problem of controversiality is especially serious when it comes to deciding on principles of interaction and because I have

4 THE PROBLEM OF FALSE SELF-ASSESSMENT: SUMMARY

It was the main aim of this chapter and the last to show that the substantive approach to the problem of self-assessment should be favored over subjectivist rationalism. It remains to make explicit how this also shows that the substantive approach to the problem of the *rationality of morality* (as this pertains to self-assessment) is superior to subjectivist rationalism. As already pointed out, the latter problem is just a version of the first: assuming that a person takes herself to have *moral* reasons, how are we to determine whether these reasons give her good reasons for action? Since I have discussed the example of *rudeness* at length, let us assume that *rudeness* is a moral concept and use this example to illustrate my argument. In that case, the problem is how to determine whether a person who guides her life by this concept (she criticizes others for being rude and tries herself to avoid being rude) has a good reason to guide her life thus.

What I have argued is that we should rather determine this by relying on substantive reasons than by trying to by-pass such reasons in the way suggested by subjectivist rationalism. This holds even if the substantive reasons which we employ to support the use of *rudeness* are themselves moral reasons. Of course, there is the worry that if these reasons are moral, then the justification of the use of *rudeness* will be *circular*. I do not think that this is a real worry. It is perfectly legitimate to have the justification of the employment of *one* substantive moral concept (in this case, *rudeness*) rest on *other* substantive moral concepts.[13] In addition, I have argued that substantive justifications are not problematic even though the use of no substantive (moral) concept can be *exhaustively* justified in terms of other concepts.[14] Thus, in the absence of any special argument to the effect that the justification of the use of particular substantive moral concepts must be based on non-moral premises, my conclusion stands. Of course, I have not shown that it would not be better to

only dealt with the problem of controversiality in the context of the question of what makes a person's life most successful. For an answer to this objection, see the answer to the fourth objection in 13.3.

[13] Of course, although the substantive approach maintains that it is not a problem if the justification does, in part, rest on moral concepts, it does not say that the justification must rest exclusively on such concepts.

[14] This circularity objection is, in effect, the bootstrapping objection mentioned in 4.3 and 5.1. For a fuller answer to this objection, see 12.3.

give a *substantive non-moral* justification of the use of rudeness.[15] I have merely argued that the substantive approach is *superior to subjectivist rationalism*: to determine whether we suffer from false self-assessment, we should rely on substantive reasons, *rather than* try to by-pass them in the way recommended by subjectivist rationalism.

It could be objected here that my argument only holds if the problem is how to determine rationally *which* moral reasons to accept (the moral alternatives problem), but not if the problem is whether we should rely on any moral reasons *at all* (the basic choice problem). In other words, my argument only holds if it has already been shown that we have a reason to be moral. And, so the objection goes, with respect to the question whether we should be moral in the first place, the subjectivist rationalistic solution should be preferred.

In my discussion, I have indeed focused on examples which pertain to the issue of which moral concepts to use, rather than the issue of whether to be moral at all. As I have already often pointed out, even if it can be shown that it is rational to be moral, it is a serious question whether it can be rationally settled which moral concepts to adopt. Thus, it is an important conclusion that which moral concepts to use should be settled substantively rather than rationalistically. Nevertheless, I think that my arguments are relevant to the question of whether to be moral at all.

I have argued quite generally that we should sometimes assess our lives with the help of substantive reasons. Thus, in the absence of arguments to the contrary, it should be expected that to answer the question of whether to be moral, we must rely on substantive reasons. And it should not be excluded that some of these substantive reasons are moral. It might be argued that, to avoid circularity, we must exclude that they are moral. Since the question is whether to be moral *at all*, this worry of circularity needs to be taken seriously. I thus defer the discussion of it until 12.3. Assuming, however, that the circularity worry can be resolved, my arguments indicate that, even with respect to the question of whether to be moral at all, the substantive approach should be favored to subjectivist rationalism.

As briefly mentioned in chapter 1, in addition to the moral alternatives problem and the basic choice problem, morality also faces the *problem of priority*. Here the question is whether moral reasons can

---

[15] This possibility will be discussed in 16.3.

be *overridden* by other reasons, and if they can, how we are to determine when they are overridden. Naturally, I think that in determining this, we should, in part, rely on substantive reasons, some of which may be moral: I think that in deciding which reasons are relevant in a particular situation, we should rely on substantive reasons; and that in deciding what we have reason to do, all things considered, we should rely on all the relevant substantive reasons we have, moral and non-moral. Now it might be argued that, in order to show that a moral reason overrides a non-moral reason, we may not rely on moral reasons. I do not think so. However, since this amounts to a circularity objection, I refer to 12.3 for the answer to this kind of objection.

What I have been arguing is that, as far as the problem of self-assessment is concerned, *morality does not need a rationalistic justification.* Without such a justification, morality would not be an entirely unjustified superstructure. To determine whether we suffer from false self-assessment in acting on a particular moral reason, we should indeed rely on substantive reasons, some of which may be moral. We can rationally settle whether to act on moral reasons at all, whether to give moral reasons priority, and which moral reasons to act on, even if there is no rationalistic justification of morality. All we need to do is to deliberate about the substantive reasons we have. In this deliberative process, we may start by relying on moral reasons without supposing that they have a rationalistic basis. If this is so, then morality surely faces no justificatory *crisis* (see 3.2). However, this does not mean that, at the end of the deliberative process, any of the moral reasons we started out relying on have indeed survived the process. Thus, I have not argued, and shall not argue, that it is indeed rational to be moral at all and that moral reasons should be given priority over other reasons. To argue this, we have to enter into a deliberative process about all the reasons we have, moral and non-moral. It is beyond the scope of this work to try to determine the correct outcome of such a process.

Of course, I have not really shown yet that morality does not need a rationalistic justification. So far, my discussion has been limited to the problem of rationality as it pertains to self-assessment. Since morality is also used to criticize others, it still remains to be seen whether rationalism is needed to justify this employment of morality. This is the topic of chapters 13–14. I now turn to a brief comparison of the substantive approach and rationalism with respect to another problem: the problem of the categorical force of morality.

5 THE PROBLEM OF THE CATEGORICAL FORCE OF MORALITY

Assuming that rationalism offers a good justification of morality, it can explain how a certain *unconditionality* of morality is possible. Rationalism shows moral demands to be unconditionally valid in that they are based on something unconditional in the sense that even a moral skeptic cannot reject it. This holds equally for subjectivist and inter-subjectivist rationalism.[16] The substantive approach cannot and does not aspire to show that morality is unconditionally valid in this sense. One might argue that these facts tell in favor of rationalism because they show that the substantive approach cannot explain one important explanandum – the unconditionality of morality – which rationalism can explain. I shall argue that this is not so.

Since the substantive approach accepts McDowell's thesis that there may be external reasons internal to ethics, this approach can certainly account for a kind of unconditionality of morality: an agent may have an external moral reason to do something, even if there is nothing in her subjective motivational set which supports doing it. It may be objected here that this does not capture the *special* categorical force of morality, since an agent may have an external reason which is not a *moral* reason and moral reasons have a peculiar force not explained by the fact that they are external reasons. I agree that the substantive approach as such does not capture it, but I think that this is not a difficulty in the present context.

The issue here is whether rationalism can capture something the substantive approach cannot – namely, the unconditionality of morality. Rationalists aim to show how morality can make demands on us independently of our desires and aims. The substantive approach can explain how morality can make such demands by invoking the idea of external reasons. And it seems that rationalism – precisely because it starts with something acceptable to the moral skeptic – also

---

[16] At least, it does not hold only for subjectivist rationalism, but also for the rationalism of Apel and Kuhlmann. As noted in 8.3, Habermas does not give a rationalistic explication of the categorical force of morality. (For a different way in which Habermas' account of the unconditionality of morality differs from Apel's and Kuhlmann's, see the Appendix.)

gives an explanation of the unconditionality of morality which equally explains the unconditionality of demands other than moral ones.[17] In the case of inter-subjectivist rationalism, one can hardly claim that the only things the rational arguer is implicitly committed to are *moral* principles. In Gauthier's case, it is shown that morality is unconditional by demonstrating that it is of necessary instrumental value. And morality may not be the only thing of necessary instrumental value. This does not mean that rationalists are unable to give an account of what is special about the unconditionality of *morality*. It just means that what is specifically rationalistic about their theories – that they are addressed to a moral skeptic – does not itself give such an account. Although the substantive approach itself does not tell a story about what is special about morality, it is certainly possible to tell such a story within the realm of the substantive approach. Thus, we must conclude that the fact that the substantive approach itself lacks an account of the special unconditionality of morality does not make it inferior to rationalism, which also does not offer such an account.

Now the rationalist might *deny* that the categorical force of morality is peculiar to morality. She might argue that morality is not the only system which addresses us as rational beings. Since it addresses us as rational beings, however, and the moral skeptic is also a rational being, morality must be understood as appealing to something which even the moral skeptic shares (even though her perception of its implications is clouded). Thus, although the substantive approach can explain how morality makes demands which are independent of our desires, it cannot capture the categorical force of morality.

Notice that the substantive approach can also say that morality addresses us as rational beings. It must only deny that morality addresses that part of our reason which we share with the moral skeptic. So what *argument* does the rationalist have for thinking that morality addresses us on the basis of assumptions we share with the skeptic? The rationalist might claim here that a moral person must assume that moral considerations always *override* all other considera-

---

[17] As I understand him, this is one reason why Habermas does not employ up-arguments to explicate the sense in which moral imperatives are categorical imperatives (see Habermas 1991f, 132–135, 187–188 [31–33, 78–81]).

tions and that only by giving a rationalistic justification can one account for this feature of morality.

I reject this claim. First, I doubt that a moral person must think of moral considerations as always overriding.[18] Thus, I do not think that a theory must be able to account for this alleged feature of morality. Second, I think that it is a serious question whether any person has a *good reason* to take moral considerations to be always overriding. In my view, there exists no rationalistic justification which successfully shows that moral considerations are always overriding. It still needs to be determined – with the help of substantive reasons – whether it is rational to let moral considerations always be overriding.

Instead of saying that the moral person must think of moral considerations as overriding, the rationalist might argue that the moral person must think of them as presenting themselves in the form of *obligations*.[19] The rationalist would then argue that nothing can have the force of an obligation unless it can be backed up by a rationalistic justification. Now it is a serious question whether it is a good idea to think of morality as presenting itself in the form of obligations.[20] Leaving that question aside, however, I do not think that a moral obligation is to be understood as something which must be given a rationalistic justification. A moral obligation is not something which is an *obligation* because it speaks to something which the moral skeptic accepts and *moral* because it demands a moral course of action. Rather, the idea of obligation at stake in moral obligations must be explained in terms of ideas which are themselves moral.[21] If

---

[18] See Foot 1978c and Brandom 1982.

[19] The moral person may think that moral considerations present themselves in the form of obligations without thinking that considerations which present themselves in this form are always overriding.

[20] See Williams' criticism of "the morality system" in Williams 1985, ch. 10.

[21] As noted in 2.3, it is not my burden to demarcate the moral and the non-moral. It is the rationalist, not I, who thinks that the use of moral concepts must, in the final analysis, be based on non-moral reasons. Thus, it is not my task to say what makes these concepts moral or these reasons non-moral. I only have to show that, even if concepts which *the rationalist* would count as moral are given justifications which *the rationalist* would not count as non-moral, there is nothing problematic about these justifications. Similar remarks apply to my comments on moral obligation. I have objected to the following idea: moral obligation is something which is an *obligation* because it can be given a non-moral basis. Since it is *the rationalist* who defends this idea, she is the one who must explain the distinction between the moral and the non-moral. I only insist that the account of moral obligation be given in terms of something which *the rationalist* surely would not count as non-moral.

that is so, then the substantive approach can and should give an account of moral obligation which differs from the one suggested here on the part of rationalism. Of course, I have not argued that moral obligation must be understood along these lines. I merely wanted to indicate why I think that the appeal to obligations does not show that only rationalism can account for the categorical force of morality.[22]

In my remarks about moral obligation, I am in agreement with Habermas. As mentioned in 8.3, he does not give a rationalistic explication of the binding force of moral norms. According to Habermas, norms are morally binding because they would be agreed to in a discourse which fulfills certain conditions, not because the principles of discourse ethics can be given a rationalistic underpinning. Now I do not mean to accept Habermas' specific account of the binding force of moral norms. The important point is that Habermas' account is an example of an account which a substantive approach could adopt, assuming that in his account discursive acceptance is understood as resting irreducibly on substantive reasons. I conclude that the explanandum "the unconditionality of morality" is something which the substantive approach can account for just as well as, or better than, rationalism.

---

[22] I think that the issue of the rationality of morality is much more important than the issue of its unconditionality. In the first case, the issue is what it is rational for us to think and do; in the latter, the question is whether we can account for the way in which we take something to speak to us. The first problem is more important because one crucial question is whether we really have a good reason to accept anything which speaks to us in unconditional demands of whatever kind. If we understand the unconditionality of morality to mean that morality presents itself in the form of obligations, then the crucial question is whether we have a good reason to accept anything which presents itself in this way.

12

Practical arguments vs. impossibility arguments

In the discussion of subjectivist rationalism, I employed a practical argument in favor of the substantive approach. In the comparison between inter-subjectivist rationalism and the substantive approach, and in my defense of (particularist) substantivism, I shall also use practical arguments. Before I actually offer any more such arguments, I want to step back and reflect on this argumentative strategy. This is what I shall do in this chapter.

One may distinguish between three different philosophical strategies. Consider, for example, some common arguments against subjectivism. According to one kind of argument, it is *impossible* to be a subjective evaluator (someone who evaluates things only in the way that subjectivism assumes they can be evaluated). For example, it could be argued that to be a subjective evaluator is not consistent with the conditions of possibility of human agency. Another philosophical strategy is to argue that even though it may be possible to be a subjective evaluator, we do *in fact* often engage in evaluation which cannot be interpreted subjectivistically. I think that as an argument against subjectivism and moral skepticism, the first strategy fails: it fails because it is indeed possible to be a subjective evaluator and a thoroughgoing moral skeptic. And arguments of the second type do not suffice: even if we in fact perform acts incompatible with subjectivism and moral skepticism, it could be argued that we should *revise* our practices to make them fit these positions. Therefore, I think that a third kind of argument is needed: it must be argued that we have a good practical reason not to revise our practices in this way. Only if there is such a practical reason do we have a good argument against subjectivism and moral skepticism.

In §1 of this chapter, I shall spell out in more detail why the first strategy fails, why the second is insufficient, and why we must therefore rely on the third. This does not mean that the second strategy is worthless. By arguing that we do in fact sometimes understand ourselves in the mode of assessive self-understanding, I myself employed an argument of the second kind against subjectivism. Since the subjectivist, however, can argue that we should revise our practices and no longer understand ourselves in this mode, I added an argument of the third kind by arguing that we have a good practical reason to rely on substantive reasons.

What, though, does the third argumentative strategy really amount to? Can I with practical arguments really show that subjectivism is *false*? After all, subjectivism is a position *about* practical reason. How, then, can an argument which *employs* practical reason rather than *reflects on* it possibly show anything concerning the truth of subjectivism? And if the practical reasons given against subjectivism are not interpreted subjectivistically, is the argument not circular? Since I have offered practical reasons against subjectivism and subjectivist rationalism and shall continue to offer such reasons against other positions, I must, before I proceed any further, clarify my argumentative strategy by answering these and related questions. This is the task of §§2–3.

I LIVING OUTSIDE STRONG EVALUATION

Is it possible to be a subjective evaluator and a thoroughgoing moral skeptic? In order to show that it is possible, I shall argue that it is possible to engage exclusively in weak evaluation. Notice that somebody who engages only in subjective evaluation need not engage exclusively in weak evaluation. To evaluate something weakly is to evaluate it according to how *strongly* one *desires* it. And if we take the agent's subjective motivational set to contain all the things that Williams includes in it, then it is certainly not plausible that the subjective evaluator evaluates things only according to the *strength* of something. Thus, it is presumably harder to show that one can engage exclusively in weak evaluation than to show that one can engage exclusively in subjective evaluation. Nevertheless, since Charles Taylor has explicitly defended the thesis that it is not possible to engage exclusively in weak evaluation, and since it is particularly enlightening to compare Taylor's arguments against weak evaluation with mine, I have chosen to focus here on weak evaluation.

Before turning to Taylor's thesis, some of the concepts he employs must be explained briefly. I have already discussed the distinction between strong and weak evaluation and it can now be employed to introduce the concept of a *qualitative distinction* and the concept of a *framework* or a *horizon*. In strongly evaluating something, we employ *qualitative distinctions*. For example, we may strongly evaluate two movies by calling one of them "authentic" and the other one "cheap," or strongly evaluate our neighbor's life as "exciting" rather than "boring." Assuming that our judgments are indeed strongly evaluative, we do in both cases draw qualitative distinctions (with respect to the films and the neighbor's life), but we do not say anything about the strength of our desires (who would not sometimes rather see a cheap movie than an authentic one?). Taylor assumes that in employing qualitative distinctions we must draw on the *horizon* or *framework* within which we exist. Frameworks – as the term indicates – are what the agent presupposes when she engages in strong evaluation. A framework is something within which we feel, think, and judge, and it incorporates qualitative distinctions.[1] With this terminology at hand, we can now move to Taylor's impossibility thesis:

> I want to defend the strong thesis that doing without frameworks is utterly impossible for us; otherwise put, that the horizons within which we live our lives and which make sense of them have to include these strong qualitative discriminations. Moreover, this is not meant just as a contingently true psychological fact about human beings, which could perhaps turn out one day not to hold for some exceptional individual or new type, some superman of disengaged objectification. Rather the claim is that living within such strongly qualified horizons is constitutive of human agency, that stepping outside these limits would be tantamount to stepping outside what we would recognize as integral, that is, undamaged human personhood.[2]

Contrary to Taylor, I believe that it is possible to do without frameworks. To support my case, I shall imagine someone who engages exclusively in weak evaluation and whose life thus moves entirely outside strong evaluation. I shall allow this person – call her the Outsider – to speak for herself and thereby to prove her own

[1] Taylor 1989, 19–20 and 26; 1985b, 18–21.
[2] Taylor 1989, 27.

existence.[3] I shall also consider how Taylor might respond to the Outsider's speeches and then allow the latter to elaborate her standpoint. In fact, at this point it is no longer possible to hold the Outsider back; after this long passage of Taylor's she is dying to state her case:

> THE OUTSIDER: I can do without any frameworks. In fact, I have *chosen* not to engage in any strong evaluation. Earlier in life I used strong evaluations, but I gave them up. Of course, I would have continued to evaluate strongly if I had desired to. But I didn't. So I stopped. This is how I lead my entire life: I am guided by my desires and nothing but my desires. I do not call my desires worthy or unworthy or strongly evaluate them in any other way. I simply let them pull me along.

If the Outsider's claims are right, then Taylor's impossibility thesis must be rejected. However, Taylor could respond by saying that he never intended to deny that individuals may exist who live outside frameworks. Rather his claim is that these individuals would inevitably be having a radical "identity crisis." Without a framework, people would be at a loss as to what is of value and importance. People would be in a state of disorientation in which they would be incapable of telling where they stand. Since "[t]o know who I am is a species of knowing where I stand," this condition would be appropriately described as an "identity crisis." And it is a "painful and frightening experience."[4] On account of these and similar remarks of Taylor's, Martin Löw-Beer has described Taylor's impossibility thesis as an assertion of *existential* impossibility. According to this interpretation, Taylor's thesis is that a life without frameworks is imaginable, but that it would be *unbearable* and in this sense existentially impossible.[5] Is it really existentially impossible?

> THE OUTSIDER: I admit that I have had a crisis. At the time, I thought that I needed values independent of my desires. But the crisis

---

[3] I do not assume that the ensuing speeches of the Outsider are a conclusive proof that it is possible to do without strong evaluation. These speeches do, however, amount to an intelligible – though sketchy – portrait of a person who lives outside strong evaluation. And assuming that the portrait is indeed plausible, the burden of proof is now on those who think that a life without strong evaluation is an impossibility.

[4] Taylor 1989, 27–28.

[5] Löw-Beer 1991, 225–226.

dissolved all by itself when I ceased desiring to engage in strong evaluation. I now take my desires for what they are: just my desires. I listen to them and assess their strength. Then I follow those that are the strongest. My crisis was simply due to the fact that I had expected something else of life. I had expected that strong values existed in the world and that it was my task to discover them. After I lost the belief in such values, I fell into a deep depression. But I got over it. I do not need any strongly evaluative frameworks any more. My disbelief in strong values and my desires exist in perfect harmony: I simply have no desire to engage in strong evaluation. I do not desire what I believe I cannot get. I am absolutely content.

I believe that there is no reason to doubt the possible existence of a person like the Outsider: a person who engages in no strong evaluation at all and is happy with her lot. In response to this speech of the Outsider, Taylor's next move could be to deny that an entity which engages in no strong evaluation at all would be a particular agent with a particular identity. According to Taylor, to be somebody who qualifies as a subject of the question "Who?" is to be one interlocutor among others. It is to be someone who can speak for herself. She must be able to answer the question "Who?" by saying where she stands. According to Taylor, this shows that "we take as basic that the human agent exists in a space of questions."[6] To have an identity is to have an orientation in this space. To lose it – to have an "identity crisis" – is to get lost in the space of questions.[7] Since existence in this space makes identity and "identity crises" possible, it does not make sense that this space itself is invented by the agent. The questions to which the strongly evaluative frameworks provide answers are there for the human agent to answer, and it does not make sense to suppose that these questions are invented by her, that these are questions that might or might not arise for her. Since for Taylor we thus answer the

---

[6] Taylor 1989, 29.

[7] This means, in effect, that Taylor should distinguish between a modest identity crisis and a radical identity crisis (a total loss of identity). To have a modest identity crisis is to be at a loss how to answer the strongly evaluative questions – to be lost in the space of questions. A radical identity crisis amounts to a total absence of such questions – amounts to an existence outside the space of questions. The former crisis can be compared with the confusion of an agent with a sense of spatial orientation who does not know, say, whether an office is upstairs or downstairs. The latter crisis is analogous to the total absence of an up–down orientation (cf. Taylor 1989, 27–31).

question "Who?" by giving strongly evaluative answers to preexisting questions, for him it is *incoherent* to suppose that identity can be defined by weakly evaluative – and thus merely de facto – desires. He must therefore conclude that we are not able to do without frameworks: it does not make sense to suppose that we can answer the question "Who?" just on the basis of weakly evaluative desires.[8] Is Taylor right, though, that it does not make sense and that we therefore cannot do without frameworks?

THE OUTSIDER: I have already admitted that I have had crises in my life. However, I have never had what people call an "identity crisis." Since many people make much of the concept of identity, I have considered how I could apply this concept to my own life. I have tried some ways of viewing it and I cannot decide which one I like the best.

Sometimes I experience myself as a person without qualities or rather as qualities without a person.[9] I have different desires and since all of these desires are had by me I suppose that there is some sense in which they are all mine. However, at these times it just does not interest me to ask which of these desires are, properly speaking, my desires and which are not. I just consider them as things that come and go, and I act on some of them and not on others.

Sometimes I feel theoretical. I spend my time thinking about my past desires and trying to come up with a story that would give them some unity. In these moods, I also play with thinking about which of my possible future desires would best fit into the story told. I then call those desires that fit into the narrative I have invented "my desires." However, this is a purely theoretical game. I don't really care whether I shall act in the future, or have acted in the past, on "my desires."

Now it should be clear why I don't have identity crises. Sometimes I am not interested in identity at all; at other times, my interest is purely theoretical. To my mind, identity is one of those things that you might or might not be interested in having.

The Outsider supposes that her existence undermines two of

---

[8] Taylor 1989, 29–31.
[9] Cf. Musil 1978, esp. Book I, Part II, chs. 39–40.

Taylor's claims. First, she suggests that identity can be defined in terms of de facto desires by offering an account of identity as a coherence or narrative structure of merely de facto desires. Second, she claims that this coherence might or might not be something that one desires to have.

I believe that the Outsider has again laid out a possible form of existence. She has also spelled out a concept of identity which we can recognize as a concept of *identity* (rather than as a concept of something else). It is possible to understand identity in this way and to lead a life that fits this understanding. Assuming that Taylor's concept of identity fits the life of the strong evaluator, the argumentative situation is thus the following: the Outsider's account and Taylor's account are two *intelligible* concepts of identity, and the Outsider's concept fits her life, whereas Taylor's concept fits the life of the strong evaluator.

Now if this is the argumentative situation, then the fact that the Outsider's concept of identity does not fit a life of strong evaluation does not give her any reason to change her life. In fact, there is no more reason to suppose the Outsider should change her life in accordance with the strong evaluator's concept of identity than to suppose that the strong evaluator should reform her life and the concept of identity which belongs to it. Unless it can be shown that the *life* which Taylor's concept of identity fits – the life of strong evaluation – is *better* or more *desirable* than the Outsider's life, it is not clear why we should accept Taylor's account of identity rather than the Outsider's.

This suggests that the right argumentative strategy against the Outsider must be different from Taylor's. Instead of trying (like Taylor) to show that the Outsider's life is *impossible* or *unintelligible*, we should offer a *strongly evaluative* argument which shows that the *life* of the strong evaluator is a better life than the life of the Outsider. In 10.5, I argued that the subjective evaluator lacks a certain way of rendering her life meaningful which is open to the substantive evaluator. Now the same could be argued for the Outsider and the strong evaluator. Since the Outsider is a subjective evaluator, what the subjective evaluator lacks she also lacks. Now if we assume that the strong evaluator is a substantive evaluator, then what is open to the substantive evaluator must also be open to the strong evaluator. Thus, I conclude that the Outsider's life lacks a certain source of meaning open to the strong evaluator. This does not show that the strong evaluator's life is, all things considered, better; but it is a first step.

It might be argued here that although I am right in pointing out that existence outside strong evaluation is intelligible, there is nevertheless a kind of unintelligibility that I have failed to draw attention to: what is unintelligible is not that an individual outside strong evaluation may exist, but rather that such an individual has *chosen* not to engage in strong evaluation. An individual outside strong evaluation would be an *a*rational being and such beings are not capable of real *choice*. Thus, since the Outsider is supposed to have chosen to abstain from strong evaluation, she is not an intelligible being.

THE OUTSIDER: If it is built into the notion of choice that choice must be based on strong evaluation, then of course I have not chosen to abstain from strong evaluation. However, there is a very real sense in which I have made a choice. I do not merely act on instinct. I am a very articulate person. And I have clearly articulated to myself what is involved in being a strong evaluator and what is involved in being a weak evaluator. (After all, I used to be a strong evaluator.) Having articulated it to myself, I find that my desires for weak evaluation are stronger. Thus, although my choice to engage only in weak evaluation is based entirely on the strength of my desires, just like all my other choices, it is not an instinctive reaction but a real choice.

What the Outsider has done is to insist that all of her choices are based on weak evaluation. Assuming that we accept that our choices are sometimes based on weak evaluation, there seems to be no reason to doubt that the Outsider makes choices. She has made intelligible not only how somebody might be a purely weak evaluator but also how she might have chosen to remain one on weakly evaluative grounds.[10]

---

[10] Of course, my portrait of the Outsider does not prove that it is intelligible that such a person is also capable of human communication. However, it seems to me that the portrait places the burden of proof on those who think that a purely weak evaluator is not capable of human communication (as Taylor does); see Taylor 1985b, 28. If somebody were not capable of human communication, this would presumably throw doubt on the view that she is capable of *choosing* to live as a purely weak evaluator. However, my argument that it is intelligible that somebody has chosen such a life does not depend on supposing that she herself – like the Outsider – is capable of and interested in showing to others that her life is intelligible.

Here it might be argued that, since the Outsider chooses on the basis of the strength of her desires, her choice is based on a principle – namely, the principle "act on the strongest desires." Now the Outsider must answer the question of why she acts on this principle rather than some other principle – for example, "act on the weakest desires." This is not an empty question. If the principle "act on the strongest desires" is to *guide* the Outsider's action, it must be possible to act contrary to this principle. If it is possible, though, then it is a serious question why one should not. Here – so the argument goes – the Outsider cannot justify acting on this principle by saying that she desires to. When the question is *which* of her desires to act on, it will not do to base the answer on some of her desires. Concerning these latter desires, it is no more clear why one should act on them than on some other desires. Rather, when the Outsider decides which of her desires to act on, she must decide which principle of action she can identify with. However, in order to do so, she must ask herself which actions are *worthy* of being undertaken.[11] Thus, the Outsider's answer to the question why she should act on her strongest desires must, in the final analysis, be based on a strongly evaluative judgment.

THE OUTSIDER: It is surely correct that I must distinguish between the desires I actually have and the desires I act on, on the one hand, and the desires I should act on, on the other. I am perfectly willing to agree that I decide the question which desires I should act on by the principle "act on the strongest desires." However, this is really the *only* principle of evaluation I accept: it is *the* principle of weak evaluation. Thus, when asked why I choose to act on the principle "act on the strongest desires" rather than "act on the weakest desires," I must answer by saying that I choose to do so because it best satisfies my strongest desires to have my strongest desires satisfied. This is a perfectly legitimate answer, because in giving the answer I am *not merely* saying that it satisfies my strongest desires to have my strongest desires satisfied, but I am *also* applying the principle of weak evaluation to itself. In other words, I am also weakly *evaluating* the principle of weak evaluation. Since this is the only principle of evaluation I accept, this is the only answer I can give

[11] Cf. Korsgaard 1996, 92–102; 1997, 220–234; cf. also Taylor 1989, 22–24, 31–32, and Hampton 1998, 136–151.

to questions as to why I should act on one principle rather than another. (It should be noted that I do not understand the principle "act on the strongest desires" as saying "act on the single most strong desire" but rather as saying "perform that action which maximizes the fulfillment of your desires given that the stronger desires have a greater weight proportionally to their strength.")

As far as I am concerned, it may be said that I thereby identify with this principle of action and that I therefore have a particular identity which I must care about. Earlier I proposed a different way of thinking about my identity. However, in neither of these cases must my identity be defined on the basis of strong evaluation. As I just explained, as all my other choices, the choice to act on the principle "act on the strongest desires" is based on weak evaluation.[12]

Now we – those who engage in both strong and weak evaluation – might want to say that the Outsider has distorted our understanding of the validity of the principle of weak evaluation. We do not – unlike the Outsider – assume that the justification of acting on this principle rather than other principles is simply that it best satisfies our strongest desires to have our strongest desires satisfied. Nevertheless, it seems to me that the Outsider has offered an account which is perfectly intelligible as an account of choice based on weak evaluation.[13] This

---

[12] This speech of the Outsider should make it clear that, by setting out to show that the Outsider's life is possible, I have set myself a task which is unnecessarily hard for my purposes. My aim here is to motivate the argumentative strategy which I employ against subjectivism and other positions. To do so, I have to show that impossibility arguments fail as arguments against these positions. Now to show this for these positions is easier than for the Outsider's position. Consider, e.g., Gauthier's subjectivistic position. As I understand Gauthier, utility maximization is a principle of practical rationality: practical reason demands that we maximize utility (Gauthier 1991a, 19–20). In arguing for constrained maximization, he uses this principle of practical reason to show that it is not rational always to be guided *directly* by the utility maximization principle. Thus, Gauthier's utility maximizer must admit that the validity of this principle is not relative to her desires. This means that Gauthier's utility maximizer may be intelligible even if it is not intelligible to take *every* evaluation to be relative to desires in the way that the Outsider proposes in this speech.

[13] Thus, although I cannot argue this here, I would also maintain that even if the argument in Korsgaard 1996 (Lecture 3) holds *for us*, it does not hold *for the Outsider*. The Outsider's choices are based on weak evaluation "all the way down."

is another indication that the best argumentative strategy against the Outsider would not be to try to argue that her position is unintelligible, but rather to give a strongly evaluative argument against acting exclusively on the principle of weak evaluation.

We have not yet covered everything which Taylor can say in defense of this impossibility thesis, however. At one point, he suggests that either a portrait of somebody who is "totally outside of any strong evaluation" cannot be painted or this portrait would disclose that the individual would be "totally reduced to the sub-human."[14] And this suggestion is meant as a remark on his impossibility thesis.[15] Of course, the Outsider is eager to sketch a portrait of herself as somebody who is anything but sub-human:

THE OUTSIDER: Now that you have failed to prove that I do not exist, you have resorted to asserting that my existence is a sub-human one. But just compare me to animals. I have many distinctly human desires and I am capable of enjoying many pleasures unavailable to animals. In fact, I would sacrifice having most of my "animalistic" desires satisfied just in order to have one of my more distinctly human desires satisfied. Of course, that is just my personal preference. As it is, I care that this preference be satisfied. If I were to develop a preference for the more "animalistic" objects, then the satisfaction of that preference would matter to me. But how "human" I am depends on the *contents* of my actual preferences. It does not depend on whether I strongly evaluate desires by, for example, judging them according to their worth. I don't. I just happen to prefer

---

[14] Taylor 1991, 251; see also Taylor 1985b, 28.
[15] There are also strands in Taylor's thinking which support interpreting his impossibility thesis as a strongly evaluative thesis. After first saying that it is not impossible to be outside the moral, and then asserting that we cannot be outside strong evaluation *without being reduced to a sub-human level* (Taylor 1991, 251), Taylor goes on to suggest that we cannot be outside the moral in the sense that we cannot *without missing a "crucial human good"* and *failing to "grow into an undamaged human being"* (252–253). Thus, it seems that the difference between being outside strong evaluation and being outside the moral is not that the one case represents an impossibility whereas the other one does not: the difference seems to have something to do with the different *prices we pay* in the two cases. Nevertheless, in each case the loss has something to do with "reduced humanity." Now, since his argument concerning morality is officially a strongly evaluative argument, it seems that Taylor should say that the claim that someone outside strong evaluation is reduced to the sub-human is also a strongly evaluative remark.

the more "human" desires. And that definitely puts me in the class of humans.

The Outsider has offered here an account of what it is to be human which we can recognize as an intelligible account of just that. Now that the Outsider has refuted yet another attempt to show that her existence is impossible or unintelligible, I think it is time to grant her that her existence is indeed possible.

The fact that the Outsider's account is an intelligible account of humanity also suggests that the claim that an individual outside strong evaluation is reduced to the *sub-human* had better be understood as a *strongly evaluative* claim. Assuming that a paradigmatic human life is the life of a strong evaluator, it may be that the Outsider's account does not fit human life in that sense. However, it is unclear why that would be a good reason not to lead a life such as the Outsider's. After all, the Outsider's account is an intelligible account of what it is to be human and it fits *her* life. The argumentative situation here is the same as it was with respect to the Outsider's intelligible account of the concept of identity: the Outsider's account of humanity (identity) fits her life, whereas Taylor's account fits the life of the strong evaluator. This much being said, no reason has been given for thinking that the Outsider should give up her mode of life in order to fit Taylor's account, rather than that the strong evaluator should change her life in order to fit the Outsider's account. If, however, the claim that the Outsider's life is sub-human is understood as a strongly evaluative claim to the effect that her life is not a worthy human existence, then this claim (if true) would give us a good reason not to lead a life such as the Outsider's and to reject her account of humanity.

The argument taken over from 10.5 can be understood as the first step in an argument intended to show that the Outsider's life is sub-human in the sense of not being a worthy human existence. If it could be shown that no elements crucial to a meaningful human existence are present in her life, then this would present a good case for saying that she leads a sub-human existence in this sense. Of course, I have not shown that, since I have only argued that a certain way of rendering life meaningful is open to the strong evaluator but not to the Outsider. Nevertheless, by thus offering a strongly evaluative reason against the Outsider's life, I have given the right *kind* of argument against her.

The point of this section was to argue that, of three possible argumentative strategies against subjectivism and moral skepticism, we must use the one which involves practical arguments. If the Outsider's life is possible, then it is surely possible to be a subjective evaluator and a thoroughgoing moral skeptic. Thus, the first argumentative strategy fails: impossibility arguments against subjectivism and moral skepticism do not hold. The Outsider showed that it cannot plausibly be claimed that her life is impossible, only at most, that she interprets certain concepts differently than we do. If the criticism of the Outsider is that she understands concepts in another way than we do, then the criticism has shifted to the second argumentative strategy. However, as I argued, if the Outsider's understanding of these concepts fits her life, then this criticism does not give us sufficient reason to reject the Outsider's interpretation of these concepts. In addition, we would need a practical reason not to lead a life such as the Outsider's. The same can now be seen to be true of arguments against subjectivism and moral skepticism. It does not suffice to show that these positions recommend an understanding of certain concepts which, from our perspective, is revisionary. It must also be shown that we have a good practical reason not to be subjective evaluators or moral skeptics.

2 MAKING SENSE OF OUR LIVES

Having argued that I need to employ an argumentative strategy which involves practical arguments, I now want to elaborate on this strategy. To do so, it is useful to compare my arguments against the Outsider with Taylor's. I start by taking a look at a revealing passage of Taylor's. After presenting the account of identity discussed in the previous section – an account which connects identity essentially with strong evaluation – he considers the objection of a naturalist:

> But the naturalist might protest: Why do I have to accept what emerges from this phenomenological account of identity? For so he might want to describe it, and he wouldn't be entirely wrong. The answer is that this is not only a phenomenological account but an exploration of the limits of the *conceivable* in human life, an account of its "transcendental conditions." It may be wrong in detail, of course; and the challenge is always there to provide a better one. But if it's correct, the objection

that arises for naturalism is decisive. For the aim of this account is to examine how we actually *make sense of our lives*, and to draw the limits of the *conceivable* from our knowledge of what we actually do when we do so. But what description of *human possibilities*, drawn from some questionable epistemological theories, ought to trump what we can descry from within our practice itself as the limits of our possible ways of *making sense of our lives*? After all, the ultimate basis for accepting any of these theories is precisely that they *make better sense of us* than do their rivals. If any view takes us right across the boundary and defines as *normal* and *possible* a human life which we would find *incomprehensible* and *pathological*, it can't be right. It is on these grounds that I oppose the naturalist thesis and say that the horizons in which we live *must* include strong qualitative discriminations.[16]

It seems that the terms I have emphasized in this passage can be divided into three categories and that Taylor can accordingly be understood as making the following kinds of claims about a life outside strong evaluation:

(1) It is inconceivable, impossible, incomprehensible.
(2) It is not a normal human life, it is pathological.
(3) We cannot make sense of such a life.

In §1, I argued that (1) is false. There is an important sense, however, in which the argument I took over from 10.5 makes a claim of type (3) about the Outsider's life and I shall now turn to explaining the sense in which the argument involves this claim. (It may also be noted that, assuming that (2) is understood as a strongly evaluative claim rather than as a psychological or sociological claim, I see no reason to dispute it.)

In order to make sense of someone's life, we need at least to make sense of her actions. And one element in making sense of someone's actions amounts to *understanding* the reasons for those actions. By reaching an understanding of the reasons for someone else's actions, I gain understanding of her actions. If another pedestrian suddenly pushed me aside, I would at first most likely be both baffled and angry. I would probably calm down, however, as soon as I realized that she pushed me aside in order to prevent me from being run over

---

[16] Taylor 1989, 32; all emphasis except for "must" added.

by a car. The same holds true of my own actions. Day after day I get up, turn on my computer, and sit all day writing and staring into the computer screen. My actions are intelligible to me because I know that I am working on a book.

Now, my understanding of my own actions isn't based simply on an "inner observation" of the reasons governing my actions. Rather, I often come to understand my actions by thinking that they are actions which I have a *good* reason to perform.[17] Of course, these two – my understanding of my own actions and my conviction that I have good reasons for them – may also come apart. Even if I fully comprehend the reasons for my actions, I may start wondering whether they are *good* reasons. For example, I know that my reason for sitting in front of the computer every day is that I am writing a book. I may start wondering, however, whether this is a good reason. Thus, understanding the reasons for my actions is one thing; thinking that they are good reasons is something else.

Nevertheless, in both cases – in trying to understand my own actions and in trying to give good reasons for them – I am trying to *make sense of* my own actions. Or rather, in trying to make sense of my own actions, I have two aspirations: I want to understand my actions and the reasons for them and I want to see these actions as supported by good reasons.[18] And these two aspirations are connected for me because I often achieve understanding of my actions by seeing them as actions supported by good reasons, and if I lose sight of any good reasons for my actions this may sometimes undermine my grasp of those actions.

Thus, if I find my actions intelligible – if I find that I have a coherent understanding of them – but cannot see them as supported by good reasons, then we may say that I have made only *partial* sense of my actions. An example of this might be a case where I fully understand the reasons guiding my actions but find my actions entirely *pointless* or *meaningless*. I have a clear comprehension of the reasons actually governing my actions, but I fail to see the point of being guided by such reasons. And this may hold not just for

---

[17] My discussion of a self-understanding which presupposes self-assessment should already have made this clear (see 10.2).

[18] In trying to see my life as supported by good reasons, I must of course strive *both* to find out in practical deliberation what the good reasons are *and* to act on these reasons.

particular actions of mine, but rather for my life: I may be able to make my life intelligible to myself by spelling out the reasons behind my actions, but I may at the same time find my life entirely meaningless. Whatever sense I can assign to my actions, it is for me a lifeless sense. In such a case, I would only have made partial sense of my own life.

This distinction between two aspects of making sense of someone's life and actions can now be used to explain the difference between my argument and Taylor's. Taylor thinks that we cannot make sense of the Outsider's life because her life is not intelligible. This I have denied. I have argued, however, that one important way of giving meaning to one's own life is not open to the Outsider. My argument for strong evaluation is thus not that life without strong evaluation would be unintelligible, but rather that strong evaluation helps us to make sense of our lives by giving us a way of rendering them meaningful.

Now we can distinguish three different points I have made in this chapter. First, employing an argument from 10.5 which concerns the notion of a meaningful life, I claimed that, because a certain source of meaning is not available to the Outsider, we have a good reason not to lead this sort of life. Second, I distinguished between saying that a life is intelligible and saying that we have a good reason to lead such a life. The fact that a certain kind of life would be more meaningful than another is an example of something which would give a person a good reason to choose to lead the first kind of life. In this section, I have added a third thesis. I have claimed that in trying to make her own life intelligible (in trying to understand it) and in trying to lead a life supported by good reasons, a person is in both cases trying to make sense of her own life. One essential component of making sense of a life is making it intelligible, but that is not enough.

So far, I have only been concerned with explaining my criticism of the Outsider's *life*. However, I have also argued against her interpretation of such *concepts* as identity and humanity. The nature of my argument against her interpretation can now be made explicit. I assume that the meaning of concepts and words depends on the role they play in life. And it may be possible to explain the *meaning of a concept* by the role it plays in a certain kind of life, even if it is *not* possible to see this kind of *life* as a fully *meaningful life*. I have, in effect, argued that this holds true of the Outsider's concepts: the concepts which derive their meaning from her kind of life are perfectly intelligible or *meaningful concepts* even though her life is *not* a fully *meaningful life*.

Having thus granted the Outsider that her concepts are intelligible, I want to argue that they should be rejected. The Outsider could be criticized for "changing the subject":[19] in order to evade Taylor's criticism, she gives the concepts *identity* and *sub-human* another meaning than Taylor. However, we cannot show that the Outsider's conceptual revisions should be rejected – we cannot show that there is anything wrong about thus changing the subject – without also rejecting the kind of life from which the Outsider's concepts draw their meaning. My argument *is* a rejection of the Outsider's concepts – a refusal to use her revised concepts – but that rejection is based on an *indirect* argument. Her concepts are perfectly intelligible or meaningful. These concepts, however, get their meaning from the kind of life she leads, and I have argued that a certain source of a meaningful life is absent from that life. *For this reason* her conceptual revisions should be rejected: her concepts get their meaning from a life which we have a good reason not to lead.

These remarks about the Outsider can now be used to throw light on the argumentative strategy of this work. I mean here the arguments used in the comparison between the substantive approach and rationalism and the comparison of substantivism and formalism.[20] I do not argue that rationalism (or formalism) is an unintelligible position. What I argue is that rationalism (and formalism) "changes the subject" in a way analogous to the Outsider. Rationalism demands that morality be given a justification from premises acceptable even to a moral skeptic. In my view, this *changes the subject* in two ways.

First, whereas we actually engage in practical deliberation by reflecting on the merits of the various substantive considerations, rationalism shifts the *subject-matter* of practical inquiry to the drawing out of the implications of a formal concept of reason acceptable even

[19] See Taylor 1989, 58–59 and 71–72.
[20] Since subjectivism is a formalistic theory of practical reason (see 2.3), my arguments against subjectivism and for the employment of substantive reasons were already a partial defense of substantivism as opposed to formalism.

to a moral skeptic. (As we saw, subjectivist rationalism turns practical inquiry into the question of what would maximize the satisfaction of our preferences *whatever their content.*)

Second, whereas we actually understand ourselves as *subjects* who care about the content of the reasons they act on, rationalism addresses us as subjects concerned with fulfilling the demands of formal rationality. (As we saw, subjectivist rationalism understands agents as utility maximizers and does not acknowledge that a dimension of the self can be understood only in the mode of assessive self-understanding.) Even if these two ways of changing the subject perhaps do not amount to conceptual revisions of the kinds proposed by the Outsider, the result is the same: in both cases, something which is at the center of our understanding of ourselves and our practical deliberations gets replaced by something else.

So far, I have only argued regarding subjectivist rationalism (in the case of self-assessment) that it changes the subject in these ways. I shall argue this for inter-subjectivist rationalism (and formalism) in the ensuing chapters. Now, as in the case of the Outsider, it is not enough to argue that these theories do *in fact* change the subject: it must also be shown that they *should not* change it. In the case of subjectivist rationalism, the argument was that we should not change the subject, because doing so would deprive us of a certain way of rendering our lives meaningful. In the case of inter-subjectivist rationalism, the argument will be different. Nevertheless, the argument is in both cases based on substantive practical reasons. These reasons are *practical* because they are reasons for living in a certain way. They are *substantive* because the considerations which speak in favor of living in that way are irreducibly substantive.

It is important to emphasize that the arguments I offer are – though practical – *not pragmatic.* Recall the discussion of earning truth from 4.2. Can senses of humor be ranked in such a way that truth can be earned for the funny? One possible way of ranking senses of humor would be according to how *useful* the different senses of humor are. If we have a narrow conception of the useful (as, say, that which leads to increased pleasure), this would be a narrowly pragmatic justification of the rankings of senses of humor. We could also, however, adopt a broader conception. On this conception, the point of saying that senses of humor are ranked according to how useful they are is just to say that the rankings are justified by appealing to something other than what counts as funny: truth for the funny is earned from outside the funny. Such a justification of the ranking of sensibilities may also be counted as pragmatic.[21]

A justification of the ranking of senses of humor would not be pragmatic if the justification itself appealed to what is and what is not funny (if truth were earned from within). This is the sense in which my justification of the substantive approach is not pragmatic. According to the substantive approach, the support for an ethical outlook is to be sought in substantive ethical reasons.[22] Now, in supporting the substantive approach itself, I am not arguing that it would be good to favor the substantive approach, where what is good about it can be understood without appeal to substantive ethical reasons. I am insisting precisely that what is good about it can only be shown by substantive reasons that may have ethical content. In other words, my justification of the substantive approach is practical but not pragmatic.[23]

Before I elaborate further on my argumentative strategy in this book, let me go briefly back to the argument against the Outsider. At the end of §1, I suggested that it would be a good criticism of the Outsider's life to say that it is sub-human, if this claim were understood as a strongly evaluative claim. It might be argued that this strongly evaluative claim cannot be a good argument against the Outsider's account of humanity if it is understood as an account of a *metaphysical* concept. Now I am willing to assume that the Outsider is offering a revision of a "metaphysical" concept, rather than a strongly evaluative concept. However, this admission in no way undermines my argument. If the Outsider's life is sub-human in the sense of not being a worthy human existence, then there is good reason to reject the "metaphysical" account of humanity which fits her life. This

---

21 Williams sees in justifications that would count as pragmatic in this sense the only way in which ethical life could intelligibly be given objective grounding (Williams 1985, 152–155).

22 Of course, as already mentioned, it does not maintain that ethical outlooks must be supported *exclusively* by ethical reasons, but rather that it is not a problem if the relevant ethical outlook cannot be given a justification based on entirely non-ethical premises.

23 It should be noted that in the construction of the justification of the substantive approach, I have been influenced by Nicholas Rescher's various "pragmatic" justifications (of values, rationality, induction, etc.) and his meta-reflections on these justifications. However, it would take me too far afield to elaborate on the similarities and differences between my practical justifications and his. See Rescher 1977; 1988, chs. 3–4; 1992, chs. 2 and 9; 1993, ch. 14.

"metaphysical" concept derives its meaning from a life which is not fully meaningful and that constitutes a good practical reason for rejecting the concept. Thus, what I have offered is a *practical* reason for rejecting a *metaphysical* concept.

It should be noted that this does not mean that I assume that practical reasons must always have priority over "metaphysical" reasons. In fact, precisely because I make no such assumption, the claim (borrowed from McDowell) that there is nothing metaphysically weird about substantive reasons plays such a crucial role in my argument. I think that there are indeed good practical reasons for employing substantive reasons. It is, however, perfectly compatible with my argument that a view or a concept should sometimes be rejected because it amounts to bad "metaphysics" even though there are good practical reasons for it.[24]

My practical argument against the account of certain "metaphysical" concepts which fits the Outsider's life is at the same time an argument for the account involved in strong evaluation. Since my argument is that strong evaluation gives us a certain way of seeing our lives as meaningful which is not open to the Outsider, the following objection against the argument might be raised: the fact that a view makes our lives seem meaningful is not necessarily a reason in its favor. Perhaps our lives *are* quite meaningless. And if they are, then a view which makes them appear meaningful would simply be false. Since I have given the same argument in favor of the substantive approach, this is also an objection against the argumentative strategy of this book.

I understand this as a "metaphysical" objection saying that the correct metaphysical view of reality shows that human life is meaningless.[25] I cannot here argue adequately against this objection. I

---

[24] For arguments to the effect that it is not possible to insulate ontological assumptions made from the standpoint of practical deliberation against ontological criticism based on what is needed to explain actions from a theoretical standpoint, see Wallace, Forthcoming, §4.

[25] Instead of understanding this objection as a "metaphysical" objection, one might understand it as a first-order value judgment about human life. The objection might be that, though metaphysically speaking it would be possible to lead a meaningful human life, it is in fact the case that all human efforts are futile. For example, so the argument might continue, despite enormous efforts on the part of people to make the world more just it continually becomes more unjust. I do not want to deny this here. It is not, however, an objection against my argument. I merely wanted to show that by relying on substantive reasons we make a certain kind of progress possible which is

simply assert that such a metaphysical view cannot possibly be available to us: it does not make sense to suppose that we can detach ourselves from all our attempts to make sense of our lives and take up an "objective" point of view from which we can decide once and for all that human life as such is meaningless.[26] If this is correct, then my argumentative strategy is exactly the right one. "Metaphysical" views relevant to our lives should be judged according to how well they enable us to *make sense of our lives*. And our attempts to make sense of our lives must always include the attempt to see our lives as meaningful ones. Thus, it is a good reason for one "metaphysical" view as opposed to another that it better enables us to lead meaningful lives and see them as such.

It could be argued here that a good substantive practical reason for changing a "metaphysical" view can never be good evidence for the *truth* of the new "metaphysical" view (or the falsity of the old one), but at most a practical reason for *adopting* the new view. For example – so the objection goes – even if by relying on substantive reasons we render our lives more meaningful, we would not thereby have a reason to think that the "metaphysical" account of human agency presupposed by subjectivism is *false*. Since I assume the test of the truth of a "metaphysical" view to be how well it succeeds in *making sense of our lives*, I must disagree. In my opinion, if the new "metaphysical" view does indeed help us to make better sense of our lives, then it is a better view of *how things are*.[27] Thus, the fact that one "metaphysical" view renders our lives more meaningful than another is a reason – though not a conclusive reason – for supposing that the former "metaphysical" view is a better view of how things are. The best view of how things are is the view which makes the best sense of our lives, but it cannot be said in advance to what extent the best view actually succeeds – without turning into bad "metaphysics" – in rendering our lives meaningful.[28]

necessary to render life meaningful in a specific way. It is a separate question whether we actually succeed in making the progress which becomes a possibility in this way. I thank Jay Wallace for pointing out the necessity of distinguishing between the two versions of the objection.

[26] See Wiggins 1991b, 108–116; Taylor 1989, 73–75; 1993.

[27] Of course, I have not really *argued* for this position. However, if (as McDowell suggests) truth can be earned by appealing to the reasons available within a practical sensibility, then this seems to be the position to take (see 4.2).

[28] This is the direction in which I would like to take Taylor (cf. Taylor 1989, 57–60) and Wiggins (cf. Wiggins 1991b, esp. 98–116). However, I am not sure that this is

3 THE BOOTSTRAPPING OBJECTION (AGAIN)

According to the bootstrapping objection raised in 4.3, the substantive approach favors *circular* justifications of ethical outlooks, since it supposes that these justifications may involve ethical reasons. Now, the same objection can be applied to my argument for the substantive approach. It could be argued that by giving substantive reasons in favor of the substantive approach in the comparison with rationalism (and in the comparison of substantivism and formalism) I am offering a *circular* argument. In this section, I shall answer this objection.

It would be a mistake to think that my justification of the substantive approach is circular just because it does not speak to something that the skeptic already accepts. That would amount to the accusation that all external reasons justifications are circular. And that is clearly wrong. There is nothing circular about saying that somebody has a reason that is not supported by anything in her subjective motivational set. Thus, the bootstrapping objection cannot rely just on the fact that I am giving external reasons to the skeptic.

Instead, the bootstrapping objection may be understood as follows: my argument offers X (substantive ethical reasons) as the justification for the employment of X (substantive ethical reasons). Thus understood, the bootstrapping objection plainly does not apply to my argument. For example, in the comparison between the lives of the subjective evaluator and the substantive evaluator, I offered a specific substantive reason in favor of the latter: I argued that, since the subjective evaluator does not employ substantive reasons, her life

really Taylor's view (see Taylor 1979, 158). The position that if, from the standpoint of first-person practical deliberation, we need to make certain ontological assumptions, then there is good reason to think that these assumptions are true, is also defended in Korsgaard 1996, 94–97, 124–125, and Wallace, Forthcoming. As stated here, this position is ambiguous because the antecedent of the conditional can be understood in two ways. On the one hand, it can mean that all first-person practical deliberation *presupposes* a certain ontology. It is not that it is the conclusion of one piece of practical deliberation as opposed to another that we have a practical reason to accept a certain ontology. It is rather that all practical deliberation – whatever its practical conclusion – presupposes a certain ontology. Understood in this way, the claim is that we have a *transcendental* reason to make certain ontological assumptions. On the other hand, the claim may be that in one piece of practical deliberation we arrive at the conclusion that we have a *practical reason* to make certain ontological assumptions. I do not want to exclude that we can have both kinds of reasons to make such assumptions. However, here I have been concerned with defending the position that we may have practical reasons for it.

lacks a certain source of meaning. This does not mean that I have simply offered X as the justification of X. Rather, I have given a *specific* substantive reason in support of the employment of *other* substantive reasons. And, of course, the former specific reason – that a certain way of giving meaning to life is not open to the subjective evaluator – must be evaluated on its own merits. However, the fact that the reasons are in both cases substantive does not make the justification circular. In the process of evaluating certain scientific reasons, a person would indeed be engaged in scientific reasoning. If she were to evaluate them positively, she would have given certain scientific reasons for accepting other scientific reasons. That, however, certainly does not make the justification circular.

According to the justificatory story told in 11.1, a good substantive justification of the use of a substantive concept appeals to the intrinsic appeal of the concept itself (the *intrinsic* element) and the relationship of the concept at stake to other substantive concepts (the *connective* element). If a justification were to rest only on the intrinsic element, then it would indeed be problematically bootstrapping. If, however, a justification rests in part on the connective element, then – as argued in 11.2 – the inclusion of the intrinsic element is merely the proper way to complete a substantive justification. What I have, in effect, just argued is that my argument for the substantive approach rests on the connective element and is thus not subject to the bootstrapping objection.

This was the short reply to this objection. However, since this brief answer does not suffice to silence the objection, I must consider two other ways in which the objection could surface. It could be objected that what is controversial is not the question of whether one substantive reason supports the use of other such reasons. Rather, the crucial question here is whether we should employ substantive reasons *at all*. And it would be circular to answer *this* question by reliance on substantive reasons.[29]

Let me start my reply by noting that the rationalist believes that substantive reasons are metaphysically suspect. If I were to give substantive reasons in favor of the substantive approach without addressing this issue, then I would indeed be offering a viciously

---

[29] The same objection could be made to the idea of using substantive *moral* reasons to argue that we should employ substantive *moral* reasons *at all* (see 11.4). My reply would be the same in this case.

circular justification. However, this is not what I do. I take myself to have dealt with this issue in 4.2–3 by employing arguments offered by McDowell. This changes the argumentative situation. If the rationalist is to stick to her position, she must of course continue to refrain from relying on substantive reasons that have not been substantiated in terms of a formal notion of reason. If, however, the rationalist has no special reason to find substantive reasons suspicious, then it must appear as a mere prejudice to refuse categorically to consider substantive reasons for and against rationalism and the substantive approach. I did not put any restrictions on my argument which would preclude the possibility that the substantive reasons could come down in favor of rationalism.[30] Thus, in the absence of special arguments against substantive reasons, it is not viciously circular to appeal to substantive reasons in favor of the substantive approach.

Here the bootstrapping objection might be reformulated as follows: one is not justified in claiming that position B is an improvement upon position A unless B can be shown to be an improvement in terms of criteria that are *neutral* between the two positions, in the sense that the acceptability of those criteria does not rest on anything that is peculiar to either position. If B can only be judged to be an improvement in the light of something that is disputed by A, are we not equally justified in claiming that A is an improvement upon B given that A would count the disputed feature to be a sign of regress rather than progress?

I answer that making neutrality of this kind a condition of improvement unnecessarily narrows our idea of improvement. In a controversy between A and B, A may have to count considerations of a certain kind for nothing: if it were to count them for something, A would cease to be the position it is. However, if there is no special reason for discounting such considerations, then we may take the fact that A must count them for nothing to be a *blind spot* of this position. It seems to limit unnecessarily the idea of progress to require that what A is blind to can always be shown to be reasonable in terms of a consideration that is not peculiar to either A or B. One advantage of B is precisely that it makes the relevance of the consideration in

---

[30] Of course, rationalists might not want to support their view by substantive reasons, since that might introduce a kind of incoherence between rationalism and its justification.

question apparent. And it may be that the neutral point of view (and not only A) is blind to its relevance. B is an improvement upon A in virtue of this consideration, even though A and the neutral position are blind to this sort of consideration.[31] It must be concluded that it is legitimate to use substantive considerations to show that the substantive approach is an improvement upon rationalism, even though rationalism and the neutral point of view are blind to this sort of consideration.[32]

The aim of this chapter was to defend and clarify the argumentative strategy of this work. I have said that my basic argument for the

---

[31] I am not assuming that there is no common ground between the positions. For example, each position is intelligible to the other. What I am assuming is that the reasons in favor of B cannot be shown to be good reasons by virtue of something whose acceptability does not depend on anything peculiar to either position.

[32] At this point, a similarity and a difference between my view and Taylor's should be noted. My argument for the substantive approach amounts to *comparing* it with rationalism and arguing that we have a good practical reason to accept the former *rather than* the latter. Here I am implicitly agreeing with Taylor's view that practical arguments are "transition arguments": "[Transition arguments] are inherently comparative. The claim is not that Y is correct *simpliciter*, but simply that, whatever is 'ultimately true,' Y is better than X . . . The argument is thus specifically addressed to the holders of X" (Taylor 1993, 225). However, my view differs from Taylor's with respect to the way in which the arguments are addressed to the holders of X. In my view, this merely means that Y is supposed to be shown to be an improvement on X. According to Taylor, "what they [transition arguments] appeal to in the interlocutor's own commitments is not explicit at the outset, but has to be brought to light" (226). It seems to me that this limits the scope of transition arguments to arguments that can appeal to something that the interlocutor already somehow implicitly accepts, and thus limits the idea of progress. Taylor also says that the transition arguments "appeal to what the opponent is already committed to, or at the least cannot lucidly repudiate" (225). The formulation in terms of what the opponent "cannot lucidly repudiate" is better, since it allows comparative arguments to appeal to considerations that the opponent is blind to, although these considerations cannot be supported by neutral considerations or be shown to be implicit in the opponent's position. This difference between my view of transition arguments and Taylor's is related to another possible difference. I have talked as if strongly evaluative reasons may be external reasons. I think that it is not clear whether Taylor believes this (see Taylor 1985b, 41–42; 1993, 210). Taylor and I both want to reject the "externalistic" view that practical reason and evaluative intuitions are suspect unless underpinned by something that lies outside our evaluative intuitions. In Taylor 1989 (71–75), the rejection of this "externalistic" view is combined with a discussion of the transition account of practical reason. I speculate that Taylor thinks that, to avoid this "externalism," one must also address practical arguments to what the interlocutor is already committed to (that is, one must also give the interlocutor internal reasons). In 4.2, I argued with McDowell that external reasons are not external to ethics: in other words, one can reject the "externalism" that Taylor and I both want to reject without denying that there are external reasons.

substantive approach and substantivism is that they *make better sense of our lives* than rationalism and formalism. I argued that in trying to make sense of our lives we are trying both to understand our lives and to lead lives supported by good practical reasons. My claim in this work is that the substantive approach makes better sense of our lives than rationalism because it better enables us to lead lives we have a good practical reason to lead. Now even if I were to give up the thesis that trying to understand our lives and trying to lead lives supported by good reasons are both ways of trying to make sense of our lives, this would not affect my argumentative strategy: even if I were to give up this thesis, my aim would still be to show that the substantive approach enables us to understand our lives at least as well as rationalism, and that there are good practical reasons to favor the substantive approach. In this chapter, I have argued both that, to demonstrate the superiority of the substantive approach, we must appeal to practical reasons, and that to offer practical substantive reasons in favor of the substantive approach is a perfectly legitimate form of argumentation. Having argued in the previous chapters that there are good substantive reasons to favor the substantive approach over *subjectivist* rationalism, I now turn to showing that there are such reasons to favor it over *inter-subjectivist* rationalism.

13

Evaluation of others

Having argued that the substantive approach to the problem of false
self-assessment should be favored over subjectivist rationalism, I now
turn to the issue of the evaluation of others. Here the central issue is
what, if anything, justifies our moral criticism of others. My aim is to
show that the substantive approach to this question should be favored
over inter-subjectivist rationalism. I shall argue that it is a mistake to
think that moral criticism of others must be justified by a rationalistic
argument revealing the presuppositions of rational argumentation.[1]
Instead, we should seek to support the criticism by substantive
reasons. In §1 of this chapter, I shall lay out the basic argument for
the superiority of the substantive approach. The rest of the chapter
consists of elaborations and answers to objections. In the next
chapter, then, I turn to the special problem of *cross-cultural* criticism of
others.

I PUTTING CRUELTY BEFORE PRAGMATIC CONTRADICTIONS[2]

The issue in this chapter is not whether rationalism and the substantive approach yield different moral judgments, but rather which
justification of those judgments should be favored. I shall thus consider
an uncontroversial judgment – the condemnation of torture – and
compare the respective justifications. My goal is not to argue that the
rationalist's conclusions do not follow from the premises (that was the
aim of chapter 9). Instead I will assume that there are good rationalistic justifications of the condemnation of torture and then argue that

---

[1] This means that my arguments in this chapter apply no less to Apel's and Kuhlmann's
rationalism than to that of Habermas. In this chapter, "rationalism" refers to this kind
of rationalism. Only when it is especially important to remind the reader what sort of
rationalism is under discussion will this be made explicit.
[2] Cf. ch. 1 of Shklar 1984, "Putting Cruelty First," though putting cruelty before pragmatic contradiction is not the same as putting it first.

we have good reasons to justify our condemnation of torture by substantive justifications rather than by rationalistic justifications.

According to the substantive approach, torture should be condemned for substantive reasons. For example, torture may be condemned on account of its cruelty, its ultimate violation of the victim, and its utter disrespect for the victim. Discourse-ethical rationalists have two options with respect to the condemnation of torture. They may justify the condemnation either *directly* by giving an up-justification of it or *indirectly* by giving an up-justification of discourse ethics (of SD and/or U) and arguing that torture would be condemned in practical discourse.[3] I will consider both options and argue that in each case the substantive approach should be favored.

Consider first the *direct* approach. In this case, the condemnation of torture is the direct result of the up-justification addressed to the moral skeptic. The moral skeptic aspires to engage in argumentation and to respect its rules. It turns out that torture is incompatible with the rules of argumentation and it is condemned on these grounds. The rational justification of the condemnation of torture is that anyone who engages in argumentation would perform a pragmatic contradiction if she were also to favor torture.

It seems to me that this is not the kind of justification of the condemnation of torture that we should give. What is deplorable about torture is the cruelty and the utter violation of the victim. Since I do not wish to argue here that there is not a good rationalistic justification of the condemnation of torture, I do not claim that torture is compatible with argumentation. However, the rationalistic emphasis on this incompatibility obscures what is deplorable about torture.[4] The condemnation of torture must not – as it were – await the resolution of the question of whether torture is incompatible with argumentation or not. Even if one could consistently both endorse the rules of argumentation and endorse torture, torture should be condemned for precisely the reasons given (and others too). This false emphasis of the rationalist stems from the fact that her justifications are meant to be acceptable to the moral skeptic on the moral skeptic's own ground. This means that the justifications may not appeal to anything the moral skeptic wishes to withhold consent from, such as the condemnation of cruelty. Precisely this limitation on the justi-

---

[3] As before, I use "up" as an abbreviation for "universal-pragmatic."
[4] Cf. Williams 1985, 115.

fications, however, means that they must leave out what is really deplorable about torture.

This does not mean that substantive justifications cannot mention what rationalistic condemnations of torture correctly emphasize, namely that torture is an "infliction of pain that substitutes screams and groans for voice."[5] Torture may be condemned for the substantive reason that it is a way of depriving the victim of the right to speak. My point is not that the rationalistic condemnation does not bring out anything of importance, but merely that its perspective on the issue is skewed.

It might be objected here that the fact that the rationalistic up-justification is addressed to the moral skeptic is only one important fact about it and that the other facts about it make it clear that the rationalist's perspective is not distorted. The up–justification unfolds what is implicit in the moral skeptic's commitment to argumentation. What it unfolds is that the moral skeptic is committed to respecting other people in much more substantial ways than she thought she was. Thus, so the argument goes, it is open to the rationalist to say that torture is deplorable not only because endorsement of the rules of argumentation is incompatible with endorsement of torture, but also because tortured people are not respected in these more substantial ways. According to this line of reasoning, this means that rationalism can offer all the reasons against torture that the substantive approach can, but it can also do more. In addition, rationalism shows that the respect which the moral skeptic wants to show others in argumentation requires that people also be paid a more substantial moral respect, and thereby rationalism gives an answer to the moral skeptic. Since the substantive approach does not address the skeptic on her own ground, it can give no such answer to moral skepticism.

It is a mistake to think that rationalism can say the *same* thing as the substantive approach and then *add* an answer to the moral skeptic. Anything the rationalist says against torture – insofar as it is to count as a *reason* against torture – must be backed up by a rationalistic

---

[5] Baier 1994b, 246. Although in this article Baier considers the protection against torture to be a right "that speech essentially entails," she is not in the business of constructing this claim so that it can be understood as a rationalistic argument; also, she says that "it seems too weak to say that the victims of torture are victims of the violation of a right. They are victims of violation itself, of violence at its most evil. If we have any responsibilities, the responsibility to prevent torture, to respond to the cries or stifled cries of the tortured, is surely the most self-evident" (246).

justification. This means that everything said against torture must be shown to be rooted in its violation of the rules of argumentation. If something someone might say against torture is not shown to be thus rooted, then – on the direct up-model – it must remain just something someone might say against torture but not a *reason* to condemn torture. Thus, if a rationalist says that torture is deplorable because it violates the victim, this (in the rationalist's view) can only count as a reason if the sense in which it is a violation can be related to the rules of argumentation. The substantive approach places no such restrictions on the sense in which it is a violation of the victim; it may elaborate on the violation of the victim as being importantly a violation of the victim's bodily and emotional (rather than intellectual) integrity.

This point can be illustrated by considering the torture of those so severely retarded that they are incapable of participating in rational discourse. There is clearly going to be some difficulty in showing by a direct up-justification, unraveling the presuppositions of rational discourse, that such torture should be condemned. Since these people are incapable of participating in argumentation, it is not clear why endorsing torturing them is incompatible with the rules for argumentation. Now, again, my point is not that there is in this case no good up-justification of the condemnation of torture. The example merely illustrates that rationalism approaches the issue from the wrong angle. It should not be a difficulty to justify the condemnation of the torture of the severely retarded. With the substantive approach, there is no difficulty. The reasons why such torture is deplorable are readily available to view, undistorted. This is the reason why we should favor the substantive approach over rationalism.

I have presented the basic case against up-rationalism by focusing on *direct* up-justifications of the condemnation of cruelty. It might be argued that by doing so I have made things too easy for myself. I argued that the up-rationalist's perspective on the reasons to be offered against torture is distorted. It could be argued, however, that this is not true if the up-justification of the condemnation of torture is *indirect*. If the up-justification is of SD and torture is then to be condemned in practical discourse, all the reasons available to the substantive approach are available in the practical discourse. Thus, indirect up-rationalism has the same perspective to offer as the substantive approach, and has in addition a rationalistic justification of SD.

To answer this objection, it is first important to emphasize what the rationalist has in effect admitted here. The justifications offered in discourse are not themselves up-justifications. If a discourse participant who accepts SD does not accept something which there is good reason to accept in the discourse, the kind of irrationality she is guilty of cannot be explained in terms of a violation of something which must be presupposed in discourse. It must be explicated in terms of a more substantive notion of reason.[6] Thus, if someone accepts SD but questions in discourse whether there are good reasons to condemn torture, she is guilty of a kind of substantive irrationality. As I have argued, these are the reasons relevant for the condemnation of torture. Since that is so, and even the up-rationalist acknowledges that they are reasons, though they are not revealed by an up-justification, I suggest that these reasons can stand on their own and that the rationalistic up-justifications are not needed.

In suggesting that the rationalistic up-justifications are not needed, I am deviating importantly from rationalism. This can be seen by reflecting on the rationalist's claim that discourse-ethical rationalism can incorporate all the considerations emphasized by the substantive approach and can then *in addition* offer a rationalistic justification. What does "in addition" mean here? There are two possibilities. One could view the rationalistic justification as a mere *fifth wheel*: the success or failure of it does not affect the justificatory status of, say, the condemnation of torture. As such an optional extra, a rationalistic justification might sometimes be useful, for example to motivate a moral skeptic who cannot be otherwise motivated. I do not object to such employment of rationalistic justifications. But these justifications are not needed to establish the validity of, say, the condemnation of torture. This is not the possibility favored by rationalism. The rationalist thinks that without a rationalistic justification of SD/U, the problems of rationality and ethnocentricity remain unsolved (see 8.3).[7] And if the justificatory status of these meta-principles is

---

[6] This is what must be assumed if rationalism wants to offer the same reasons as the substantive approach and *additionally* a rationalistic justification of SD. In any case, Habermas assumes that the reasons offered *in* discourse are not to be understood rationalistically (see 8.1 and 8.4).

[7] As far as I know, Habermas never says this in so many words. However, there is good reason to believe that this is what he thinks. He clearly thinks that these problems are serious difficulties and he consistently responds to them by offering a rationalistic justification of morality (see Habermas 1988d, 86–89 [76–78]; 1988e, 127 [116]; 1991b,

jeopardized in this way by the absence of a rationalistic justification, the same must hold for the substantive results (for example the condemnation of torture) reached under the guidance of these meta-principles.

It is this insistence of rationalism on the necessity of the rationalistic justification which makes the substantive approach superior to it. Although the rationalistic justification is not to be applied directly to the condemnation of torture, the call for it obscures the force of the substantive reasons against torture. The call for it makes the issue of whether there is good reason to condemn torture dependent on the question of what is presupposed in argumentation. And as urged before, the judgment that torture is deplorable should not have to wait for the results of an investigation into the presuppositions of argumentation.

In this section, my aim was to state as succinctly as possible the most important advantage of the substantive approach over rationalism. What I have, in effect, argued is that inter-subjectivist rationalism goes wrong in the same way as subjectivist rationalism: both of them change the subject. Inter-subjectivist rationalism changes the subject-matter by shifting the focus to the presuppositions of argumentation. As a result of this change of focus, the substantive reasons for which we condemn torture are no longer properly in view. And we are addressed as subjects who are interested in respecting the presuppositions of argumentation, rather than as subjects who care whether other people are treated with cruelty (and in other substantively specified ways).

I am not merely saying that rationalism *in fact* changes the subject, but also that it *should not* change it in this way. In saying that we should condemn torture because it is cruel, I am making a claim as to how we *should* lead our lives: we should condemn cruel actions because of their *cruelty*. This claim is in accordance with the account of substantive critique given in 11.1: one part of a substantive justification must be the intrinsic appeal of the substantive concept itself. In other words, I am claiming that we have a good substantive

12–13 [197–198]; 1991f, 133–134, 185–186 [31–32, 76–77]; 1996, 59–61). Thus, we may at least assume that he thinks that these difficulties remain unresolved unless a justification can be offered which accomplishes the same as his rationalistic justification. Both Apel and Kuhlmann make it very clear that they think that only rationalistic justifications can resolve such difficulties (see Apel 1989; Kuhlmann 1992c, 181–201).

reason to condemn cruel actions and that this reason consists irreducibly, in part, in the *cruelty* of those actions. Rationalism does not allow that we guide our actions by nothing more "fundamental" than cruelty and other substantive considerations. By insisting that we must guide it by something more "fundamental," it distorts our view of the substantive reasons we have. Therefore, it should be rejected.

2 MORAL CRITICISM AND RATIONAL WARRANT

Here it might be objected that in my argument I have wrongly assumed that indirect rationalism makes the *deplorability* of torture dependent on the analysis of the presuppositions of argumentation. On the contrary, the point of this analysis is merely to show that the subjective reaction of abhorrence towards torture is *rationally warranted*: if the meta-principles (SD and U) which guide our substantive moral judgment are not beyond rational doubt, then those judgments themselves are not beyond rational doubt.

According to this objection, indirect rationalism distinguishes between that which makes torture deplorable and that which rationally warrants criticism of torture. If this is how indirect rationalism is to be understood, it seems to me that the substantive approach is in any case superior to it. It is precisely a virtue of the substantive approach that it locates both that which makes the deplorability of torture apparent and the rational warrant of the criticism of torture in the same place: in the substantive reasons for the condemnation of torture.

The substantive approach must here be distinguished from a third view – the kind of view taken by Richard Rorty (see chapter 14). Rorty shares with the substantive approach the intuition that it is dubious to suppose that the substantive criticism of torture – it is cruel and utterly violates the victim – is somehow wanting in the absence of a rationalistic justification. However, Rorty does away with the idea of rational warrant itself and says that all we need are these substantive considerations. In other words, torture is criticized by appeal to substantive considerations, but the idea that this criticism is rationally warranted is discarded.

The route taken by the substantive approach makes it superior to both Rorty's view and rationalism. By not giving up the idea of rational warrant, the substantive approach – unlike Rorty's view –

meets the justified worry that, without being rationally warranted, the criticism of torture would indeed be wanting. By not splitting up the rational warrant and that which makes the deplorability of torture apparent, the substantive approach – unlike rationalism – does justice to the intuition that the criticism of torture is not wanting in the absence of an analysis of the presuppositions of argumentation.

At this point, the objection might be reformulated as follows: the indirect rationalist does not have to say that the cruelty of torture only reveals the *deplorability* of torture; rather, she can say that cruelty also gives us a *reason* against torture. The point of indirect rationalism is to explain *why* the cruelty of an action provides a reason against it. An explanation of this does not have to distort our reasons for opposing torture. In fact, such an explanation presupposes that it is *cruelty* which gives us a reason to oppose torture. Otherwise it would not even be possible to set out to explain why cruelty gives us such a reason. Thus, indirect rationalism is superior to the substantive approach because it can acknowledge the reasons we have and, in addition, explain the justificatory force of those reasons.[8]

In answer to this objection, it must first be noted that the substantive approach can explain why the cruelty of actions provides a reason against them. According to the account of substantive justi-fications given in 11.1, the justification of the use of substantive concepts rests on an *intrinsic* and a *connective* element: (1) the intrinsic appeal of the substantive concept itself and (2) the relationship of the concept in question to other substantive concepts. Applying this account to cruelty, we get a two-part answer to the question of why the cruelty of actions provides a reason against them. First, cruelty provides a reason against cruel actions on account of what it is – namely, cruelty: we have a reason not to perform cruel action precisely because those actions are cruel. Second, because *cruelty* is related in a certain way to other substantive concepts which provide us with reasons against actions, it borrows part of its justificatory force from those other concepts: since the fact that actions are painful and humiliating for the victim provides a reason against those actions, and since cruel actions are often also painful and humiliating for the victim, the cruelty of actions provides us with a reason against them.

Of course, the indirect rationalist will not be satisfied with this

---

[8] Here, and in the ensuing reinforcement of this objection, I have attempted to formu-late an objection raised by Jay Wallace.

reply. Let us even suppose that she – for the sake of argument – grants me that the two-part justificatory story is correct as far as the justifications given *in discourse* are concerned. Both parts in the justificatory story are elements of *first-order practical justifications*. She may grant me that the intrinsic element reveals that there is a sense in which the first-order justification comes to an end with the appeal to cruelty: we have a reason to oppose cruel actions precisely because they are *cruel*.[9] Of course, the connective element correctly emphasizes that there may be *other* practical reasons for opposing cruel actions. Nevertheless, the intrinsic element rightly brings to light that part of what is wrong with cruel actions is nothing other than that they are cruel. Thus, it would be distorting to go beyond cruelty in the first-order practical justification. However – so the indirect rationalist will argue – even if the first-order practical justification comes to an end with the appeal to cruelty, there remains the *philosophical* question as to what the source of the reason-giving force of cruelty is. Since this question asks what gives first-order considerations their reason-giving force in the first place, it cannot be answered by giving an additional first-order justification. Contrary to the substantive approach, rationalism has an answer to this question. And it is an answer which does not distort our first-order practical reasons, since the rationalist can fully acknowledge that the first-order justification comes to an end with the appeal to cruelty.[10]

Before answering this objection, it must be stressed that the debate between the substantive approach and indirect rationalism concerns the issue of whether morality needs a rationalistic *justification*. Thus, the rationalist cannot understand the answer to the philosophical question to consist in an explanation as opposed to a justification. The rationalist claim must be that a rationalistic justification is the source of the reason-giving force of cruelty and that, in the absence of such a justification, cruelty would be wanting in reason-giving

---

[9] I leave aside the issue of whether these concessions are really consistent with *discourse-ethical* rationalism. Here I am interested in a certain rationalistic response to my arguments and, for this purpose, it is not important whether this response is consistent with a discourse-ethical understanding of moral justification, or whether Apel, Habermas, or Kuhlmann would actually endorse this response.

[10] Cf. Korsgaard's distinction between showing that it would be a *good idea* to perform an action and that one is *obligated* to perform it (see Korsgaard 1996, 23–27, 103–113).

force. Since this must be the rationalist claim, I think it does indeed obscure the force of the substantive reasons we have.

As I see it, the indirect rationalist faces here a dilemma: *either* the rationalistic justification concerns only the intrinsic element in the justificatory story told by the substantive approach *or* this justification amounts to a first-order practical justification which belongs to the connective element.[11] In the first case, the rationalistic justification obscures the force of the substantive reasons we have. In the second case, rationalism does not – contrary to the claim made in the objection – give an answer to a philosophical question which the substantive approach cannot answer. Let me explain.

As the intrinsic element brings out, what is partly wrong with cruel actions is that they are cruel and nothing else.[12] If that is so, the rationalistic claim that cruelty derives its reason-giving force from a rationalistic justification must be rejected. If cruelty were to derive its reason-giving force from a rationalistic justification, then it would simply not be true that it was only cruelty which was wrong with these actions. Thus, it is a mistake to suppose that with respect to the intrinsic element there is room for the philosophical question of what else except cruelty gives cruelty its reason-giving force. If the intrinsic element is properly understood, there is no room for such a philosophical question. However, as far as the connective element is concerned, there is plenty of room for a question about the source of the reason-giving force of cruelty. After all, the connective element concerns the first-order question of what else except cruelty supports criticizing actions for their cruelty. But as already explained, the substantive approach can supply answers to this question. Thus, here it is possible to trace the reason-giving force of cruelty beyond cruelty itself, but this is something which the substantive approach can also do.

According to the substantive approach, it makes perfect sense to

---

[11] As I have defined the connective element, it concerns the relationship between the substantive concept in question and other *substantive* concepts. Of course, this is not how the rationalist can understand it, since she wants to support the use of the concept in question by a rationalistic justification. I speak of the connective element here simply in order to indicate that the rationalist is giving a *first-order practical justification* which rests on *something else* than the intrinsic appeal of the concept in question.

[12] The use of the phrases "partly" and "nothing else" in this sentence does not lead to a contradiction. "Partly" is used here merely to indicate that the story must be complemented by the connective element.

ask "Why not be cruel?" The answer to the question will have two elements. The intrinsic element will say that we should not perform cruel actions because they are cruel. The connective element will rely on other (substantive) considerations than cruelty. What does not make sense is to suppose that we can retain the intrinsic element as a response which differs from the connective element, while tracing the reason-giving force of cruelty (as it pertains to the intrinsic element) to something else. The mistake of the objection under discussion is to suppose that this makes sense.[13]

Contrary to the suggestion made in the objection, the claim that morality needs a rationalistic justification amounts to saying that the intrinsic element must be eliminated from the justifications of the use of substantive moral concepts. According to the substantive approach, such justifications should contain both an intrinsic and a connective element. Moreover, the connective element presupposes the intrinsic element in the following sense: if we give a connective justification of the use of the concept of cruelty with the help of the concept of humiliation, then the question arises of whether the use of the latter concept is justified; and the justification of the latter concept will also contain an intrinsic element.

Not only rationalists think that the intrinsic element must be eliminated. For example, one might claim that the justification of the use of a substantive concept rests ultimately on its *coherence* with other substantive concepts. In order to argue that the intrinsic element should not be eliminated *in this way*, I have to consider in detail what such an elimination would amount to.[14] My arguments in this chapter are directed against the elimination proposed by up-rationalism. Nevertheless, my thesis is perfectly general: practical justifications should always, in part, rest on the intrinsic appeal of substantive concepts.[15] This thesis, however, cannot be made plau-

---

[13] According to a common interpretation of Prichard 1912, there H. A. Prichard argues that it does not make sense to ask the question "Why be moral?" I do not agree that this does not make sense. The question can be answered by asking – for the different moral stances there are – "Why take up this moral stance?" and then giving an answer consisting of the intrinsic and the connective element. However, perhaps Prichard can be understood as arguing that the intrinsic element cannot be preserved while its justificatory force is traced back to something else. In that case, I would be in agreement with him.

[14] This I shall do in the discussion of formalism in chapter 15.

[15] I say "should" because – in accordance with the argumentative strategy discussed in ch. 12 – this thesis is itself a practical judgment.

sible without considering the plausibility of the different ways of eliminating the intrinsic element.[16] One might say that the whole book is an argument for and an elaboration on this thesis.

Let me turn to a different defense of rationalism: if there is a good rationalistic justification of something, must it not *in the case of conflict* with a substantive justification *take precedence* over the substantive justification? If the arguments in chapters 10–11 are sound, then the answer is "no" for the case of subjectivist rationalism. What about up-justifications which take argumentation as such as their starting point, though? Since they take argumentation *as such* as their starting point, would they not take precedence over substantive justifications? Before answering this question, I should emphasize that in this chapter I have been concerned with cases in which there is not such a conflict. I did not suppose that there are good rationalistic justifications for torturing the severely retarded. I merely pointed out that rationalists have difficulties justifying the condemnation of torture in such cases, and that this is a sign of the distorted perspective of rationalism.

Even if there are cases of conflict between the conclusion of a substantive justification and an up-justification, this is not a problem for the substantive approach. First, it is by no means obvious that, even if something is a presupposition of argumentation as such, it should also be respected in situations which are not cases of argumentation. If there are good substantive reasons for not respecting it in these situations, then these justifications may well take precedence

---

[16] Christine M. Korsgaard offers a transcendental argument for moral obligation. She argues that rational action is possible only if the rational agent is under moral obligation (see Korsgaard 1996, 113–125, 160–164). This is a rationalistic argument. The starting point of the argument is supposed to be thin enough to be acceptable to a moral skeptic who wants to fulfill all the conditions of rational agency while disputing that she has any moral obligations. The transcendental argument is then supposed to reveal to her that having moral obligations is among the conditions of the possibility of rational agency. If my thesis is correct, then the supposition that morality needs a Korsgaardian justification distorts our view of the reasons we have in the same way as the supposition that morality needs a rationalistic justification starting from the presupposition of rational argumentation. However, I cannot take the thesis as a premise which has been established through the discussion of up-rationalism, and then deduce from this premise that Korsgaardian justifications are distortive in this way. On the contrary, showing that they are indeed distortive in this way would be one part of an "inductive" argument for the plausibility of this thesis. The thesis can only be made plausible by showing that the different attempts to eliminate the intrinsic element are distortive in this way.

over the rationalistic up-justifications. Second, if I am right that substantive justifications represent the appropriate justificatory ideal and that we can do entirely without rationalistic justifications, then there will be a good substantive justification for any moral position worth holding. Thus, if there is indeed a conflict between the conclusion of a good rationalistic up-justification and a substantive justification we currently favor, this does not show that we need to give up the substantive approach in this case; it shows at most that we may have to search for another substantive justification.[17]

This section and the last have made clear what the advantages of the substantive approach are. However, the rationalist may still think that the substantive approach comes at too high a price. She may argue that, despite the appeal of the substantive approach, it comes with severe disadvantages, such as making it impossible to make sense of cross-cultural moral criticism. This is a serious objection to the substantive approach and it will be addressed in the next chapter. Before I turn to it, however, I shall conclude this chapter by answering four less severe objections.

3 FOUR OBJECTIONS

1. In the basic argument for the substantive approach, I focused on the torture of humans. It might be argued that I could just as well have discussed cruelty to animals and made all the same points. The fact that I could have done that, however – so the argument goes – reveals the questionable structure of my argument. It is not that cruelty to animals should not be condemned. However, it is questionable to assume that a moral theory must treat our relations to animals precisely like our relations to humans. Thus, it would not as such have been an objection against up-rationalism that it has "more difficulties" (given that it takes argumentation as its starting point) accounting for the wrongness of cruelty to animals than does the substantive approach. It is the substantive approach which is problematic, because it is not discriminative enough. If substantive reasons are

---

[17] It must be noted that, in urging that we do entirely without subjectivist and inter-subjectivist rationalisms, I am not saying that utility-maximizing reasoning should be given up and that there are no formal conditions of argumentation. All I have been arguing is that the analysis of the utility-maximizing conception of rationality and of the formal conditions of rational discourse should not be elevated into a rationalistic justification of morality.

all we are to appeal to, then we will be unable to distinguish between our relations to humans, animals, and inanimate nature.

Quite the contrary: in considering what substantive reasons we have, we should certainly take some differences to be relevant and others not. It must be emphasized that in offering a substantive approach, I am being very unspecific about the correct approach to morality (for example, I have not made any commitment as to whether our relations to non-human animals are morally different in an important way from our relations to other humans). To say that the account is substantive is just supposed to set it aside from rationalism (or, more generally, formalism). And the example of torture is merely supposed to illustrate a very general point. This point is that rationalism puts artificial constraints on what can count as a good reason. The example was supposed to be a case in which the question of whether something is a good reason does not depend on an investigation into the presuppositions of argumentation.

Of course, in giving this example I took a specific moral stance and thus went beyond merely offering the substantive approach without any specific substantive commitments. Doing so, however, is part and parcel of my argumentative strategy. It is not because it would be dubious for me "as a philosopher" to take a particular substantive stance that I am being so unspecific about what specific substantive approach to offer. It is just that in this work I am in the business of defending the very idea of a substantive approach against rationalism, rather than developing a specific substantive approach. Though it is not dubious, however, to offer substantive reasons without rationalistic underpinnings, getting the substantive reasons right is a messy and complicated affair (see 11.1–2). Thus, I took the example of torture to illustrate my point, not because other examples would have been philosophically dubious, but rather because I feel secure in my substantive judgment about this case.

2. In the last section, the focus was on the condemnation of torture. But it is one thing to condemn torture, so to speak, for oneself, another thing to *demand* that torture be stopped, and yet another thing to back up the demand by a *threat* of *enforcement*. It might be argued that, even if I have succeeded in showing that the substantive approach does as well as rationalism in justifying the condemnation itself, only rationalism is capable of justifying the demand, the threat, and the actual enforcement. The substantive

approach allows that the justification of the condemnation of torture may have to appeal to moral considerations which simply leave the torturers cold. How, though, could such a justification ever suffice to justify demands and enforcements of them? In such a case, would we not simply be imposing our opinions on others? If the demands and the enforcements are given a rationalistic justification, things look different. At least if the torturers are willing to support their practice by reasons, if they are willing to engage in argumentation about it, we can show that they must implicitly assume the illegitimacy of torture. Thus, in demanding that they stop the torture, we would only be demanding that they act on something which they themselves implicitly accept. Thus, we would not simply be imposing our opinions on them.

Before answering this objection, let me first note that the fact that the arguing torturers must implicitly condemn torture by no means guarantees they will give up their practice. They might accept that by both arguing and torturing they are involved in a pragmatic contradiction and go on to say that they are willing to live with the contradiction. Torture may be too important for maintaining their political power to give up. If they were to give up torture, they would be acting against their own interests. They may admit that they have lost the argument, but that this is of no consequence. Since living with a performative contradiction of this sort is in their self-interest, they have a good reason to live with it and are not likely to give up torture on account of it.[18]

As already argued, the reasons why torture is deplorable are substantive reasons such as that it is cruel and that it is a complete violation of the victim. Now it seems to me that if we are going to demand that torture be stopped and to enforce that demand, then these should be the reasons we give in support of our actions. After all, this is why torture is deplorable. Of course, some additional reasons are needed to move from condemnation of something to enforcement.[19] However, by suggesting that the justification of the demand and its enforcement be the implicit commitment of the arguing torturer, rationalism both draws attention away from the

[18] Cf. Nozick 1981, 406–409; Williams 1985, 23; Debruin 1988, 54–63.
[19] As argued in Baier 1994c, a morality which treats cruelty as the worst vice should be wary of a morality eager to command and enforce.

reasons I think should be given for demanding that torture be stopped and at the same time creates for itself a new problem.

The new problem is analogous to the problem of justifying paternalistic demands. The problem with paternalistic demands is that the person on whom the demand is made is not harming others, only herself. Of course, the torturers are harming others. However, in suggesting that the justification of the demand be the torturers' implicit commitment to the condemnation of torture, rationalism suggests that the justification of the demand (as in the case of paternalistic demands) is not the harm done to others. Like the paternalistic demand, the rationalist's demand is not based on the harm done to others but on the person's irrationality (that is, the irrationality of a performative contradiction). Thus, rationalism is faced with a problem analogous to the problem of paternalism: what justification do we have for demanding that someone act rationally when we cannot base our justification on harm to others? Of course, I do not mean that paternalism is always indefensible. The problem is that the up-rationalist cannot appeal to the most natural defense of paternalism: that the irrational person's actions go against her own interests, that she is harming herself. As already argued, it may be in the self-interest of the arguing torturer simply to live with the pragmatic contradiction.

Rather than giving a better justification of making demands on others than the substantive approach does, the proposal made on behalf of up-rationalism in this objection (1) ignores the substantive reasons that should be appealed to, were such demands to be made, and (2) creates for itself a new justificatory problem analogous to the problem of paternalism, but which up-rationalism is unable to solve in the way that the problem of paternalism is most naturally solved.

3. It might be argued that, to avoid being *dogmatic* in offering substantive reasons in support of the substantive approach, I must understand my arguments as contributions to a Habermasian discourse. And the fact that these arguments must be understood as contributions to discourse makes it explicit that my approach *cannot be purely substantive*. After all, it makes no sense to talk of substantive content except as the counterpart to form. And this form is expressed by the discourse rules for the discourse in which the substantive considerations are offered. Then, since the substantive reasons are

offered in discourse, it also becomes clear that the *justifications of the discourse rules themselves cannot be substantive.*

I agree that, to avoid dogmatism, I must submit my arguments to critical examination. However, though I cannot argue for this here, I do not think that submitting something to critical examination amounts to submitting it (implicitly) to an examination in a Habermasian discourse.[20] Be that as it may, I have no objections to the idea that the critical examination to which substantive reasons are to be subjected must fulfill certain formal conditions.[21] And it is no part of my view that *all* justifications must rest on substantive reasons. Thus, I have no objection to the supposition that the formal constraints on critical examination must be given an up-justification.[22] I have not been arguing that up-justifications are never needed, but merely that it is a serious mistake to think that moral views must be given an up-justification acceptable even to a moral skeptic.

4. It might be argued that the substantive approach faces a severe practical problem. If the substantive approach is to be of help in fighting the forces of evil – say, Nazism – it must be capable of generating agreement on principles which show the forces of evil to be wrong. This, however, the substantive approach cannot do very well: substantive moral agreement is hard to get. In this respect, rationalism does much better. It is capable of generating universal agreement, since it reveals principles which any rational being must accept. Here we have the problem of controversiality coming back to haunt the substantive approach. As admitted in 11.1–2, the substantive approach does not deliver a clear-cut method for settling disputes about practical reasons. Thus, it might be argued that if there is ever

---

[20] Cf. Walzer 1990, and Gunnarsson 1995b, 124–127.

[21] I do object, however, to the formalistic idea that good reasons are to be identified with those reasons that would be the outcome of a certain procedure (see chapter 15).

[22] I have said that my basic argument for the substantive approach is that it makes better sense of our lives than rationalism. I have also said that, at one extreme, attempts to make sense concern intelligibility. Thus, it fits my argumentative strategy to say that there are some constraints on critical examination, without which it would no longer be intelligible to call something a critical examination. If this supposition of the unintelligibility of critical examination without certain constraints were to be called a supposition to the effect that these constraints are up-presuppositions of critical examination, I would have no objections. (See the Appendix, however, for my reservations about Habermas' interpretation of up-justifications.)

to be agreement on moral matters, morality must be given a rationalistic justification.

This argument suffers from a fundamental ambiguity, and once the ambiguity is dissolved the argument collapses. Either the argument is that *correct* substantive reasoning will not lead to agreement whereas correct rationalistic reasoning will, or it amounts to a *prediction* to the effect that, by appealing to substantive reasons, we will *in fact* never reach agreement, whereas by appealing to rationalistic justifications we will. In the former case, it will trivially be true that if everybody engages in correct substantive reasoning there will be agreement on those issues where everybody has a substantive reason to accept the same conclusion. In the second case, the argument turns out to be an empirical prediction. And it is entirely unclear whether it is more likely that everybody will agree if we appeal to rationalistic reasons than if we appeal to substantive reasons: given the persistence of philosophical disagreement, there is no reason to think that people are more likely to come to agree on a rationalistic justification of human rights than to agree on human rights on account of a substantive justification.

14

Universality without neutrality

How are we to justify cross-cultural moral criticism? According to an objection raised in the last chapter, the substantive approach is unable to justify such criticism, whereas rationalism is. Contrary to the substantive approach, rationalism justifies cross-cultural criticism by *neutral* criteria. They are neutral in the sense that they are not in dispute between the critics and the criticized.[1] Substantive justifications often draw on criteria which are in dispute between the two sides. Now – so the objection goes – cross-cultural criticism cannot be shown to be justified unless it is based on neutral criteria. Therefore, the substantive approach is unable to justify such criticism.

In this chapter, I shall argue that, even with respect to the justification of cross-cultural moral criticism, the substantive approach is superior to rationalism. It should be emphasized that this does not amount to showing that moral criticism of other cultures is ever justified. To do so, I would have to embark upon a discussion of relativism about reason and morality which would take me beyond the scope of this study. All I want to show is that *if* cross-cultural criticism is ever justified, it is a mistake to demand that it must be justified by rationalistic reasons rather than only by substantive reasons.

In §1, I shall argue that there are good reasons to reject the demand for neutral criteria. In my view, this argument suffices to show that the substantive approach should be favored over rationalism even in the case of cross-cultural criticism. However, since the substantive approach shares some claims with Richard Rorty's ethnocentrism, it

---

[1] I am really making this objection on behalf of inter-subjectivist rationalism, rather than subjectivist rationalism. Since Gauthier's argument concerns a contract among utility maximizers who interact for mutual advantage, it is not immediately clear how his theory could justify criticism of the members of another culture with whom we are not engaged in an interaction for mutual benefit.

could mistakenly be thought to be subject to the same criticism as Rorty. Thus, it is important to show how the substantive approach differs from his view, and why a common criticism of his account of cross-cultural criticism therefore does not apply to the substantive approach. This is what I shall do in §§2–3.

I REJECTING NEUTRALITY

Cross-cultural moral criticism is only one example of a claim to the effect that one position is superior to another one. In this section, I shall argue *generally* that the criteria for the superiority of one of two positions should sometimes be substantive and non-neutral, rather than neutral. Now I see no reason to treat the case of cross-cultural moral criticism as an exception to this rejection of the demand for neutrality. Thus, to show that the substantive approach must be preferred to rationalism, even in the case of cross-cultural criticism, all I need to do is to offer general arguments for a rejection of the demand for neutrality. I give three such arguments.

(1) Rationalism achieves neutrality by offering a justification acceptable even to a moral skeptic. Now I have already argued in the last chapter that to demand that moral criticism be justified in this way distorts our view of the reasons we have. Thus, the arguments of the last chapter already show that the neutrality which rationalism aspires to is not an ideal against which we should measure the adequacy of the justification of our criticism of others. Instead this justification should sometimes consist of substantive reasons.

(2) In 10.5, I argued that the life of a substantive evaluator can be meaningful in a way that the life of a subjective evaluator cannot. Now this argument can also be used to show that one should not demand that the criteria by which the quality of a change in attitudes is judged be *neutral* criteria. To allow a change which according to neutral criteria would count as neither progress nor regress to be nevertheless counted as improvement gives the agent's attempts to make sense of her life a certain purpose that they would otherwise lack. In times when neither the criteria which the agents currently accept nor neutral criteria can help agents make sense of their lives, they sometimes make changes which, when assessed according to neutral criteria, would count as neither progress nor regress. If these changes were not allowed to count as improvement, the agents'

efforts to make sense of their lives would in a way have been pointless or meaningless: those agents might as well have made a different change. Thus, it must be concluded that the substantive evaluator who counts something as improvement on the grounds of criteria which the change itself brings with it has access to a source of meaning which is not available to the one who only relies on neutral criteria. And this is a good reason for allowing oneself to judge a change as an improvement by criteria which the change itself brings with it.[2]

This argument against the demand for neutral criteria directly concerns the meaning a person can give her *own life* rather than the criteria for her criticism of *others*. Nevertheless, it is also an argument for not demanding neutral criteria for the criticism of others. After all, if a person regards it as regress if she were to take up a new position, she would have to criticize others for having this position.[3] Thus, since my argument shows that a person should not restrict evaluation of changes in her own position to neutral criteria, it also shows that the criticism of others should not be limited to such criteria.

(3) Arguments (1) and (2) are based on substantive practical reasons in favor of employing substantive criteria rather than solely neutral criteria. As in 12.3, it could be objected that such arguments in favor of the use of substantive criteria are circular. It could be argued that the dispute over whether to use substantive criteria or only neutral criteria must itself be settled by criteria which are neutral towards these two possibilities. In 12.3, I answered this objection in part by saying that, to reveal the *blind spot* of one position, we sometimes need to rely on criteria which are more discriminative than neutral criteria. Now this not only answers an objection to arguments (1) and (2) but itself amounts to an argument against the demand for neutrality: to suppose that all improvements can be revealed by neutral criteria is to ignore that not only one of the two alternative positions, but also the neutral criteria, may be *blind to* certain important considerations which only become visible if we adopt the other position. To require that all improvements must be

---

[2] It should be noted that, even though the substantive evaluator can only accept the new criteria after she has made the change, she of course views them as criteria whose validity does not depend on their now being accepted by her. This makes it possible for her to understand the revision as a change for the better.

[3] Unless, of course, her criticism of herself depends on some facts peculiar to her.

revealed by neutral criteria thus arbitrarily limits the kinds of changes which can count as progress.

These three arguments show that the neutrality requirement should be rejected. Since I do not see any reason to make an exception to this rejection for the case of cross-cultural criticism, I conclude that the substantive approach is superior to rationalism for this case.[4]

2 RORTY'S ETHNOCENTRISM

Rorty defends a view which he understands as *ethnocentric* but *not relativistic*. He argues that it is misguided to think that we have a choice between relativism and an approach according to which the issue between conflicting moral positions is to be settled by criteria which are neutral in the sense that their validity can be determined independently of these moral positions.[5] It is misguided because both relativism and "neutralism"[6] assume that there is a standpoint outside moral positions from which moral positions can either be judged to be relatively valid or be evaluated on neutral grounds. And since no sense can be made of such a standpoint, and relativism and "neutralism" must therefore both be rejected, the absence of neutral criteria does not lead to relativism. Rather, the absence of neutral criteria inevitably means that the justification of a moral position will be *ethnocentric* precisely in the sense that it must rest on reasons which cannot be validated in terms of neutral criteria: in considering cruelty to be horrible and condemning torture on those grounds, *we* – those who take cruelty to be horrible – base our condemnation on a reason which is *ours* in the sense that there may be no way to show cruelty to be horrible on neutral grounds.[7]

The substantive approach is ethnocentric in exactly this way.[8] The

---

[4] It would be a mistake to suppose that the substantive approach opens up the road to dogmatic criticism of other cultures. It is a difficult question exactly when cross-cultural criticism is justified. And it must be answered with the help of substantive reasons.

[5] I focus here on the issue of moral/ethical relativism, but Rorty also wants to distance himself from relativism more generally.

[6] This is my term.

[7] Rorty 1989, xv, 49–57, 197–198; 1991b, 22–30; 1991c, 194–195.

[8] Of course, there is a sense in which it is misleading to call the substantive approach "*ethno*centric." The substantive approach does not appeal to criteria that are neutral in the sense that they can be shown to be valid independently of substantive (ethical)

crucial difference between the substantive approach and Rorty's ethnocentrism surfaces in the different explications of claims to the effect that a change is an *improvement*, a change for the *better*.

According to the substantive approach, the standard against which we judge something to be an improvement may itself be new to us and be part of the improvement. It is in light of this new standard that we judge the move from our old position to the new position as an improvement. For example, if *tolerance* were our new standard of correctness, we might judge the move to the new position as an improvement because it is more tolerant than the old position. In each case where we claim that something is an improvement, we owe a justification of some form like "the new position is an improvement because it is _____" (e.g., "the new position is an improvement because it is more tolerant"). According to the substantive approach, the sense in which something is an improvement is to be explained by filling in such blanks with the respective substantive evaluative standards.

This explanation precludes another possible understanding of improvement. When we say that the new view is an improvement upon the old one, we do not mean that it now *seems* to us to be a superior view.[9] In relying on substantive standards to explain why something is an improvement, we assume precisely that some other standards might show that what now seems to us an improvement is in fact not one.[10]

views. To say that something is not neutral in this sense is compatible with saying that it is neutral in the sense that it can be shown to be valid independently of being acceptable to a certain group (identified ethnically or otherwise). Lack of neutrality in the former sense means that the justification of validity must be substantive, and this is compatible with assuming that this substantive justification shows something to be neutrally valid in the second sense, namely valid independently of being acceptable to a certain group.

[9] Of course, the substantive approach is compatible with assuming that I am justified in accepting something in a particular situation which I would not be justified in accepting if my epistemic situation were better (see Stout 1988, 21–32). And it is surely also compatible with assuming that something is valid in one set of (cultural or natural) circumstances which would not be valid in other circumstances. This has nothing to do with epistemic deficiency; it is just that something may be appropriate in one situation which is not appropriate in another (see Stout 1988, 85–86). In addition, the substantive approach is compatible with assuming that, even if the validity of something is not relative to circumstances, there may be ties for first place. Two proposals may claim to be valid for all circumstances, and these two proposals may be equally good (see Stout 1988, 96–99).

[10] Cf. Putnam 1990, 23–26, and 1992, 36.

The germ of Rorty's understanding of improvement is to be found in a remark from his *Consequences of Pragmatism*: "[The pragmatist] does think that in the process of playing vocabularies and cultures off against each other, we produce new and better ways of talking and acting – not better by reference to a previously known standard, but just better in the sense that they come to *seem* clearly better than their predecessors."[11] Hilary Putnam has used this remark as a basis for criticizing Rorty as a relativist.[12] In his reply to Putnam in "Putnam and the Relativist Menace," Rorty denies that he is a relativist and goes on to elaborate in an ethnocentric vein on the remark just quoted. He does this by saying that he wants to understand the phrase "come to seem clearly better than their predecessors" as "come to seem *to us* clearly better than their predecessors."[13] Here "us" is to be understood as "language users whom we can recognize as better versions of ourselves." He then goes on to explain that we recognize them as better versions of ourselves by recognizing them as "people who have come to hold different beliefs from ours by a process that we, by *our present* notions of the difference between rational persuasion and force, count as rational persuasion." Given that we have an interest in such things as avoiding brainwashing and that we value liberal education and a free press, actualizations of these interests and values are understood to play an appropriate role in this process.[14]

Rorty clearly realizes that, for something to be an improvement, it is not enough that it comes to *seem* better *to us*. Thus, he imposes substantive restrictions – "our" substantive restrictions – on how the new position may be arrived at. These restrictions are wrong-headed in two ways, however. (For the sake of simplicity, let me call the old and new positions "p1" and "p2" respectively, and the times at which they are accepted "t1" and "t2.")

First, it is neither a necessary nor a sufficient condition on progress that it be arrived at by rational persuasion rather than by force. We may condemn brainwashing, but we nevertheless allow that even if we arrive at p2 by brainwashing it may be better than p1, and it may be the case that we would probably not have arrived at p2 by rational persuasion. If asked why it is better, we may then produce a reason, such as that p2 is more tolerant. Here Rorty's mistake is to focus on

11 Rorty 1982, xxxvii.   12 See Putnam 1990, 21–26.
13 Rorty 1993, 453.   14 Rorty 1993, 454.

the process by which the change took place rather than on the outcome of the change.[15]

Second, it is also a mistake to place substantive restrictions on either the process or the outcome. It is true that, at each time, we use "our" notions to judge whether something is an improvement. But it is a mistake to build into the idea of improvement itself the standards that we *at t1 (or at any other time)* use to judge whether something is an improvement. Of course, we use these at t1 to judge whether something is an improvement. We should, however, allow that these standards may themselves be improved. Since we cannot say how they are going to be improved, it is a mistake to fix our understanding of the idea of improvement by reference to our standards at t1.

By thus connecting the idea of improvement and our standards at t1, Rorty distorts the understanding we have of improvement *as practical deliberators*. According to the substantive approach, as practical deliberators, we justify the superiority of p2 by reference to substantive standards while at the same time assuming that these standards themselves may need to be improved. These standards are *ours* in a trivial sense: they are not neutral and they are rejected by those who accept p1. According to the substantive approach, however, the fact that these standards are ours should not be used to explicate the idea of improvement. As practical deliberators, we justify the superiority of p2 by saying that *tolerance* or some other substantive consideration speaks in its favor, not by saying that *our* standards speak in favor of it.

Rorty, in contrast, understands the superiority of p2 to lie in the fact that it is judged to be superior by *our* standards. It is the fact that p2 is judged to be superior by *our* standards which accounts for its superiority, where what counts as our standards is identified by their connection with certain standards we accepted at t1. For the reasons just given, this kind of ethnocentrism must be rejected.[16]

---

[15] Rorty says that he is not offering a meaning-analysis of "better," or necessary and sufficient conditions for something's being better (Rorty 1993, 455). My criticism does not depend on assuming that this is what he is offering. The point of my criticism is not to come up with isolated counter-examples to his analysis, but to show that, in his explication, it is wrong-headed of Rorty to focus only on the process.

[16] In fact, it may be that *no* general explication of the idea of improvement is possible. It may be that such explications are always either circular or false. To say that an improvement is a change for the better is circular. To identify improvement with changes made according to certain standards is probably false, since we thereby exclude by definition the possibility that these standards themselves may need to be improved. In any case, no such general explication is offered by the substantive

3 SUBSTANTIVE TRANS-CULTURAL CRITERIA

Because of its understanding of improvement, the substantive approach has – in contrast to Rorty – no problems accounting for cross-cultural criticism. Rorty explicitly gives up "transcultural criteria of rationality."[17] Karl-Otto Apel argues that by doing so he is thereby giving up the possibility of the critical comparison of traditions.[18] According to the substantive approach, there is a perfectly clear sense in which we appeal to cruelty as a trans-cultural criterion, when we criticize torturers in another culture for cruelty. Cruelty is being used as a *criterion* in the sense that it is that which we appeal to in the justification. And it is a *trans-cultural* criterion in the sense that cruelty should be condemned whether or not it happens to be condemned in this or that culture.[19] As I argued in §1, however, this does not mean that cruelty needs to be a *neutral* criterion.[20] In

approach. However, the objection against Rorty is not that he offers a *general* account of improvement. The objection is rather this: on each occasion, the explanation why something is an improvement must appeal to evaluative standards. Rorty, in contrast, turns the explanation into an appeal to the fact that these standards are *our* standards.

[17] Rorty 1991d, 208; see also 1991b, 26–27.

[18] Apel 1988d, 402–404, 408–409. Rorty's response to Apel is to be found in a paper written in response to Thomas McCarthy (see Rorty 1990).

[19] This use of the word "criterion" certainly does not imply that rationality or morality should be thought of as the application of criteria (see Rorty 1991b, 26), where the phrase "application of criteria" is meant to express something which is undermined by Wittgenstein's remarks on rule-following. Also, to say that something is a trans-cultural criterion in the sense explained in the text is not to say that it is relevant in all contexts. It is just to say that its relevance does not depend on whether it is taken to be relevant in this or that culture. Rorty works with the contrast between choice within language games which may be based on *criteria* and choice between language games or vocabularies which is based on *re-descriptions* in whose light one alternative looks better than another (Rorty 1989, 5–7, 73–78). Even if we were to say that the clash of two cultures is the clash of two language games, it seems to me that if we do not reserve the word "criteria" for neutral criteria and if we do not understand the way in which a re-description shows something to be better according to Rorty's interpretation of "better," Rorty's contrast between criteria and re-descriptions loses its importance, and there is no reason not to say that cross-cultural criticism may be based on trans-culturally valid criteria.

[20] MacIntyre correctly argues (MacIntyre 1977, and 1988, 349–369) that the lack of such neutral criteria to evaluate different traditions does not mean that one tradition cannot count as an improvement upon another one (and he does not fall into the trap of reinterpreting "improvement" in the way that Rorty does). Although I cannot elaborate on MacIntyre's position here, I want to say a word to defend his position, or a cousin of it, against some of Habermas' criticism of MacIntyre. Habermas attributes to MacIntyre the view that there is "no context-transcending rationality" and takes this to be in tension with MacIntyre's view that one tradition can learn from

contrast to the substantive approach, Rorty cannot make sense of this talk of trans-cultural criteria: given his ethnocentric understanding of improvement, it would have to count as improvement if cruelty were to come to be condoned in a culture which had been transformed from "our" culture by a process of rational persuasion.

For Rorty, the rejection of trans-cultural criteria is of a piece with adopting what Rorty takes to be Rawls' approach to political theory: it is of a piece with bracketing such philosophical topics as "an ahistorical human nature, the nature of selfhood, the motive of moral behavior, and the meaning of human life."[21] It should be clear from what I said that such bracketing of philosophical issues is compatible with invoking trans-cultural criteria in the way I explained. It is just that these criteria will not be justified by an appeal to views about these philosophical issues.

This is not to say that the substantive approach rejects appealing to views about these issues as a way of justifying these criteria. Whether it rejects it or not depends on what is meant by the bracketing of these topics. If what is being bracketed are attempts to come up with non-moral accounts of something, say, human nature, which can then serve as criteria for settling moral issues, then the substantive approach does indeed bracket, or better, reject, these attempts as misguided. However, if the theories to be bracketed do not aspire to such neutrality, then their bracketing is not part of the substantive approach. Within moral conceptions, Rawls wants to bracket "comprehensive" conceptions to leave us with a "political" conception.[22] The substantive approach itself neither endorses nor rejects this kind of bracketing. It is a substantive question whether it is a good idea to proceed in this way in political theory. The substantive approach is perfectly compatible with an approach to political issues based on a

another (Habermas 1991f, 209–218). Leaving aside the issue of whether MacIntyre himself believes that there is *no* "context-transcending rationality," I see no reason why MacIntyre's position – or its cousin – should not admit that there is *some* "context-transcending rationality" in the sense that the very assumption that two traditions are *comprehensible* to each other involves the assumption that these traditions share *some* standards of rationality. However, this does not imply that the standards by which one of the traditions is judged to be superior with respect to some issues – say, moral issues – are not special to that tradition but neutral. And these tradition-specific standards may be trans-culturally valid (or have a validity transcending tradition) in the sense explained in my text.

[21] Rorty 1991c, 180. See 1991c, 176–186.
[22] Rawls 1993, 11–15.

theory about the nature of selfhood, if that theory does not aspire to be morally neutral. It is no part of the substantive approach to exclude terms like "human nature," "self," etc. The substantive approach is motivated by the insight that trying to give morality a neutral foundation distorts our view of what matters. It does not follow, however, that moral or political views are not best phrased in terms like "human nature" where such terms are non-neutrally understood.[23]

4 SUMMARY OF PART III

The aim of this part of the book was to show that *even if* there are successful rationalistic justifications of morality, it is a mistake to assume that morality *needs* such a justification. Rationalistic justifications are not an ideal against which we should measure the success of justifications of moral judgments. I argued that this ideal must be rejected because to make it our ideal would be to distort and ignore the substantive reasons which we need to employ to make full sense of our lives. In the case of subjectivist rationalism, the argument was that rationalism must falsely assume that there is no such thing as assessive self-understanding and that rationalism cannot account for the kind of progress which is part and parcel of a meaningful life, where substantive reasons are needed to capture what it is about a change that makes it progress. In the case of inter-subjectivist

---

[23] Rorty often says things such as that the "philosophical superficiality and light-mindedness" of his approach "helps make the world's inhabitants more pragmatic, more tolerant, more liberal, more receptive to the appeal of instrumental rationality" (Rorty 1991c, 193; cf. 1991b, 32–33). However, it seems that the substantive approach incorporates any "light-mindedness" worth having. It urges that we give up the "narrow-minded" focus on neutral criteria which characterizes rationalism. And the substantive approach is surely compatible with, e.g., a tolerant attitude towards criticism and new suggestions. If "light-mindedness," however, is supposed to include Rorty's understanding of improvement, it is unclear that it introduces any "light-mindedness" worth having. (If "light-mindedness" is supposed to amount to ironism where one defining characteristic of an ironist is that "[s]he has radical and continuing doubts about her final vocabulary" [Rorty 1989, 73], "light-mindedness" is not part of the substantive approach itself. Although the substantive approach is not uncritical, it is itself a substantive question whether to have "radical and continuing doubts." This means that, contrary to what Rorty takes to be the case for ironism [Rorty 1989, 87–88], there is no reason to think that the substantive approach should be considered to be a private matter.)

rationalism, I used torture to illustrate how rationalism distorts the reasons for which torture should be condemned.

My arguments rested on the fact that rationalistic justifications must by-pass substantive reasons and appeal solely to a formal concept of reason acceptable to a moral skeptic. Since this is what my arguments were based on, these arguments do not show that morality does not need a *substantive* non-moral justification. This issue will be discussed in chapter 16.

The main topic of this part of the book was the question of how to justify morality and moral standpoints.[24] The substantive approach offers a specific answer to this question. Now the substantive approach assumes a certain theory of practical reason – namely, *substantivism*. According to substantivism, some of the good reasons we have are substantive, not formal reasons (see 2.3 and 3.1). Since the substantive approach assumes substantivism, I must also defend the latter. This shifts the topic from the justification of morality to theories of practical reason. In this part, I have in fact already offered a partial defense of substantivism. I have demonstrated the critical potential of substantive reasons. And I have argued that we have a good reason to employ substantive reasons rather than just subjective reasons. This is, in effect, an argument for substantivism and against subjectivism. Now since subjectivism is only one version of formalism (see 2.3), I must also offer arguments against non-subjectivistic formalism. This I shall do in the next chapter. In the sixteenth and final chapter, then, I shall show what kind of substantivism we should favor.

---

[24] As already noted, however (in 11.4), I have not tried to decide whether we actually have a good reason to be moral.

PART IV

For particularist substantivism

15

Against formalism

What does the rationality and irrationality of actions consist in? What settles the question of whether a person has a good reason to do something? It is the task of theories of practical reason to answer such questions. I take myself to have already shown (in chapter 10) that we should reject one such theory – namely, subjectivism. This means that we should also assume that we sometimes have external reasons to perform certain actions. In this part of the book, I shall take this as an established result. I have also argued (in 11.1–2) that the criteria for determining whether we have a good external reason to do something should be, in part, substantive. I said that *cruelty* and *rudeness* were examples of such substantive criteria. Now it could be argued that such substantive criteria should not be the final criteria for deciding whether someone has a good reason to do something. Rather, this issue should be settled by formal criteria.

Now if these formal criteria were meant to be rationalistic, I take myself to have already offered good arguments against this proposal. It is easy, however, to imagine formal criteria which are not acceptable to a moral skeptic. Thus, it still needs to be discussed whether the question of whether somebody has a good reason to do something should be settled by *non-rationalistic formal* criteria. In this chapter, I want to undermine formalism by arguing that this question should be settled by substantive criteria rather than only by formal criteria (be they rationalistic or not).

I FORMALISM

Before saying more about formalism, I must explain what I take formalism to be a theory of. To do this, I must distinguish between the reasons a person *really* has and the reasons she has *epistemically speaking*. *Given her epistemic situation*, a person may have a good reason to suppose that she has a good subjective or external reason to do something, even though the person does not *really* have a good subjective or external reason to do something. For example, given her epistemic situation, a person may have a good reason to suppose that the glass on the table in front of her contains wholesome orange juice, and therefore to think that she has a good subjective or external reason to drink out of the glass. However, if the glass in fact contains deadly poison, the person presumably really has a good subjective reason and/or external reason not to consume its contents. In that case, *epistemically speaking*, the person has a good reason to drink out of the glass, but *not really*.

The formalisms I shall discuss are theories about the *external* reasons a person *really* has.[1] In other words, they provide an answer to the question "What criteria decide when a person really has an external reason to do something?" This means that they are not supposed to answer the question "What criteria decide when a person has, epistemically speaking, a good reason to do something?" It is important to keep in mind that this is how I understand formalism, because in the literature the terms I use to refer to the different kinds of formalism (for example "coherentism") are surely often used to denote theories which address the second question. My ensuing criticism of formalism is *not* intended as a criticism of theories answering the second question.

According to formalism, only formal criteria can decide whether a person really has an external reason to do something. Substantivism denies this. Thus, a theory does not count as formalistic simply because it defends some formal principles or criteria. What makes a theory formalistic is the claim that formal criteria are the *only* test of external reasons.[2] Accordingly, substantivism allows that there may be some such formal criteria; it just maintains that substantive criteria are also needed.

When I first introduced the contrast between formalism and substantivism (in 2.3), I said that it was not my job as a substantivist to define the contrast between form and content, between formal and substantive considerations. After all, it is the *formalist* who thinks that

---

[1] Since I am assuming that subjectivism has already been refuted, by "formalism" I mean here *non-subjectivistic* formalism.

[2] Thus, simply defending a series of formal principles (like, e.g., Gensler 1996), does not make one a formalist in my sense.

formal criteria are the only test of external reasons. In my view, such considerations as the adventurousness, rudeness, cruelty, boldness, superficiality, or coolness of actions sometimes decide whether a person has an external reason to perform these actions. The formalisms known to me would count these considerations as substantive and would want to show that formal criteria are the only means of deciding whether a person has an external reason to perform such acts. My aim is to show that the test of external reasons sometimes consists in such "substantive" considerations rather than the considerations which the formalisms known to me would count as formal. Let me thus start by mentioning the most important examples of the formalisms I have in mind.

According to *coherentism*, a person really has a better reason to perform one action rather than another one if the first action belongs to a set of aims and actions which is more coherent than the set to which the second action belongs.[3] As stated, this coherentist thesis is somewhat vague. The important point is that the rationality of an action does not depend on its content, but rather on the coherence of the set of actions and aims to which it belongs. Of course, whether an action coheres with other actions depends on its content, but it is the *coherence* of the set which determines how good the reasons for the action are.[4]

Proceduralism holds that an agent has a good reason to perform those actions which would be recommended if a certain rational procedure were followed – *whatever the content* of those actions happens to be. There are many very different kinds of proceduralism, depending on

---

[3] This is not a subjectivistic thesis. If one action is supported by the agent's subjective motivational set whereas another action is supported by another and more coherent set, then coherentism must say that the person has a good reason to choose to perform the latter action.

[4] Since the formalisms I discuss here are meant to answer the question "What criteria decide when a person really has an external reason to do something?" it is not always easy to determine whether a particular author is a formalist in this sense. Some defend a formalistic theory only for moral reasons, rather than practical reasons in general. In other cases, it is hard to determine whether a particular theory is supposed to answer this question or rather the question "What criteria decide when a person has, epistemically speaking, a good reason to do something?" Thus, I hesitate to attribute this coherentism to anyone. Brink 1989 (100–104, 122–143) defends a position he calls "moral coherentism." If this position were generalized so as to apply to external reasons in general and understood as an answer to the first question, I suppose that it would count as a coherentism in my sense. However, this is by no means to say that Brink's actual position is coherentist in my sense.

what the relevant procedure is taken to be. Contractarianism (the agent has a good reason to perform those actions which would be recommended by a rational contract) and discourse theory (the agent has a good reason to perform those actions which would be recommended by a rational discourse) are two examples of proceduralism. There are also individualistic theories such as rational desire theory (the agent has a good reason to perform the actions recommended by the desires she would adopt under certain idealized conditions) which are proceduralistic.[5]

Reflective equilibrium theories (the agent has a good reason to perform those actions which would be recommended by a theory in reflective equilibrium) can also be interpreted formally (see §2). They can then be understood as containing both coherentist and proceduralistic elements. Only coherent theories can be in reflective equilibrium, but in formally interpreted reflective-equilibrium theories, at least two procedural elements are present: the state of reflective equilibrium is conceived as the outcome of a certain process, and the "inputs" to this process are identified with judgments which would be made under certain conditions.

Certain versions of *Kantian ethics* are obviously formalistic. According to such theories, the categorical imperative amounts to a formal test of action maxims. If accepting a certain maxim involves one in a contradiction, then the acceptance of this maxim must be rejected as irrational (and immoral). This test is formal: maxims with different contents are all rejected only because accepting them involves one in a contradiction.[6]

Given how many versions of formalism there are, it would be

[5] As with coherentism, I hesitate to attribute these positions to particular authors. It is not my aim to refute a theory which anyone actually holds. Rather, my aim is to show that, insofar as authors who understand themselves as "proceduralists" (or as some other sort of "formalists") take their theories to provide a test of external reasons, these authors face a dilemma. Either they must understand their theories as proceduralistic (or coherentist, etc.) in my sense, or they must admit that the test of external reasons must sometimes be substantive. In the first case, these theories must be rejected. In the second case, they have accepted the substantivist thesis. Thus, I leave aside whether anybody is actually a contractarian, a rational discourse theorist, or a rational desire theorist in the sense just defined in the text.

[6] If the account of the categorical imperative as a test of maxims offered in O'Neill 1989 were to be understood as a test of *external reasons in general* and as the *only* such test, this would be a formalistic test in my sense. I do not mean to say that O'Neill's position is formalistic in my sense; I just want to indicate what kind of a position I have in mind. Obviously, given R. M. Hare's prescriptivism about morality, his aim is not to

foolish to try to refute all of them in one chapter. I have thus chosen to focus here on only one kind: formal reflective equilibrium theories. Such theories are clearly not, as such, rationalistic, since the "inputs" to the process may not be acceptable to a moral skeptic. As just indicated, they are nevertheless formal (see also §2). Although I shall (in §3) only develop my argument for such theories, I shall also indicate why I think that it applies to proceduralism and coherentism. And I think that the reasons I shall give for substantivism do in fact tell against all versions of formalism as well, but here I cannot demonstrate this general conclusion.

By focusing on reflective equilibrium theory (for short, "RET"), I also hope to contribute to the clarification of such theories and to provide substantivism with an epistemic story. To accomplish this, I shall discuss what role substantive evaluators can give the method of reflective equilibrium. I shall argue that, though they cannot use it as a test in the way that formalists do, substantive evaluators can have reflective equilibrium as an *epistemic goal* (§4).

2 SUBSTANTIVE VS. FORMAL REFLECTIVE EQUILIBRIUM

In introducing the term "reflective equilibrium" in his *A Theory of Justice*, Rawls mentions that Nelson Goodman offers the same kind of justification in another context.[7] According to Goodman, the process of the justification of particular inferences and inference rules consists in amending the rules in the light of particular inferences and vice versa. Using Rawls' terminology, the rules and the particular inferences are in *reflective equilibrium* when no further adjustments are taken to be needed on either side. Goodman holds that *both* the rules *and* the particular inferences are justified when they are in reflective equilibrium.[8] This general form of justification can be applied to other subject-matters. For example, one could say that our moral principles and considered moral judgments have been justified if they can be shown to be in reflective equilibrium.

This kind of equilibrium has been called "*narrow* reflective equilibrium" in order to contrast it with *wide* reflective equilibrium. A wide reflective equilibrium is an equilibrium of three, not two, items:

---

offer a formal test of external moral reasons. Nevertheless, his theory is, broadly speaking, Kantian and formalistic in orientation; see, e.g., Hare 1981, ch.1.
[7] Rawls 1971, 20.   [8] Goodman 1973, 64.

moral principles, considered moral judgments, and the relevant back-ground theories.[9] The relevant background theories are – unlike the other items – not limited to morality. In fact, adding background theories to narrow reflective equilibrium will give us wide reflective equilibrium for any subject-matter: the first two items will be specific to the subject-matter (moral principles, moral judgments; inference rules, particular inferences) and the background theories will not. Here I am interested in a reflective equilibrium achieved by an agent reflecting on how to lead her life: it will consist of practical (moral or not moral) principles, considered practical judgments, and the rele-vant background theories.

In wide reflective equilibrium, none of the three kinds of input out of which it is formed has priority over any of the other ones. For example, the considered judgments do not form a fixed starting point to which the principles and the background theories must adhere. Rather, each of the three can be modified in light of the others. Nevertheless, reflective equilibrium justifications are not to be equated with coherentist justifications. According to coherentism, a necessary and sufficient justification of something is that it form a part of (or be) a coherent system. There is no external justification of the system itself or anything in the system.[10] In contrast, coherence is a necessary but not a sufficient condition for reflective equilibrium justifications. For example, reflective equilibrium justifications are constrained by the considered judgments, and the justification of the considered judgments is not simply a matter of cohering or being in equilibrium with the other elements of the system. The considered judgments are surely modified in light of the other elements in reflective equilibrium, but one element of the equi-librium must always be the – partially independently justified – considered judgments.[11]

[9] I have drawn the distinction between wide and narrow reflective equilibrium in es-sentially the same way as it is drawn in Daniels 1979. Rawls introduces the terms "wide reflective equilibrium" and "narrow reflective equilibrium" in Rawls 1974. I leave aside the issue of whether Daniels and Rawls are using the terms in the same way.

[10] Of course, there are other theories that can meaningfully be called "coherentism," e.g. the theories of Rescher and Susan L. Hurley. See Rescher 1992, ch. 10; 1993, 81–85; 1988, 128–132; Hurley 1989, 11. For the sake of clarity, I reserve the term for the meaning given to it in the text.

[11] In thus distinguishing reflective equilibrium justifications from coherentist justi-fications, I follow Ebertz 1993.

Wide RET can be thought of as holding that an "output" represents a justified conclusion if and only if the "input" (the considered judgments, the principles, the background theories) satisfies certain conditions and the output is the result of a process that brings the three kinds of input into reflective equilibrium. The output can be of many kinds: it can be a principle (perhaps a modified version of an input principle); a considered judgment (perhaps a modified version of an input considered judgment); it can be a considered judgment about what to do in a particular situation, all things considered; it can be a considered judgment of a greater generality, etc. For example, the output of reflective equilibrium may give an answer to any of the following questions. Should I be loyal to my family? Does loyalty to my family require that I do not betray the values of my family? Does loyalty to my family require that I go to weddings in the family? Should I go to this particular wedding even if it conflicts with other important commitments?

I can now distinguish between two versions of RET: formal and substantive. These amount to two different answers to the question of when the output represents a justified conclusion.

What conditions must the input fulfill if the output is to count as justified? Let us take considered judgments as an example of input. *Formal RET* identifies the considered judgments which serve to justify the output with those judgments – whatever their content is – that the agent would reach under certain conditions or in a certain way. In other words, it is only required that the considered judgments have been arrived at by a certain *process*, rather than that they are supported by certain substantive reasons. Thus, it is important that this process be characterized purely formally. For example, it may not be described as a process in which the agent accepts certain substantive reasons. Rather, the considered judgments must be identified with, say, those judgments that the agent would reach if she were to reflect calmly on the matter. Formal RET conceives of all of the inputs which serve to justify the output in this way. The process of aiming for reflective equilibrium takes these inputs as its starting points. It is a process of mutual adjustments. The answer to the question "Should I be loyal to my family?" which is in reflective equilibrium after those mutual adjustments counts as the justified answer – whatever that answer is. This is clearly a *formal* RET: the input is identified as something which is the outcome of a certain process, and the justified output is identified with that which comes out of the process of mutual adjustments (whatever its content is).

Substantive RET differs from formal RET in that, according to the former, the output only counts as justified if the various inputs are supported by certain substantive reasons and the process of mutual adjustments is itself guided by substantive reasons. Substantive RET shares with formal RET the assumption that three kinds of inputs are to be mutually adjusted. However, the two theories differ radically in their account of the justification of the output. In substantive RET, the idea of a *reflection process* does not really play any role. In the justification of the output, such a process does not need to be mentioned. The justification is that all the inputs and the mutual adjustments are supported by substantive reasons. According to formal RET, however, the justification of the output is that it is the result of a process of adjustments – whatever the content of the output happens to be.

3 AGAINST FORMAL REFLECTIVE EQUILIBRIUM

As stated in chapter 12, I shall continue to view matters from the standpoint of the agent engaged in practical deliberation. I have already argued that the practical agent has a good practical reason to assume there are external reasons (10.5). Now the question is what criteria the practical agent should use to decide whether she has an external reason to do something. In this section, I shall argue that she must reject formal RET as a test of external reasons and instead assume that these criteria are sometimes substantive.

It is common to distinguish between different versions of RET, according to *whose* reflective equilibrium is taken to be important. According to the *individualistic* version of RET, it is the reflective equilibrium of a single person which is of relevance. *Social RET* assumes that it is the reflections of a certain group which are in equilibrium.[12] I start by arguing against the individualistic version of formal RET.

Let us assume that the individual whom the individualistic RET has in mind is the agent deliberating what to do. Let us further

[12] Hahn 1996, 410–411; cf. Daniels 1979, 281–282. Depending on what the group is, further versions of RET could be distinguished. I leave such further distinctions aside.

assume that the agent has brought all the inputs into equilibrium and has made a certain output judgment. Since we are concerned here with *formal* RET, the input judgments are *identified* with the judgments which the agent would arrive at under certain formally specified conditions. And the output is identified with the judgment which happens to come out of the mutual adjustment process, whatever its content. Now this must cast doubt on the correctness of the output. The agent cannot assume that the judgments she would make under certain formally specified conditions amount to correct judgments as to what she has an external reason to do. For example, judgments which she makes when she "reflects calmly" on the matter may be quite false.[13] Since this holds for all the inputs, and the mutual adjustment process merely brings the inputs into accordance with each other, the agent must deny that formal RET delivers an appropriate test for deciding what she has an external reason to do.

It could be objected that the output in reflective equilibrium only deviates from the correct judgment if we are talking about a *preliminary* reflective equilibrium. The agent, however, may at any time call this preliminary result into question and aim to reach a new reflective equilibrium. Thus, the correct judgment should not be identified with the output of a reflective equilibrium which the agent *has actually reached*. Instead, it should be identified with the output of a reflective equilibrium which the agent *would finally reach* if she were to revise her preliminary reflective equilibria until she reaches a definite end.

The proposal does not solve the central difficulty of the individualistic formal RET. The problem is not that the agent does not have enough time to reflect and revise her judgments. Rather, the problem lies in the formal characterization of the process leading to reflective equilibrium. The fact that the agent reaches her judgments under formally speaking optimal circumstances (for example she reflects calmly, she is not subject to coercive forces, etc.) does not guarantee that her judgments are correct. This problem remains no matter how often the agent is allowed to revise her judgments until she reaches a "definite end." The defender of formal RET cannot characterize this "definite end" as the point at which the agent reaches correct judgments. Instead, formal RET must understand it as the point at

---

[13] Cf. Richardson 1994, 187–188.

which the agent *would actually* not make any more revisions, even if there are no temporal constraints or other constraints. However, the judgments which the agent would reach at this end-point need not be correct.

It could now be objected that I have been falsely assuming that formal RET takes the output judgment to be identical with the judgment which is really correct. However – so the objection goes – this is only one possible interpretation of formal RET. One does not have to understand RET as saying that being an output judgment of a reflective equilibrium is *constitutive* of the correctness of judgments. Instead, one can interpret it as saying that the fact that something is the output of a reflective equilibrium is good *evidence* for its correctness. The objection is that my argument does not undermine formal RET in this evidential interpretation: I have only shown that the output judgment is not necessarily correct. However, this is compatible with assuming that the fact that something is the output of a reflective equilibrium is good *evidence* for its correctness.[14]

It is not my aim to dispute that formal RET provides good *evidential* criteria of external reasons. To decide whether something amounts to a good evidential criterion, however, we must appeal to a constitutive criterion. For example, to decide whether the celebration of the fans of a football team is good evidence for the team's victory, we need to know what is constitutive of winning a football game. Thus, to decide whether formal RET provides good evidential criteria of external reasons, we would have to appeal to constitutive criteria – criteria telling us what makes something an external reason. And I have been arguing that formal RET cannot offer such criteria.

It cannot give such criteria because there is always a possible discrepancy between the output of a formal reflective equilibrium and the external reasons that a person really has. This holds not only

---

[14] In Daniels 1979, 276–278, Daniels leans towards the evidential reading. Since Rawls says that rational intuitionism can take reflective equilibrium as indicative of how things stand in an independent order of values, it seems that he also favors the evidential reading (Rawls 1993, 95–96). (This does not mean that Rawls himself – as a private person endorsing a comprehensive doctrine – does not favor the constitutive reading. It just means that, in its role as the test for the validity of a political conception – a test that is to be compatible with rational intuitionism – reflective equilibrium should not be interpreted constitutively; see Rawls 1993, 126–129.) The constitutive reading forms the basis of Stich's criticism of RET; Stich 1990, 78.

for the *individualistic* formal RET, but also for the *social* one. The possible discrepancy arises because formal RET understands the inputs as judgments which would be made under certain formally specified circumstances. Even if we are talking about the judgments of a group of people, rather than just the agent's judgments, the problem remains that the judgments which people would make under such circumstances are not necessarily correct. Therefore, the social model fares no better than the individualistic one.

I conclude that formal RET must be rejected, because it cannot explain what about an action gives an agent an external reason to perform it. Substantive criteria, in contrast, can explain it. Substantive criteria sometimes explain precisely what is attractive or unattractive about actions. To show this, let me take an example.

Let us assume that a person has a serious disease which is likely to kill her in the next months. However, this disease is neither painful nor causing any of her mental or physical capacities to diminish. She can be just as sure that she will die painlessly and suddenly as that she will die soon. Her only other option is to undergo a difficult and painful therapy with uncertain results. If successful, she has good chances of living for another ten or twenty years, but perhaps with seriously limited mental and physical capacities. In her thinking about whether to undergo the treatment, substantive considerations are likely to play a crucial role. In favor of the treatment, such considerations as the following may be important. She would prevent her own *premature death*. Not to undergo the treatment would be a *cowardly* way of giving up without a *fight*. And it would be to ignore that life is a *priceless gift* which one may not give up at any price. It would be *irresponsible* and *inconsiderate* to leave those who love her behind by willingly choosing to die. Against the treatment, such considerations might play a role. The treatment is *painful* and *humiliating*. Life after the treatment is likely to be *bland* and *boring* – a life not *worth* living. It would in any case be more *dignified* to die a *natural* and sudden death while still being perfectly fit.

Assuming that the person does indeed have an external reason to undergo treatment, such substantive considerations will explain why she has an external reason to act in this way. Having taken all these considerations into account, she might say that she has a good reason to undergo the treatment because it may prevent a premature death, because she can live and die with more dignity if she faces the hardship of such a treatment with a determination to live, etc. Leaving aside the question of whether it can be completely articulated why some substantive considerations are more important than others, such substantive considerations are clearly the right sort of explanation why the person has a good reason to act in this particular way. It is *these considerations* – not the fact that the agent would accept these considerations under certain formally specified circumstances – which explain what is good about acting in this way.[15]

It must be remembered that at this point the issue is what the criteria of external reasons are. The issue is no longer whether all reasons are subjective. Thus, I can at this point assume that the explanation why the agent has a good reason to do something does not have to be based on something in her subjective motivational set. What I have argued is that, given this assumption, it must sometimes be based on *substantive* criteria.

It should also be noticed that to assume that the person has an external reason to undergo treatment does not amount to assuming that *all* persons in the same situation have an external reason to undergo treatment. Whether somebody has an external reason to do something depends on the circumstances of the case, and her own physical and psychological make-up may be counted as part of the circumstances. Thus, other persons would perhaps have an external reason not to undergo treatment.[16]

In my arguments against formal RET and for substantivism, I have occupied the point of view of the agent engaged in practical deliberation. In claiming that we should reject formal RET as a test of

[15] The examples of substantive considerations I have given in this work are in one sense extremely misleading. I have always talked as if the relevant substantive considerations could be expressed in a word or two; for example, by saying that something is *cruel* or *humiliating*. This is *very* misleading. First, and more trivially, it may be quite a complicated matter to explain the relevant substantive concept. Second, and more importantly, a substantive concept may be bound to a certain form of expression. For example, it may not be possible to express a particular substantive concept expressed in a poem or a novel in standard philosophical prose or in another poem or novel (cf. Nussbaum 1990). Thus, in my view, substantive justifications may often have to make use of other forms of expression than standard philosophical prose. It is often only by using other forms of expression that we can give expression to the subtle substantive differences which are crucial for substantive justifications. This is an important point, because, as already argued (in 11.2), it is precisely one of the main virtues of substantivism that it makes substantive differences in all their multiplicity directly relevant to the reasons we have.

[16] See Smith 1994, 168–171.

external reasons and should sometimes rely on substantive considerations to explain why we have a good reason to do something, I have myself been making a claim about how we should engage in practical deliberation. I have, in effect, claimed that formal RET – just like rationalism – changes the subject in a way in which we should not change it. If we follow formal RET, then the subject-matter is no longer the substantive reasons which I have been suggesting should guide our conduct. Rather, the subject gets shifted to the question of what conclusion we *would accept* – whatever its content – if we were to follow a particular procedure. This change of subject should be rejected because it is often such substantive considerations as that an action would be humiliating or lead to death which tell us why not to perform the action.

It might be argued here that *substantive* RET is no less problematic than formal RET, because both merely aim to systematize our intuitions.[17] I surely agree that an ideal is not acceptable just because it would be justified according to a certain notion of justification embedded in everyday thought and language.[18] However, it does not follow that we should cast away all common-sense notions and try to figure out what is valuable without any appeal to such notions. What I have been arguing here and in the last chapters is that we make the best sense of our lives by relying on substantive reasons. And we should not shy away from the use of substantive notions just because these notions are part of common sense. Nevertheless, we should not consider the common-sense notions acceptable just because they are part of common sense. These notions must be evaluated, even though in the evaluation we may never move completely beyond the space of substantive reasons. It is just as mistaken to think that because something is a common-sense intuition we cannot appeal directly to it as it is to think that because something is a common-sense intuition we must respect it.

I suspect that all theories which aim to stand outside common-sense intuitions – assuming that these theories are also formalistic – are problematic for exactly the same reasons as formal RET. This holds at least for rational desire theories. Such theories propose a formal test which is essentially a richer version of the process Gauthier

---

[17] Brandt 1979, 18–22.   [18] Stich 1990, 89–93.

describes as terminating in considered and coherent preference: the test amounts to asking what people would want or prefer under some conditions that are "idealized" in the sense of granting the agents, for example, full information.[19] Ironically, rational desire theories – which are meant to provide a standpoint from which to evaluate the common-sense notions that are part and parcel of reflective equilibrium – fall prey to the same objections as formal RET: telling us what would be accepted under certain conditions, they still leave us with the task of evaluating whether we should accept it – a task that I have suggested should be carried out by substantive reasons.[20]

I would go even further and claim that not only rational desire theory, but also all other proceduralistic theories as well as coherentism fall prey to the same objection as formal RET. Proceduralism, coherentism, and formal RET all have a common goal and a common method. The goal is to offer a test of external reasons without invoking substantive reasons, and the method is to abstract from the contents of the reasons and declare those reasons to be good that would be the outcome of a certain procedure: the good reasons are those that would be accepted in a contract, in a rational discourse, or by an appropriately situated and fully informed rational deliberator, or those that fit into a coherent system, or those that would be in formal reflective equilibrium. The crucial issue for all of these justifications is formal rather than substantive. Would it be accepted in a rational discourse or contract (*whatever its content*)? Would it be accepted by an appropriately situated and fully informed rational deliberator (*whatever its content*)? Does it form part of a coherent whole (*whatever its content*)? Is it in formal reflective equilibrium (*whatever its content*)? As I already argued for formal RET, theories which abstract from content in this way shift the subject away from the substantive reasons we should rely on. Therefore, they should all be rejected.[21]

---

[19] See Brandt 1979, 10–13, 110–129; a modified version of Brandt's test is part of the formal test defended in Gosepath 1992, 365–377. Again, I am not assuming that these authors themselves intend the test as a test of *external reasons*.

[20] For criticism of rational desire accounts, see Gibbard 1990, 18–22; Anderson 1993, 129–140; Ripstein 1993.

[21] Of course, this does not show that we should reject other versions of formalism, such as Kantian ethics. However, given what I have said about the way in which substantive criteria explain what gives someone an external reason to do something, these formalists would have to argue that this explanation is faulty or incomplete and that their formalism offers a better explanation.

This concludes the argument against formalism. In the final section, I shall argue briefly that substantivism is not *epistemologically* questionable.

4 AN EPISTEMIC GOAL FOR SUBSTANTIVE EVALUATORS

I have said that RET is not simply a version of coherentism. Thus, although all the inputs of a substantive reflective equilibrium – the principles, the considered judgments, the background theories – can be used to correct each other, their justification cannot consist merely in the fact that they cohere with each other. And since we are talking here about *substantive* reflective equilibrium, part of the justification of the different inputs must be the intrinsic appeal of the substantive considerations involved (see 11.1).

Now this can be used to argue that substantive RET – and substantivism more generally – must be *epistemically foundationalistic* in the following sense: it must assume that there are two groups of beliefs. On the one hand, there are beliefs about the intrinsic appeal of substantive considerations which are epistemically privileged and do not derive this privilege from their evidential or inferential connection with other beliefs. On the other hand, there are beliefs which derive their justification from their evidential or inferential connection with the privileged beliefs.[22] If substantivism is foundationalistic in this sense, however, it must be rejected. There is namely no plausible way of epistemically privileging a group of beliefs. All such stories of epistemic privilege must make false assumptions, such as that certain beliefs are infallible, that certain beliefs can be directly confirmed through a special faculty of intuition, etc.

This objection introduces a new topic. So far, I have been arguing that we sometimes need substantive considerations to explain why people *really* have an external reason to do something. This objection does not directly doubt that we need substantive considerations to explain this. Rather, the objection concerns the *epistemic* justification of a person's *belief* to the effect that certain substantive considerations tell her that she has an external reason to do something. According to the objection, substantivism must assume that some such beliefs are epistemically privileged and that the justification of all other such

---

[22] See the characterization of foundationalism in Sayre-McCord 1996, 149.

243

beliefs must be based on the privileged beliefs. In this section, I shall argue that substantivism does not need to assume this. In the course of my argument, I shall suggest what substantive evaluators might take as their epistemic goal. It is not my aim to show that this is the only possible epistemic goal which substantive evaluators could reasonably adopt. I sketch this goal merely to show that substantivism does not need to make any questionable assumptions about epistemic privilege.

I have argued that, in seeking to determine what she has an external reason to do, the agent relies on substantive criteria. Now it is possible that she thereby relies on the wrong criteria – criteria which recommend that she do something she does not really have a good reason to do. Nevertheless, given her epistemic situation, she may be justified in believing that these are the correct criteria. Now the question is what epistemic steps the agent should take to try to make her beliefs correspond better to the correct substantive criteria.

If we grant our objector that the agent's aim should not be to gain some epistemically privileged beliefs on which all her other beliefs can then be based, what should her aim be? Let us assume that the agent has just accepted a new substantive input judgment. Her justi-fication of accepting this judgment is, in part, the intrinsic appeal of the substantive considerations involved. Before she made this judg-ment, all her inputs were in reflective equilibrium, and she did not accept the new input judgment in order to solve any difficulties or tensions in her reflective equilibrium.[23] Now what steps should the agent take to ensure that she is not mistaken in her acceptance of the new input judgment? Substantive RET here has specific recommen-dations to the agent. According to substantive RET, to determine whether her new input judgment is mistaken, the agent has no option but to rely on her other beliefs. *None* of the agent's beliefs is epistemically privileged. *Each* of these beliefs can be used to correct the others. Thus, the agent's only way of testing the new input judgment is to try to bring it into a reflective equilibrium with her other beliefs. This may lead her to reject or modify the new input

---

[23] Since substantive RET allows that agents may accept new input judgments even if they are not based on her old reflective equilibrium in this way, substantive RET favors the *radical* over the *conservative* conception of reflective equilibrium (for the distinction between these two conceptions, see DePaul 1993, 35–43).

judgment or to change her other beliefs.[24] In any case, it is the only epistemic test available to her.[25]

Substantive RET must therefore hold that the substantive evaluator has two kinds of goals: her *"objective"* goal must be to have her actions guided by the *external reasons she really has*. Since she does not have an epistemically privileged access to these reasons, however, she must set herself a second, *epistemic* goal: she must try to bring her beliefs into reflective equilibrium. And since new input may always make her current reflective equilibrium unstable, she must continually be looking for a new equilibrium.

In pursuing these goals, the agent wants her beliefs and actions to be both *really* and *epistemically speaking* based on good reasons. To explain why she *really* has an external reason to do something, she must in part appeal to substantive criteria. To show that her beliefs are justified epistemically speaking, she must show that these beliefs are the output of a reflective equilibrium. This does not mean, however, that the agent must understand epistemic justification here in the way that formal RET does. The agent does not take her judgments to be epistemically justified because she has brought these judgments into reflective equilibrium, but rather because these judgments are supported by substantive criteria in reflective equilibrium.[26] (For a schematic presentation of these ideas, see Fig. 3.)

It would take me too far afield to say more about the epistemic justification of beliefs. I just wanted to show that substantivism does not have to make questionable epistemological assumptions. In the next chapter, I shall address the question of whether substantivism must assume that all substantive justifications must be based on a list of basic substantive reasons. I shall argue that it must not. However, the issue will not be how our *beliefs* concerning the reasons we have

[24] However, it seems that substantive RET should not demand that the agent must strive to reach perfect reflective equilibrium in the sense that all conflict between inputs has been eliminated; it may sometimes be reasonable to live with a conflict between substantive inputs which are "intrinsically appealing" (cf. Richardson 1994, 179–183).

[25] I am not assuming that substantive RET provides the agent with the appropriate epistemic test. I have just used substantive RET to demonstrate that substantivism is not committed to questionable epistemological assumptions. To determine what exactly the agent should take as her epistemic goal, a long discussion would be necessary which would take me too far away from the topic of this study. I thus leave this issue aside.

[26] Sayre-McCord 1996, 158, 170–172.

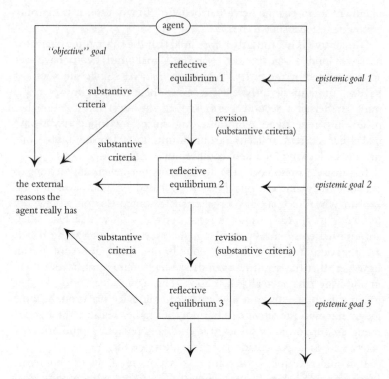

Fig. 3. The "objective" and epistemic goals of the agent according to substantive RET

are to be *epistemologically* justified. Rather, the issue will be this: assuming that we *know* what *really* justifies our actions, what is the structure of the justification we have knowledge of? Must the substantive justification which *really* justifies our actions be based on a list of basic substantive reasons?

16

Particularist substantivism
vs. list-substantivism

We may distinguish between two kinds of substantivism: *particularist substantivism* and *list-substantivism*. In this chapter, I shall explain why I think we should favor particularist substantivism. This also enables me to complete the argument in favor of my thesis that morality does not need a non-moral justification. As I shall argue, the rejection of list-substantivism in favor of particularist substantivism gives us a reason to reject the assumption that morality needs a substantive non-moral justification. It should be emphasized that this chapter is not supposed to give an adequate defense of particularist substantivism. I shall indeed offer some arguments against list-substantivism. However, an adequate defense of particularist substantivism would require that I take up many issues which I have chosen to set aside. This work is already long enough. I have said plenty in defense of substantivism and the substantive approach. This final chapter is merely meant to indicate the direction in which one would have to go in the further development of these views.

I TWO VERSIONS OF SUBSTANTIVISM

Substantivism maintains that actions are sometimes rational or irrational on account of substantive considerations rather than formal ones. According to one version of substantivism, there is a certain specifiable set of ends which it is rational to pursue or irrational to sacrifice. In other words, it is distinctive of this theory – which may be called "*list-substantivism*" – that the content on which the rationality of actions depends can be laid down in a list of possible ends or actions.[1] To be more precise, list-substantivism may be defined as the theory which holds the following two theses:

[1] Of course, list-substantivism must be distinguished from those theories which are sub-

247

List thesis: There esists a list of things which either always count for or
always count against the rationality of an action.

Dependence thesis: The rationality and irrationality of all actions can be
traced back to the things on this list.

To explain better what list-substantivism amounts to, let me consider
Bernard Gert's theory as an example. Gert offers two lists. He offers a
list of things which it would be irrational not to avoid (for the agent
herself or those for whom she is concerned) without an adequate
reason. The things on the list are death, pain, disability, loss of
freedom and loss of pleasure.[2] And he offers a list of the basic reasons
which can make an otherwise irrational action rational. These basic
reasons are conscious beliefs to the effect "that someone will avoid
suffering any of the items on the previous list or that they will gain
greater ability, freedom, or pleasure."[3] Gert distinguishes between
rationally prohibited (irrational), rationally required, and rationally
allowed actions. For him, irrational actions are fundamental and serve
to define the other categories. The rationally required actions are the
actions it would be irrational not to do.[4] The rationally allowed
actions are the actions which are neither rationally required nor
prohibited.[5]

Since the items on Gert's first list always count against the rationality
of an action and the items on the second list always count for the
rationality of an action, he clearly accepts the list thesis. His relation-

---

jectivistic, but which make the additional assumption that all agents have certain basic
desires in common. According to those theories, if a certain action is rational because
it satisfies these basic desires, then the action is rational because it satisfies desires
which the agent has, not because those desires have a certain content.

[2] A complication should be noted. Although Gert thinks that it is always irrational to act
on a desire for one of the items on this list, he thinks that it is only irrational not to
avoid an increase in the risk of suffering the harms on the list if the increase is *significant*
and the harm *non-trivial* (Gert 1998, 52–53).

[3] Gert 1990, 280; see Gert 1998, 56; Gert has now added consciousness to the list of
things whose attainment can make an otherwise irrational action rational (see Gert
1998, 56, 92). It should be noted that, according to Gert, the agent's actions can only
count as irrational if *she herself or those for whom she is concerned* are to suffer the harms
on the first list. However, the basic reasons on the second list concern the harms and
benefits which *someone* might suffer – whether or not that someone is the agent herself
or someone for whom she is concerned (see Gert 1998, 59–61, 71–73). Since this
complication is not relevant for my criticism of list-substantivism, I shall ignore it.
There are also other features of Gert's account which I ignore, such as his account of
what makes a reason adequate (see Gert 1998, 57–58).

[4] Gert 1990, 281.   [5] Gert 1998, 30.

ship to the dependence thesis is a bit more complex. He accepts it for rationally prohibited and rationally required actions without qualification and for rationally allowed actions with a qualification. According to Gert, the irrationality of an action can always be traced back to the fact that the action increases the chances of suffering one of the items on the first list.[6] And the agent can only be rationally required to do something if doing it is a way of avoiding one of the items on the first list. Thus, Gert holds that, to show that an action is irrational or rationally required, we must appeal to the first list.

For rationally allowed actions, there are two cases. If the agent knows that the action increases the chances of suffering one of the items on the first list, then it can only count as rationally allowed if it can be supported by some of the basic reasons on the second list. For this case, Gert accepts the dependence thesis, since he holds that the rationality of the action must be traced back to the second list.[7] However, according to Gert, there is also another case. If the agent's action is not a way of increasing the chances that she, or those for whom she is concerned, suffer the items on the first list, then the action is rationally allowed, even if it is not supported by items on the second list.[8] Since Gert accepts the list thesis and the dependence thesis for all other cases, I nevertheless count him as a list-substantivist.[9]

Particularist substantivism denies the dependence thesis. To explain this further, let me call a consideration *"invariably relevant"* if it always speaks for, always against, or is always neutral with respect to the rationality of an action. In these terms, the dependence thesis amounts to the claim that an action can be shown to be rational or irrational only if it can be justified or criticized on the basis of an invariably relevant consideration. Particularist substantivism holds that, to show that an action is rational or irrational, it is enough to appeal to substantive considerations which are variably relevant.

The difference between particularist substantivism and list-substantivism may be further clarified by an example. Let us assume that a particularist substantivist and a list-substantivist agree that it is nor-

---

[6] Gert 1990, 280; Gert 1998, 39.   [7] Gert 1998, 56.   [8] Gert 1998, 59–60.

[9] List-substantivism is also defended in Rescher 1988 (esp. ch. 6 and ch. 10). If we were to reformulate list-substantivism into a thesis about prudential values, it seems that Griffin 1996 (29–31) would accept it. Understood as a theory about prudential values, list-substantivism would also be one way of fleshing out what Parfit 1984 (493, 499–501) means by an "objective list" theory.

mally irrational to choose one's own painful death, and that in the case that the painful death is part of a religious ritual it may not be irrational. The list-substantivist would have to account for the irrationality with reference to something which has an invariable relevance. For example, she could assume that pain and death have a negative invariable relevance: that they always speak against the rationality of something. If so, the list-substantivist would have to assume that, in the case of the religious ritual, they are *outweighed* or *overridden* by something which also has invariable relevance. The particularist substantivist, in contrast, does not have to assume that there is anything of invariable relevance at stake in either case. For example, she may maintain that pain and death normally have a negative relevance, but that in the context of a religious ritual they do not. It is not that pain and death have a negative relevance in the religious case and are outweighed. In that case, they may speak for the choice of engaging in the religious ritual or be neutral.

This does not mean that the particularist substantivist must assume that there are no criteria which decide whether actions are rational or irrational.[10] There are two points of importance here. First, particularist substantivism does not reject the list thesis. It leaves it as an open possibility that there are indeed some criteria of invariable relevance. Particularist substantivism only rejects the dependence thesis – the thesis that the rationality of actions *must* be traced back to considerations with invariable relevance.[11]

Second, even when there are no invariable criteria involved, this

---

[10] Here I am responding to an objection of Bernard Gert's. In the exposition and criticism of Gert's views given in this chapter, I have greatly benefited from the comments he made to me at the 1997 Eastern Division Meeting of the American Philosophical Association and at a 1998 workshop on Gert's moral philosophy in Essen.

[11] In Gunnarsson 1996, I defend a version of particularism about morality which parallels particularist substantivism about practical reason. This version of particularism allows that a thesis analogous to the list thesis may be true – namely, the thesis that there exists a set of invariably relevant moral principles. And this version of particularism rejects a thesis analogous to the dependence thesis – namely, the thesis that the justification of every moral judgment must appeal to invariably relevant moral principles. As I understand Jonathan Dancy, when he writes "that the moral relevance of a property in a new case cannot be predicted from its relevance elsewhere" (Dancy 1993, 57), he means to be rejecting both of these theses. However, in Dancy, Forthcoming, he explicitly allows that something like the first thesis may be true. For a discussion of the different versions of moral particularism, see Shafer-Landau 1997.

does not mean that criteria play no role or that the decision as to which actions are rational is arbitrary. A particularist substantivist who denies that pain is of invariable relevance can nevertheless maintain that pain is *normally* of negative relevance.[12] She would just have to maintain that pain may change its relevance from one situation to another. But the particularist substantivist could say that this change is in no way arbitrary. She may argue that a painful experience which is part of a religious ritual does not necessarily speak against the rationality of the ritual. If it is part of the *point* of the religious ritual that I inflict pain on myself, then it would be odd to say that the negativity of pain is outweighed by whatever is positive about the ritual. It seems to make more sense to say that pain is not bad in this case. When I go to the dentist, the situation is different. Suffering pain is not a part of the point of going to the dentist. That I suffer pain speaks against going, but it is normally outweighed by the benefits. Thus, the particularist substantivist can say that the person considering whether to go to the dentist would be wrong not to assign pain a negative relevance. And the change in the relevance of pain from one situation to the other is in no way arbitrary. There is an explanation why pain changes its relevance: in one case, pain is part of the point of the activity taken to be rational; in the other case, it is not.[13]

This is how I understand the particularist substantivism I favor. Although it rejects the dependence thesis, it assumes that there must always be an explanation of the change in relevance from one situation to another. In this way, it avoids arbitrariness.[14] And I see no good reason for supposing that this explanation must be based on something which has invariable relevance. Of course, more would

[12] Thus, it would be quite consistent for a particularist substantivist to take reflective equilibrium as her epistemic goal in the manner suggested in 15.4. She would just have to deny that the principles involved in a reflective equilibrium must be of invariable relevance.

[13] Cf. Dancy 1993, ch. 4.

[14] Because this is so, because particularist substantivism does not reject the list-thesis, because a moral particularism corresponding to particularist substantivism can take either side in the "ethics of care" debate (see Gunnarsson 1996, 133), and because substantivism does not make the validity of practical judgments relative to cultural practices (see my criticism of Rorty's account of improvement in 14.2–3), much of what falls under "particularism" in O'Neill 1996 does not apply to my position. It would take me too far afield, however, to discuss whether none of what she says in her elaborate criticism of the range of positions she describes as particularist is a good criticism of my view.

have to be said about such explanations. However, since it is not my goal to offer an adequate defense of particularist substantivism, I let this suffice as a characterization of the particularist substantivism I favor.

2 THE IRREDUCIBLE PLURALITY OF SUBSTANTIVE REASONS

I think that the dependence thesis should be rejected for the following reason: there are indeed substantive considerations with variable relevance and the variability of their relevance cannot be explained in terms of something with invariable relevance. Since the rationality of actions sometimes depends on such substantive considerations, rather than on considerations with invariable relevance, the dependence thesis must be rejected. In this section, I shall argue that there are substantive considerations for which this holds. I start by arguing that the rationality and irrationality of actions cannot always be traced back to the things on Gert's lists.

I take it that the *beauty* and *magnificence* of a waterfall normally provide good reasons against ruining the waterfall for commercial purposes. Now we may imagine that a person may risk all the things on Gert's first list (risk dying, suffering pain, etc.) to prevent the destruction of the beautiful site. And she may do this without believing that anybody would ever benefit in any of the ways specified on Gert's second list (avoid pain, loss of pleasure, etc.) if she were to die and save the waterfall. The waterfall may be in a secluded area where no one can enjoy its beauty or no one may care about its beauty. Thus, nothing on Gert's second list speaks in favor of her sacrificing herself for the waterfall. Nevertheless, the person thinks that, because of the waterfall's beauty and magnificence, it makes sense for her to risk all the things on Gert's first list to try to save it. Would it be irrational of her to do so?

To answer this question, we would have to decide what is rational for her to do, *all things considered*. To do so, we would have to know more about the case. Thus, I do not want to try to determine what is rational for the person to do, all things considered. It is clear, however, that the beauty and the magnificence of a waterfall normally provide reasons against its destruction *and* that these reasons cannot be traced back to anything on Gert's second list. Even if it may not be rational for the person to make the sacrifice if nothing else but the beauty and the magnificence speak for it, these two substantive considerations make a contribution to the rationality of the sacrifice which cannot be traced back to anything on the second list. These two considerations may tip the balance in favor of the sacrifice, assuming that enough other things speak in favor of it. Thus, I conclude that Gert has not offered a complete list of the things which can make an (otherwise irrational) action rational.

If this were the only counter-example against Gert's list-substantivism, it might be tempting to think that we merely need to revise the theory a bit. However, it seems to me that there is a plurality of substantive considerations which can make actions rational or irrational *and* cannot be traced back to his lists. I mention some here, though I will not try to show for all of them that Gert's theory cannot accommodate them. The following adjectives refer to such substantive considerations: funny, boring, ugly, erotic, scary, perverted, vulgar, demeaning, cheerful, melancholic, saddening, truthful, honest, joyful, spontaneous, barbaric, eccentric, creative, daring, shocking, provocative, passive, aggressive, superficial, banal, bland, square, ironic, etc.

Let me take a closer look at two of these substantive considerations. It may be a good reason for wearing a mask that one looks *funny* with the mask.[15] The reason-giving force of this substantive consideration can surely not be traced back to anything on Gert's second list. It suffices to mention that the reason-giving force does not depend on the fact that the agent gets pleasure from wearing the mask or gives others pleasure by wearing it. Perhaps the agent or others get pleasure from it, perhaps they do not. In any case, the humor of the situation is an independent consideration in favor of wearing the mask.[16]

[15] The subjectivist would object here that the agent would not have a reason to do something funny unless doing so is supported by something in her subjective motivational set. Since I have already offered a general argument against subjectivism, I take it as established that an agent may have a good reason to do something on substantive grounds, even though doing so is not supported by anything in her subjective motivational set. Of course, this does not show that the *humor* of an action can ever give us an external reason to do something. Here I have two replies. First, I do not see why the humor of an action should never give an agent an external reason to do something. Second, even if humor never gives us such a reason, surely some of the other indefinitely many substantive considerations which cannot be traced back to anything on Gert's lists can give us such a reason.

[16] It could be objected here that *finding something funny* is a way of getting pleasure, just as finding something comfortable is a way of getting pleasure, and that it is the pleasure which one gets which gives one a reason to do what one finds funny. In order to

For particularist substantivism

It could contribute to making an action irrational that this action would be *banal*, that it would be a confirmation of the banality of the agent's existence. In some cases, we would surely say that it would be *irrational* of the agent to choose an action *because it is banal and for no other reason*.[17] What makes this action irrational cannot be traced back to anything on Gert's first list. Clearly the agent may here be choosing an action which does not risk death, disability, loss of freedom, or loss of pleasure. (Banal actions may indeed be quite pleasurable.) It is equally implausible to explain the irrationality of the choice by saying that choosing a banal action on account of its banality amounts to choosing to suffer some kind of pain. The banality of an action has nothing to do with any sensations the agent is having, let alone with sensations which she experiences as painful. I conclude that it is not anything on Gert's first list which makes the choice irrational, but rather the *banality* of the action.

What I have said here for the substantive considerations *funny* and *banal* could be repeated for a plurality of other substantive considerations. Thus, it seems fair to conclude that there are multiple cases in which the rationality or irrationality of actions cannot be traced back to anything on Gert's lists, even if slightly revised.

answer this objection adequately, I would have to discuss the concept of pleasure in some detail. Let me briefly consider three possibilities. (1) Pleasure is a separate sensation with a special phenomenal quality which one gets from finding something funny. If so, the pleasure is surely not the reason for doing what is funny. (2) To feel pleasure is not to have a special kind of sensation, but rather to have some sensation which one wants to go on. Why though does the fact that the agent wants the sensation to go on give her a reason for having it continue? One possibility would be to give a subjectivistic answer. Since Gert and I both reject subjectivism, this is not an option I need to discuss. Another possibility would be to say that one has some non-subjectivistic reason for wanting it to continue. If, however, pleasure is to account for the reasons we have, then this reason must rest on the fact that we are getting pleasure. In that case, we are back either to the subjectivistic interpretation, to (1), or to some other account of pleasure. Thus, let me turn to a third account. (3) Pleasure is not a separate feeling, but rather consists of its components (finding something funny, finding something comfortable, etc.). In this case, it would not be an objection to my argument to say that the pleasure is the reason. The pleasure would simply be a reason in the sense in which the whole is a reason if one of its components is a reason. (By this component model of pleasure, I have in mind something like Mill's account of happiness; see Mill 1863, ch. 4.)

[17] Of course, particularist substantivism does not deny that some failures of rationality are formal, it merely denies that all of them are. On this and other points, particularist substantivism is in agreement with the position defended in Kambartel 1989. However, it would take me too far afield to discuss at what points particularist substantivism may differ from Kambartel's complex view.

Now it should be noticed that the substantive considerations *funny* and *banal* have a *variable* relevance. The fact that something is funny is normally a reason for doing it; at funerals, however, it is usually a reason against doing it. It is irrational to choose something because it is banal and for no other reason. Sometimes, though, we have a good reason to choose something because it is banal. For example, the banality of activities may be a good reason for engaging in them because their banality enables us to relax after a stressful week.

I have argued that when actions are rational or irrational because they are funny or banal, their rationality or irrationality cannot be traced back to anything on *Gert's* lists. Now I have argued that these substantive considerations have a variable relevance. This brings me one step closer to showing that the dependence thesis should be rejected. If I can show that there are *no other* lists of things with invariable relevance to which the rationality or irrationality of funny and banal actions can be traced, then I will have shown that the dependence thesis is false. I will have shown that the rationality of actions sometimes depends only on things with variable relevance.

Gert says that his lists are lists of harms and benefits.[18] It might be suggested that though he offers an incomplete or a wrong list of harms and benefits, he is right in insisting that rationality and irrationality must always be traced back to harms and benefits. An action is rational because it is beneficial and irrational because it is harmful. Thus, the explanation why banal actions are sometimes rational and sometimes irrational is that in the first class of cases they are beneficial and in the second class of cases harmful. This means that the rationality and irrationality of actions is always based on something with invariable relevance: either on the beneficial or on the harmful.

The suggestion here is that we should not say that the list of things with invariable relevance is a list of harms and benefits (such as death, pain, etc.), but rather a list of two things: the harmful and the beneficial. This proposal can now be used to show what the problem is with all versions of list-substantivism – whatever the relevant list is. The defender of this proposal faces a dilemma. She must say what she means by "the beneficial" (and "the harmful"). She can either maintain that to say that something is beneficial *just is to say* that it is

18 Gert 1990, 286.

255

rational; or she can maintain that "the beneficial" and "the rational" do not mean the same, but that to say that something is beneficial *explains* why something is rational. Both horns of the dilemma lead to difficulties.

First horn. If "the beneficial" and "the rational" mean the same, then there is no reason to doubt that the two things on the list – the beneficial and the harmful – are invariably relevant. However, the list will have lost its point as part of a substantive theory of rationality. If to say that something is beneficial just is to say that it is rational, we will no longer be able to refer to the list to give a substantive answer to the question of why something is rational.

Second horn. If "the beneficial" and "the rational" do not mean the same, then a different problem arises. I do not want to dispute that "the beneficial" will in this case be of invariable relevance. After all, my aim here is to reject the dependence thesis, not the list thesis. Let me thus assume that the beneficial is of invariable relevance. The question is what the relationship of the beneficial is to all the indefinite number of variably relevant substantive considerations there are. When we employ a variably relevant substantive consideration to account for the rationality of an action, must we always also say that the action is rational because it is beneficial? I think not. If it is, for example, the humor and creativity of an action which make it attractive, then it seems simply wrong to account for its rationality by saying that it is beneficial. To say that an action is funny or creative is quite different from saying it is beneficial, and sometimes an action's rationality seems to consist in the former aspects, rather than the latter.[19]

[19] It could be objected here that the list-substantivist can allow that variably relevant considerations may *partially* account for the rationality of the action, but that invariably relevant considerations are needed to explain why a variably relevant consideration is positively relevant in one situation and negatively or neutrally relevant in another. In the discussion of pain at the end of §1, I suggested that the substantivist can offer explanations of the change in relevance without resorting to invariably relevant considerations. However, as I said, a longer discussion would be needed to settle the matter. Among other things, in this discussion the following list-substantivist proposal would have to be dealt with: to decide what relevance a variably relevant consideration has in a particular case, we need to know more about the case. For example, if we know more about the context in which a banal action is embedded, we can decide whether *banality* is positively or negatively relevant in this case. Now the list-substantivist proposal is that by adding these specifications of the context to *banality*, we arrive at considerations with invariable relevance. Thus, though *banality* may not always speak for an action, *banality which serves the purpose of*

I think that all versions of list-substantivism will face the same dilemma. As I have suggested, there is an indefinite number of substantive considerations with variable relevance which we use to account for the rationality and irrationality of actions. It is highly implausible that for all of these considerations there will always be a substantive consideration with *invariable* relevance which also accounts for the action's rationality. When we account for their rationality with the help of such variable substantive criteria, it is precisely *these criteria* which are supposed to account for the rationality of the action.[20] By insisting that there must always be invariable criteria involved, we shall in many cases plainly be giving the wrong account of the action's rationality. Therefore, the dependence thesis must be rejected.

3 A SUBSTANTIVE NON-MORAL JUSTIFICATION OF MORALITY?

Having argued that we should reject list-substantivism in favor of particularist substantivism, I am now in a position to return to the main question of this work: does morality *need* a non-moral justification? I already showed in Part III that it does not need a *formal* non-moral justification. The question remains whether it needs a *substantive* non-moral justification. Such a justification would show that, to be substantively and non-morally rational, one must accept certain moral judgments.[21]

relaxation may. Presumably, a more complex addition to the variable considerations is needed to arrive at invariance. However, it seems that we will eventually arrive at invariance. Would those invariable considerations then not be the complete account of what makes an action rational? As I said, I shall not try to refute this proposal here. In this sense, my defense of particularist substantivism remains incomplete. However, it should be noticed that this proposal stands for a version of list-substantivism which is very different from Gert's theory. Gert provides a short list of easily specifiable items. If we follow the current list-substantivist proposal, the list will not only be indefinitely long, but the specification of each item is also likely to be very complex. In fact, the potential problem which this list-substantivist proposal faces is that the specification of the considerations which are supposedly invariably relevant will be so specific that these considerations will apply to only one situation (see Dancy 1993, 81; Shafer-Landau 1997, 593–595).

20 It does not as such help the list-substantivist to propose that the list of things with invariable relevance is not fixed, but rather essentially incomplete. The problem is that the substantive considerations with variable relevance are *different* from the considerations with invariable relevance, and that sometimes only one of the variable ones captures what is rational or irrational about an action.

21 It should be noted that Gert does not offer such a justification of morality. Although

Someone who accepts list-substantivism, assumes that all the items on the relevant list are non-moral, and wants to show that we are rationally required to be moral, would have to believe that morality needs a substantive non-moral justification. What this list-substantivist assumes, in effect, is that no action can count as rationally required unless it can be justified on the basis of a list of non-moral goods. This means that morality cannot count as rationally required unless it can be justified in this way. In other words, without a substantive non-moral justification, morality cannot count as rationally required.

Now if, as I have recommended, we reject list-substantivism, then this reason for supposing that morality needs a substantive non-moral justification evaporates. It would simply not be true that morality can only count as rationally required if it can be justified on the basis of a list of goods (whether moral or non-moral). This reason for thinking that morality needs a substantive non-moral justification rests on a list-substantivist assumption about practical *rationality*. It is important to remember that this reason disappears with the rejection of list-substantivism. However, there may be other reasons for supposing that morality needs a substantive non-moral justification. One might suppose this not because of any assumptions about *rationality*, but rather because of an assumption about *morality*. One might suppose that there is something especially problematic or characteristic about morality which requires that it be given a non-moral justification based on considerations with invariable relevance.

It should be remembered that the issue here is not whether there *is* any such successful justification of morality. The question is whether morality *needs* such a justification. In Part III, I argued that morality does not need a *formal* non-moral justification by considering *specific* justifications of this kind.[22] To argue that morality does not need a *substantive* non-moral justification, I would need to do the same for such justifications. This I cannot do here. However, I suspect that morality indeed does not need a substantive non-moral justification, and I want to indicate why.

he offers a substantive justification of moral rules, he does not start with a non-moral concept of reason and try to show that a moral skeptic who aspires to be rational in this sense *must* also accept some moral rules (see Gert 1998, 72–73, 76–83, 167–170, 343–344, 348–349, 355–360).

22 Thus, I could only *suggest* that this holds for formal non-moral justifications other than the specific ones I actually considered.

In discussing the question of whether morality needs a non-moral justification, in this work I have been assuming that the question is whether such a justification is needed to resolve the problem of the rationality of morality.[23] Thus, the assumption that morality needs such a justification means that without it, it could not be settled whether it is rational to accept one moral view rather than another, or whether it is rational to be moral at all.

Now recall my argument against the dependence thesis in the last section. I argued that the correct account of the rationality of some actions appeals only to *variably* relevant substantive considerations. If some of these actions are moral actions, then we would give a wrong account of the rationality of these moral actions by insisting that they must be justified on the basis of non-moral *invariably* relevant considerations. This is the danger inherent in the assumption that morality needs a substantive non-moral justification based on invariably relevant considerations. The danger is that this assumption – just like the assumption that morality needs an up-justification – distorts our view of the reasons for action which we have (see 13.1). To show that this assumption does in fact distort our view of the reasons we have, I would have to consider particular examples of such justifications. My suspicion is, however, that this assumption leads to such a distortion no matter what the particular substantive non-moral justification based on invariably relevant considerations happens to be.[24]

Here it might be suggested that what morality needs is a substantive non-moral justification based, in part, on *variably* relevant considerations. I think that this suggestion is not an option for the defenders of the need for a substantive non-moral justification. To see why this is so, let us imagine that the variably relevant consideration at stake is the fact that an action *brings the agent pleasure*. Performing a moral action, for example a *fair* action, would then be justified by the fact that doing so brings the agent pleasure. Assuming that morality needs a substantive non-moral justification then involves assuming that the fact that the relevant action brings the agent pleasure is what makes

---

[23] As I argued in 11.5, the problem of the rationality of morality is more fundamental than the problem of its categorical force.

[24] It might be argued that morality needs a justification based on invariably relevant principles because *moral justification* must be based on invariably *morally* relevant principles. I think that moral justification does not have to be based on such principles (see Gunnarsson 1996), but this is not something I can argue here.

the action rational and that being fair is rational only because it brings the agent pleasure.

Now, given the variable relevance of the agent's pleasure, why should we assume that only the *agent's pleasure* rather than the action's *fairness* can make it rational? I see no rationale for assuming this. And I think that the defenders of the need for a substantive non-moral justification can offer no rationale for assuming it.[25] They are searching for a secure foundation of morality. They think that, for any moral action, one can always doubt whether one should perform it. They suppose that only when we reach a non-moral basis is there no longer room for such doubt. However, if the non-moral turns out to be something of variable relevance, there surely seems to be room for doubt: if the agent's pleasure does not always speak for the rationality of an action, why does it speak for it in the case at hand? Even if there is an answer to this question, it is no longer clear why there should be a difference between the agent's pleasure and fairness with respect to the rationality of actions. There is no longer any rationale for letting the non-moral consideration set the criteria of rationality and for giving the moral consideration a derivative status.

I conclude that it is not an option for the defenders of the need for a substantive non-moral justification to maintain that morality needs a basis which is, in part, variably relevant. And I have already argued that my argument against list-substantivism shows that it is a mistake to assume that morality needs a substantive non-moral justification based on invariable considerations. I have thus finally reached the goal of this work. I have shown that *it is a mistake to think that morality needs a non-moral justification*.

This work began with the worry that in behaving morally we are being stupid. One way of understanding the book is that it has argued against a false motivation of this worry. This motivation consists in the assumption that morality needs to be based on something more rationally basic than morality; otherwise morality will be entirely without rational support. This assumption I have undermined. However, the worry itself has not disappeared. A critical substantive

---

[25] I myself would also not think that there would be any rationale for assuming this if the agent's pleasure were *invariably* relevant. However, the defenders of the need for a substantive non-moral justification of morality would think that there would be such a rationale if pleasure were invariably relevant.

review of a moral standpoint should draw on all the substantive resources available. Some of these resources may be moral, others non-moral. There is no guarantee that the substantive review will come down in favor of this moral standpoint rather than some other standpoint, moral or immoral.

If I am right, the assumption that morality needs a non-moral justification distorts our perspective on the substantive reasons we have. This holds no less for the substantive reasons which may speak for morality than for the reasons which may speak against it. The aim of this book was to free ourselves from this assumption and thus to clear the way for an unprejudiced investigation into the substantive reasons we have. I have argued that we may in this investigation rely on substantive moral reasons. The result of this investigation, however, cannot be predicted in advance. It is still possible that we moral mortals are indeed fools.

Appendix

Transcendental vs. universal pragmatics

Habermas, Apel, and Kuhlmann all try to show that the skeptic's willingness to engage in rational argumentation unavoidably commits her to assume implicitly the validity of a certain moral principle.[1] Thus, for all of the three philosophers, the *structure* of the argument is the same: it is in all cases a rationalistic argument. However, Habermas understands his argument as a universal pragmatic argument (or a weak transcendental pragmatic argument), whereas Apel and Kuhlmann understand their respective arguments as (strong) transcendental pragmatic arguments amounting to an ultimate justification (*Letztbegründung*).

It might be argued that because of this difference, Apel and Kuhlmann would have been more appropriate targets of my criticism in this book. I disagree. The aim of the book was to criticize the rationalistic assumption which they share. For this purpose, the difference between universal and transcendental pragmatic arguments is simply irrelevant. In addition, there is an important sense in which my own argumentative strategy in this book has more in common with transcendental pragmatic arguments than universal pragmatic arguments. The aim of this appendix is to explain the sense in which this is so. This will also allow me to explain how my approach and Habermas' represent two very different ways of allowing morality to be contingent in a way that Kuhlmann and Apel do not allow.

Kuhlmann argues that Habermas' theory is "empiricist" in a way which makes it impossible for Habermas to account for the unconditionality of morality. Although every human being who engages in

---

[1] Habermas 1988d, 102–104, 109 [92–94, 99]; Apel 1988d, 352–354; Kuhlmann 1992c, 200–201; see also my 8.4. For issues concerning the skeptic who rejects engaging in argumentation and/or communicative action, see Habermas 1988d, 109–112 [99–102]; 1991f, 185–189 [76–79]; Apel 1988d, 345–357; 1989, 57–59 [156–157].

argumentation must, in fact, make certain presuppositions which amount to the acceptance of a certain moral principle, according to Habermas it is a *contingent empirical fact* about humans that they must engage in argumentation with these presuppositions. Thus, this moral principle is not an unconditional demand of reason; rather, its validity depends on a contingent empirical fact which could one day no longer hold.[2]

In my view, Habermas' theory is indeed "empiricist" in an important sense. He thinks that there is only one form of rational argumentation; but he thinks that there could have been another form of rational argumentation with different presuppositions. It is not that the existence of other forms of rational argumentation is excluded because no sense can be made of the supposition that there is another practice which would also count as rational argumentation. Rather, it is a contingent empirical fact that there is no other form of rational argumentation. In my view, this position turns the issue of which presuppositions we must accept into an empirical matter: the final answer to the question of why we must accept certain presuppositions is not that these are presupposed by a practice which is constitutive of rationality; rather, the final answer is that they are implicit in a form of rational argumentation to which there happens to exist no alternative.[3]

Habermas wants to avoid a certain kind of moral relativism. According to this relativistic view, the ultimate answer to the question "Why should we accept this moral principle?" is "The acceptance of it is implicit – whether we realize it or not – in our actual practices." In other words, a moral principle is valid only for those who (implicitly) accept it in their practice or form of life. This means that even though this principle may tell us to make moral demands even on those who do not accept the principle, it cannot be *valid* for them. Thus, the validity of the principle is contingent (on [implicit] acceptance) and relative (perhaps to culture).

---

[2] Kuhlmann 1992c, 187–189; 1993, 218–219; cf. Apel 1989, 44–52 [147–153].

[3] See Habermas 1991f, 194–195 [83–84]. It is a delicate matter to formulate precisely what Habermas' empiricism amounts to. This I have formulated in more detail in Gunnarsson 1995b, 275–280. Of course, I do not mean to suggest that Habermas turns every kind of justification into an empirical justification. For example, it is certainly not his view of the justification of substantive moral norms in practical discourse. I think that there are strong indications, however, that this must be his view of justification "at the fundamental level," e.g., at the level where U is to be justified.

Habermas' position may be viewed as an attempt to keep the contingency of U while insisting on its universality:[4] its validity is contingent in the sense that it is only valid for those who must implicitly presuppose it, but its validity is universal in the sense that everyone must presuppose it. This is a response to moral relativism which shares with relativism the empiricist assumption that the final answer to the question "Why should we accept this principle?" is that this principle is implicit in a practice which happens to be ours: according to Habermas, rational argumentation is the practice in which U is presupposed. As a matter of empirical fact, there exists no other form of rational argumentation and everyone – or almost everyone – is willing to engage in rational argumentation. Thus, this principle must be presupposed by everyone.[5]

Now we can see why the ambition to defend universalism against cultural relativism leads Habermas to rationalism. If validity is contingent in the sense that it ultimately rests upon implicit acceptance, then it is not promising for a moral universalist to look to moral practices. These are not universally shared. Everyone, however, is willing to engage in rational argumentation. Thus, up-rationalism – the attempt to uncover the moral presupposition of rational argumentation – becomes the natural way of arguing for moral universalism.

Rationalism is one way of avoiding moral relativism. There is another way, however. One can simply reject the empiricist assumption on which it is based. And if one does that, then rationalism is not needed to avoid immediately implying relativism. One may instead defend a non-empiricist, non-rationalistic position. This is precisely the position that I have defended. According to this view, the answer to the question "Why should we accept this moral principle?" is *neither* that this principle is implicit in a practice which happens to be ours, *nor* that the principle can be founded on a non-moral notion of reason.

My view concurs with Apel's and Kuhlmann's approach in rejecting Habermas' empiricist assumption. Instead of arguing that the moral skeptic rejects a principle which she must, *due to the factual*

---

[4] Cf. McCarthy's contention that Rorty falsely opposes contingency to universality rather than to necessity (McCarthy 1991, 36).
[5] This also makes it clear why cases of people who refuse to argue (or communicate) might seem to threaten universal validity; cf. Habermas 1988d, 109–112 [99–102].

lack of an alternative, accept, I agree with Apel and Kuhlmann that the way to argue against moral skepticism is to urge that we cannot make rational sense of it. However, there are important differences between my approach and theirs. Since they think that the validity of a certain moral principle can be demonstrated by uncovering the presuppositions of rational argumentation, their argument is a rationalistic transcendental pragmatic argument. Since I assume that it is possible to respect the rules of rational argumentation without having to presuppose any particular moral principle, and thus that the moral skeptic cannot be refuted on her own ground, the kind of argument that I recommend is neither rationalistic nor a transcendental pragmatic argument.[6] I admit that there is a sense in which the moral skeptic is indeed rational, and I must therefore spell out what it could mean to say that we nevertheless cannot make rational sense of moral skepticism. This is what I have done in 12.2.

My rejection of rationalism has the implication that I, like Habermas, cannot suppose that morality is unconditional in the way that Apel and Kuhlmann assume. However, I interpret the contingency of morality very differently from Habermas. If he is indeed an empiricist in the way I have explained, then he must assume that not only moral principles, but all rational principles, are in a sense empirically contingent. And it seems to me that this is a misguided position both for moral principles and for other principles. On my account, morality is *contingent* in the sense that the moral skeptic is indeed rational in the sense required by rational argumentation. In other words, it is *not necessary* to accept moral principles as being rational in this way. Thus, in my view, morality is not an unconditional demand of reason in the sense that it is demanded by this formal sort of rationality. As I argued in 11.5, however, this does not exclude that it is an unconditional demand of reason.

---

[6] I also think that they wrongly suppose that philosophical analysis of the presupposition of argumentation must in a sense be *infallible*; see Apel 1987, 174–184; 1989, 19–21n [163–164 (endnote 9)]; Kuhlmann 1985, 138–140; 1993, 214–216. I argue for this in Gunnarsson 1995b, 277–279.

Bibliography

Abel, Günter 1993, *Interpretationswelten. Gegenwartsphilosophie jenseits von Essentialismus und Relativismus*. Frankfurt-am-Main: Suhrkamp.

1999, *Sprache, Zeichen, Interpretation*. Frankfurt-am-Main: Suhrkamp.

Alexy, Robert 1978, "Eine Theorie des praktischen Diskurses," in Willi Oelmüller (ed.), *Materialen zur Normendiskussion*, Vol. II, pp. 22–58. Paderborn: Schöningh.

Altham, J. E. J., and Ross Harrison (eds.) 1995, *World, Mind, and Ethics: Essays on the Ethical Philosophy of Bernard Williams*. Cambridge University Press.

Anderson, Elizabeth 1993, *Value in Ethics and Economics*. Cambridge, Mass.: Harvard University Press.

Anscombe, G. E. M. 1957, *Intention*. Ithaca and New York: Cornell University Press.

Apel, Karl-Otto 1973, "Das Apriori der Kommunikationsgemeinschaft und die Grundlagen der Ethik. Zum Problem einer rationalen Begründung der Ethik im Zeitalter der Wissenschaft," in Apel, *Transformation der Philosophie*, Vol. II, pp. 358–435. Frankfurt-am-Main: Suhrkamp. English: "The *a priori* of the Communication Community and the Foundations of Ethics: The Problem of a Rational Foundation of Ethics in the Scientific Age," in Apel, *Towards a Transformation of Philosophy*, pp. 225–300. Trans. Glyn Adey and David Frisby. London: Routledge and Kegan Paul, 1980.

1975, "The Problem of Philosophical Fundamental-Grounding in Light of a Transcendental Pragmatic of Language," *Man and World* 8: 239–275. Trans. Karl Richard Pavlovic.

1987, "Fallibilismus, Konsenstheorie der Wahrheit und Letztbegründung," in Forum für Philosophie (ed.), *Philosophie und Begründung*, pp. 116–211. Frankfurt-am-Main: Suhrkamp.

1988a, *Diskurs und Verantwortung. Das Problem des Übergangs zur postkonventionellen Moral*. Frankfurt-am-Main: Suhrkamp.

1988b, "Verantwortung heute – nur noch Prinzip der Bewahrung und Selbstbeschränkung oder immer noch der Befreiung und Verwirklichung von Humanität," in Apel 1988a, pp. 179–216.

1988c, "Die transzendentalpragmatische Begründung der Kommunikationsethik und das Problem der höchsten Stufe einer Entwicklungslogik des moralischen Bewußtseins," in Apel 1988a, pp. 306–369.

1988d, "Zurück zur Normalität? – Oder könnten wir aus der nationalen Katastrophe etwas Besonderes gelernt haben? Das Problem des (welt-) geschichtlichen Übergangs zur post-konventionellen Moral in spezifisch deutscher Sicht," in Apel 1988a, pp. 370–474.

1989, "Normative Begründung der 'Kritischen Theorie' durch Rekurs auf lebensweltliche Sittlichkeit? Ein transzendental-pragmatisch orientierter Versuch, mit Habermas gegen Habermas zu denken," in Axel Honneth *et al.* (eds.), *Zwischenbetrachtungen im Prozeß der Aufklärung. Jürgen Habermas zum 60. Geburtstag*, 2nd. edn., pp. 15–65. Frankfurt-am-Main: Suhrkamp. English: "Normatively Grounding 'Critical Theory' through Recourse to the Lifeworld? A Transcendental-Pragmatic Attempt to Think with Habermas against Habermas," in Axel Honneth *et al.* (eds.), *Philosophical Interventions in the Unfinished Project of Enlightenment*, pp. 125–170. Trans. William Rehg. Cambridge, Mass.: MIT Press, 1992.

1990, "Ist Intentionalität fundamentaler als sprachliche Bedeutung? Transzendentalpragmatische Argumente gegen die Rückkehr zum semantischen Intentionalismus der Bewußtseinsphilosophie," in Forum für Philosophie (ed.), *Intentionalität und Verstehen*, pp. 13–54. Frankfurt-am-Main: Suhrkamp. English: "Is Intentionality more Basic than Linguistic Meaning?" in Ernest Lepore and Robert Van Gulick (eds.), *John Searle and his Critics*, pp. 31–55. Oxford: Basil Blackwell, 1991.

Baier, Annette C. 1994a, *Moral Prejudices: Essays on Ethics*. Cambridge, Mass.: Harvard University Press.

1994b, "Claims, Rights, Responsibilities," in Baier 1994a, pp. 224–246.

1994c, "Moralism and Cruelty: Reflections on Hume and Kant," in Baier 1994a, pp. 268–293.

Benhabib, Seyla 1986, *Critique, Norm, and Utopia: A Study of the Foundations of Critical Theory*. New York: Columbia University Press.

1989, "Liberal Dialogue Versus a Critical Theory of Discursive Legitimation," in Nancy L. Rosenblum (ed.), *Liberalism and the Moral Life*, pp. 143–156. Cambridge, Mass.: Harvard University Press.

1990, "In the Shadow of Aristotle and Hegel: Communicative Ethics and Current Controversies in Practical Philosophy," in Kelly 1990, pp. 1–31.

Blackburn, Simon 1981, "Reply: Rule-Following and Moral Realism," in Steven H. Holtzmann and Christopher M. Leich (eds.), *Wittgenstein: To Follow a Rule*, pp. 163–187. London: Routledge and Kegan Paul.

1984, *Spreading the Word: Groundings in the Philosophy of Language*. Oxford: Clarendon Press.

1993, "How to Be an Ethical Anti-Realist," in Blackburn, *Essays in Quasi-Realism*, pp. 166–181. Oxford University Press.

1998, *Ruling Passions: A Theory of Practical Reasoning*. Oxford: Clarendon Press.

Brandom, Robert 1982, "Points of View and Practical Reasoning," *Canadian Journal of Philosophy* 12: 321–333.

1988, "Inference, Expression, and Induction," *Philosophical Studies* 54: 257–285.

1994, *Making It Explicit: Reasoning, Representing, and Discursive Commitment*. Cambridge, Mass.: Harvard University Press.

Brandt, Richard B. 1979, *A Theory of the Good and the Right*. Oxford: Clarendon Press.

Brink, David O. 1989, *Moral Realism and the Foundations of Ethics*. Cambridge University Press.

Buchanan, James M. 1975, *The Limits of Liberty: Between Anarchy and Leviathan*. University of Chicago Press.

1988, "The Gauthier Enterprise," *Social Philosophy and Policy* 5: 75–94.

Dancy, Jonathan 1993, *Moral Reasons*. Oxford: Blackwell.

Forthcoming, "The Particularist's Progress," in B. W. Hooker and M. Little (eds.), *Moral Particularism*. Oxford University Press.

Daniels, Norman 1979, "Wide Reflective Equilibrium and Theory Acceptance in Ethics," *Journal of Philosophy* 76: 256–282.

Danielson, Peter 1988, "The Visible Hand of Morality," *Canadian Journal of Philosophy* 18: 357–384.

1992, *Artificial Morality: Virtuous Robots for Virtual Games*. London and New York: Routledge.

Davidson, Donald 1980, *Essays on Actions and Events*. Oxford: Clarendon Press.

Davis, Felmon John 1994, "Discourse Ethics and Ethical Realism: A Realist Realignment of Discourse Ethics," *European Journal of Philosophy* 2: 125–142.

Debruin, Debra A. 1988, "Justifying Morality to Fooles." Dissertation, University of Pittsburgh.

DePaul, Michael R. 1993, *Balance and Refinement: Beyond Coherence Methods of Moral Inquiry*. London and New York: Routledge.

Dummett, Michael 1981, *Frege: Philosophy of Language*, 2nd. edn. Cambridge, Mass.: Harvard University Press.

Ebertz, Roger P. 1993, "Is Reflective Equilibrium a Coherentist Model?" *Canadian Journal of Philosophy* 23: 193–214.

Fishkin, James S. 1988, "Bargaining, Justice, and Justification: Towards a Reconstruction," *Social Philosophy and Policy* 5: 46–64.

Foot, Philippa 1978a, *Virtues and Vices and Other Essays in Moral Philosophy*. Berkeley and Los Angeles: University of California Press.

1978b, "Moral Arguments," in Foot 1978a, pp. 96–109.

1978c, "Are Moral Considerations Overriding?" in Foot 1978a, pp. 181–188.

Frankfurt, Harry G. 1988, "Freedom of the Will and the Concept of a Person," in Frankfurt, *The Importance of What We Care About: Philosophical Essays*, pp. 11–25. Cambridge University Press.

Frey, R. G., and Christopher W. Morris (eds.) 1993, *Value, Welfare, and Morality*. Cambridge University Press.

Gauthier, David 1986, *Morals by Agreement*. Oxford University Press.

1988a, "Morality, Rational Choice, and Semantic Representation: A Reply to My Critics," *Social Philosophy and Policy* 5: 173–221.

1988b, "Moral Artifice," *Canadian Journal of Philosophy* 18: 385–418.

1991a, "Why Contractarianism?" in Vallentyne 1991a, pp. 15–30.

1991b, "Rational Constraints: Some Last Words," in Vallentyne 1991a, pp. 323–330.

1993a, "Value, Reasons, and the Sense of Justice," in Frey and Morris 1993, pp. 180–208.

1993b, "Uniting Separate Persons," in Gauthier and Sugden 1993, pp. 176–192.

1994, "Assure and Threaten," *Ethics* 104: 690–721.

1996, "Individual Reason," in J. B. Schneewind (ed.), *Reason, Ethics, and Society: Themes from Kurt Baier, with his Responses*. Chicago and La Salle: Open Court.

Gauthier, David, and Robert Sugden (eds.) 1993, *Rationality, Justice and the Social Contract: Themes from Morals by Agreement*. Ann Arbor: The University of Michigan Press.

Gensler, Harry J. 1996, *Formal Ethics*. London and New York: Routledge.

269

Bibliography

Gert, Bernard 1990, "Rationality, Human Nature, and Lists," *Ethics* 100: 279–300.

1998, *Morality: Its Nature and Justification*. Oxford University Press.

Gewirth, Alan 1977, *Reason and Morality*. University of Chicago Press.

Gibbard, Allan 1990, *Wise Choices, Apt Feelings: A Theory of Normative Judgment*. Cambridge, Mass.: Harvard University Press.

Goodman, Nelson 1973, *Fact, Fiction, and Forecast*, 3rd. edn. Indianapolis: Bobbs-Merrill.

Gosepath, Stefan 1992, *Aufgeklärtes Eigeninteresse. Eine Theorie theoretischer und praktischer Rationalität*. Frankfurt-am-Main: Suhrkamp.

Griffin, James 1996, *Value Judgement: Improving our Ethical Beliefs*. Oxford: Clarendon Press.

Gunnarsson, Logi 1994, "Diskurs ohne Konsens," *Deutsche Zeitschrift für Philosophie* 42: 313–326.

1995a, "A Discourse about Discourse," in Mikael M. Karlsson and Ólafur Páll Jónsson (eds.), *Law, Justice and the State IV* (= *Archiv für Rechts- und Sozialphilosophie*, Beiheft 61), pp. 66–83. Stuttgart: Franz Steiner.

1995b, "Making Moral Sense: Substantive Critique as an Alternative to Rationalism in Ethics." Dissertation, University of Pittsburgh.

1996, "Universalgültigkeit und kontextuelle Relevanz," in G. Abel and H. J. Sandkühler (eds.), *Pluralismus – Erkenntnistheorie, Ethik und Politik* (= *Dialektik* 1996/3), pp. 119–133. Hamburg: Felix Meiner.

1997a, "Að skilja lífið og ljá því merkingu," *Skírnir* 171: 111–141.

1997b, "Dimensions of Morality," *Philosophy and Social Criticism* 23: 125–130.

Habermas, Jürgen 1973, *Legitimationsprobleme im Spätkapitalismus*. Frankfurt-am-Main: Suhrkamp. English: *Legitimation Crisis*. Trans. Thomas McCarthy. Boston: Beacon Press, 1975.

1984a, *Vorstudien und Ergänzungen zur Theorie des kommunikativen Handelns*. Frankfurt-am-Main: Suhrkamp.

1984b, "Wahrheitstheorien," in Habermas 1984a, pp. 127–183.

1984c, "Was heißt Universalpragmatik?" in Habermas 1984a, pp. 353–440. English: "What Is Universal Pragmatics?" in Habermas, *Communication and the Evolution of Society*, pp. 1–68. Trans. Thomas McCarthy. Boston: Beacon Press, 1979.

1984d, "Replik auf Einwände," in Habermas 1984a, pp. 475–570. English: "A Reply to my Critics," in J. Thompson and D. Held (eds.), *Habermas: Critical Debates*, pp. 219–283. Trans. Thomas McCarthy. Cambridge, Mass.: MIT Press, 1982.

1984e, "Erläuterungen zum Begriff des kommunikativen Handelns," in Habermas 1984a, pp. 571–606.

1987a, *Theorie des kommunikativen Handelns*, Vol. I, 4th. edn. Frankfurt-am-Main: Suhrkamp. English: *The Theory of Communicative Action*, Vol. I. Trans. Thomas McCarthy. Boston: Beacon Press, 1984.

1987b, *Theorie des kommunikativen Handelns*, Vol. II, 4th. edn. Frankfurt-am-Main: Suhrkamp. English: *The Theory of Communicative Action*, Vol. II. Trans. Thomas McCarthy. Boston: Beacon Press, 1987.

1988a, *Moralbewußtsein und kommunikatives Handeln*, 3rd. edn. Frankfurt-am-Main: Suhrkamp.

1988b, "Die Philosophie als Platzhalter und Interpret," in Habermas 1988a, pp. 9–28. English: "Philosophy as Stand-In and Interpreter," in Habermas 1990, pp. 1–20.

1988c, "Rekonstruktive vs. verstehende Sozialwissenschaften," in Habermas 1988a, pp. 29–52. English: "Reconstruction and Interpretation in the Social Sciences," in Habermas 1990, pp. 21–42.

1988d, "Diskursethik – Notizen zu einem Begründungsprogramm," in Habermas 1988a, pp. 53–125. English: "Discourse Ethics: Notes on a Program of Philosophical Justification," in Habermas 1990, pp. 43–115.

1988e, "Moralbewußtsein und kommunikatives Handeln," in Habermas 1988a, pp. 127–206. English: "Moral Consciousness and Communicative Action," in Habermas 1990, pp. 116–194.

1988f, "Handlungen, Sprechakte, sprachlich vermittelte Interaktion und Lebenswelt," in Habermas *Nachmetaphysisches Denken. Philosophische Aufsätze*, pp. 63–104. Frankfurt-am-Main: Suhrkamp.

1990, *Moral Consciousness and Communicative Action*. Trans. Christian Lenhardt and Shierry Weber Nicholsen. Cambridge, Mass.: MIT Press.

1991a, *Erläuterungen zur Diskursethik*. Frankfurt-am-Main: Suhrkamp.

1991b, "Treffen Hegels Einwände gegen Kant auch auf die Diskursethik zu?" in Habermas 1991a, pp. 9–30. English: "Morality and Ethical Life: Does Hegel's Critique of Kant Apply to Discourse Ethics," in Habermas 1990, pp. 195–215.

1991c, "Was macht eine Lebensform rational?" in Habermas 1991a, pp. 31–48.

1991d, "Gerechtigkeit und Solidarität. Eine Stellungnahme zur Diskussion über 'Stufe 6,'" in Habermas 1991a, pp. 49–76. English: "Justice and Solidarity: On the Discussion Concerning Stage 6," in

Thomas E. Wren (ed.), *The Moral Domain: Essays in the Ongoing Discussion between Philosophy and the Social Sciences*, pp. 224–251. Trans. Shierry Weber Nicholsen. Cambridge, Mass.: MIT Press, 1990.

1991e, "Vom pragmatischen, ethischen und moralischen Gebrauch der praktischen Vernunft," in Habermas 1991a, pp. 100–118. English: "On the Pragmatic, the Ethical, and the Moral Employments of Practical Reason," in Habermas 1993, pp. 1–17.

1991f, "Erläuterungen zur Diskursethik," in Habermas 1991a, pp. 119–226. English: "Remarks on Discourse Ethics," in Habermas 1993, pp. 19–111.

1993, *Justification and Application: Remarks on Discourse Ethics*. Trans. Ciaran Cronin. Cambridge, Mass.: MIT Press.

1994, *Faktizität und Geltung. Beiträge zur Diskurstheorie des Rechts und des demokratischen Rechtsstaats*. 4th. edn. Frankfurt-am-Main: Suhrkamp. English: *Between Facts and Norms: Contributions to a Discourse Theory of Law and Democracy*. Trans. William Rehg. Cambridge, Mass.: MIT Press, 1996.

1995, "Reconciliation through the Public Use of Reason: Remarks on John Rawls's Political Liberalism," *Journal of Philosophy* 92: 109–131.

1996, "Eine genealogische Betrachtung zum kognitiven Gehalt der Moral," in Habermas, *Die Einbeziehung des Anderen: Studien zur politischen Theorie*, pp. 11–64. Frankfurt-am-Main: Suhrkamp.

1998, "Richtigkeit vs. Wahrheit: Zum Sinn der Sollgeltung moralischer Urteile und Normen," *Deutsche Zeitschrift für Philosophie* 46: 179–208.

Hahn, Susanne 1996, "Überlegungsgleichgewicht und rationale Kohärenz," in K.-O. Apel and M. Kettner (eds.), *Die eine Vernunft und die vielen Rationalitäten*, pp. 404–423. Frankfurt-am-Main: Suhrkamp.

Hampton, Jean E. 1998, *The Authority of Reason*. Cambridge University Press.

Hare, R. M. 1981, *Moral Thinking: Its Levels, Method, and Point*. Oxford: Clarendon Press.

Harman, Gilbert 1988, "Rationality in Agreement: A Commentary on Gauthier's *Morals by Agreement*," *Social Philosophy and Policy* 5: 1–16.

Harsanyi, John C. 1982, "Morality and the Theory of Rational Behaviour," in Sen and Williams 1982, pp. 39–62.

Heath, Joseph 1995, "The Problem of Foundationalism in Habermas's Discourse Ethics," *Philosophy and Social Criticism* 21: 77–100.

Helm, Bennett W. 1996, "Integration and Fragmentation of the Self," *Southern Journal of Philosophy* 34: 43–63.

Bibliography

Hintikka, Jaakko 1962, "*Cogito, Ergo Sum*: Inference or Performance?" *Philosophical Review* 71: 3–32.

Hurley, Susan L. 1989, *Natural Reasons: Personality and Polity*. Oxford University Press.

Kambartel, Friedrich 1989, "Vernunft: Kriterium oder Kultur? Zur Definierbarkeit des Vernünftigen," in Kambartel, *Philosophie der humanen Welt: Abhandlungen*, pp. 27–43. Frankfurt-am-Main: Suhrkamp.

Karlsson, Mikael K. Forthcoming, "Hume, Reid and Rational Ends."

Kelly, Michael (ed.) 1990, *Hermeneutics and Critical Theory in Ethics and Politics*. Cambridge, Mass.: MIT Press.

Kettner, Matthias 1992, "Bereichsspezifische Relevanz. Zur konkreten Allgemeinheit der Diskursethik," in Karl-Otto Apel and Matthias Kettner (eds.), *Zur Anwendung der Diskursethik in Politik, Recht und Wissenschaft*, pp. 317–348. Frankfurt-am-Main: Suhrkamp.

1999, "The Disappearance of Discourse Ethics in Habermas' *Faktizität und Geltung*," in R. v. Schomberg (ed.), *Reading Habermas' Recent Philosophy of Justice*. Albany: State University of New York Press.

Korsgaard, Christine M. 1986, "Scepticism about Practical Reason," *Journal of Philosophy* 83: 5–25.

1997, "The Normativity of Instrumental Reason," in G. Cullity and B. Gaut (eds.), *Ethics and Practical Reason*, pp. 215–254. Oxford: Clarendon Press.

Korsgaard, Christine M., with G. A. Cohen *et al.* 1996, *The Sources of Normativity*. Cambridge University Press.

Kuhlmann, Wolfgang 1985, *Reflexive Letztbegründung. Untersuchungen zur Transzendentalpragmatik*. Freiburg/Munich: Karl Alber.

1992a, *Sprachphilosophie – Hermeneutik – Ethik. Studien zur Transzendentalpragmatik*. Würzburg: Königshausen and Neumann.

1992b, "Ethik und Rationalität," in Kuhlmann 1992a, pp. 150–163.

1992c, "Ethikbegründung – empirisch oder transzendentalphilosophisch?" in Kuhlmann 1992a, pp. 176–207.

1993, "Bemerkungen zum Problem der Letztbegründung," in Andreas Dorschel *et al.* (eds.), *Transzendentalpragmatik. Ein Symposium für Karl-Otto Apel*, pp. 212–237. Frankfurt-am-Main: Suhrkamp.

Leist, Anton 1989, "Diesseits der 'Transzendentalpragmatik': Gibt es sprachpragmatische Argumente für Moral?" *Zeitschrift für philosophische Forschung* 43: 301–317.

Lewis, David 1989, "Dispositional Theories of Value," *Proceedings of Aristotelian Society*, suppl. vol. 63: 113–137.

273

Lovibond, Sabina 1983, *Realism and Imagination in Ethics*. Minneapolis: University of Minnesota Press.

Löw-Beer, Martin 1991, "Living a Life and the Problem of Existential Impossibility," *Inquiry* 34: 217–236.

MacIntyre, Alastair 1977, "Epistemological Crises, Dramatic Narrative and the Philosophy of Science," *Monist* 60: 453–472.

1988, *Whose Justice? Which Rationality?* University of Notre Dame Press.

Mackie, J. L. 1977, *Ethics: Inventing Right and Wrong*. Harmondsworth: Penguin.

McCarthy, Thomas 1991, *Ideals and Illusions: On Reconstruction and Deconstruction in Contemporary Critical Theory*. Cambridge, Mass.: MIT Press.

McDowell, John 1978, "Are Moral Requirements Hypothetical Imperatives?" *Proceedings of the Aristotelian Society*, suppl. vol. 52: 13–29.

1979, "Virtue and Reason," *Monist* 62: 331–350.

1983, "Aesthetic Value, Objectivity, and the Fabric of the World," in Eva Schaper (ed.), *Pleasure, Preference, and Value: Studies in Philosophical Aesthetics*, pp. 1–16. Cambridge University Press.

1985, "Values and Secondary Qualities," in Ted Honderich (ed.), *Morality and Objectivity*, pp. 110–129. London: Routledge and Kegan Paul.

1986, "Critical Notice: *Ethics and the Limits of Philosophy*. By Bernard Williams," *Mind* 95: 377–386.

1995a, "Might there Be External Reasons?" in Altham and Harrison 1995, pp. 68–85.

1995b, "Two Sorts of Naturalism," in Rosalind Hursthouse *et al.* (eds.), *Virtues and Reasons: Philippa Foot and Moral Theory*, pp. 149–179. Oxford: Clarendon Press.

1996, *Mind and World: With a New Introduction*. Cambridge, Mass.: Harvard University Press.

1998, "Projection and Truth in Ethics," in McDowell, *Mind, Value, and Reality*, pp. 151–166. Cambridge, Mass.: Harvard University Press.

Mill, John Stuart 1863, *Utilitarianism*. London: Parker, Son, and Bourn.

Morris, Christopher 1988, "The Relation Between Self-Interest and Justice in Contractarian Ethics," *Social Philosophy and Policy* 5: 119–153.

Musil, Robert 1978, *Der Mann ohne Eigenschaften*. Ed. Adolf Frisé. Hamburg: Rowohlt.

Niquet, Marcel 1991, *Transzendentale Argumente. Kant, Strawson und die Aporetik der Detranszendentalisierung*. Frankfurt-am-Main: Suhrkamp.

Nozick, Robert 1974, *Anarchy, State, and Utopia*. New York: Basic Books.
  1981, *Philosophical Explanations*. Cambridge, Mass.: The Belknap Press of Harvard University Press.
Nussbaum, Martha C. 1990, *Love's Knowledge: Essays on Philosophy and Literature*. Oxford University Press.
O'Neill, Onora 1989, "Consistency in Action," in O'Neill, *Constructions of Reason: Explorations of Kant's Practical Philosophy*, pp. 81–104. Cambridge University Press.
  1996, *Towards Justice and Virtue: A Constructive Account of Practical Reasoning*. Cambridge University Press.
Ott, Konrad 1996, "Wie begründet man ein Diskursprinzip der Moral? Ein neuer Versuch zu 'U' und 'D,'" in Ott, *Vom Begründen zum Handeln*, pp. 12–50. Tübingen: Attempto Verlag.
Parfit, Derek 1984, *Reasons and Persons*. Oxford University Press.
  1997, "Reasons and Motivation," *Proceedings of the Aristotelian Society*, suppl. vol. 71: 99–130.
Prichard, H. A. 1912, "Does Moral Philosophy Rest on a Mistake?" *Mind* 21: 21–37.
Putnam, Hilary 1990, *Realism with a Human Face*. Ed. James Conant. Cambridge, Mass.: Harvard University Press.
  1992, "Truth, Activation Vectors and Possession Conditions for Concepts," *Philosophy and Phenomenological Research* 52: 431–447.
Quinn, Warren 1993, "Putting Rationality in Its Place," in Quinn, *Morality and Action*, pp. 228–255. Cambridge University Press.
Rawls, John 1971, *A Theory of Justice*. Cambridge, Mass.: Harvard University Press.
  1974, "The Independence of Moral Theory," *Proceedings and Addresses of the American Philosophical Association* 48: 5–22.
  1993, *Political Liberalism*. New York: Columbia University Press.
  1995, "Reply to Habermas," *Journal of Philosophy* 92: 132–180.
Rehg, William 1991, "Discourse and the Moral Point of View: Deriving a Dialogical Principle of Universalization," *Inquiry* 34: 27–48.
  1994, *Insight and Solidarity: The Discourse Ethics of Jürgen Habermas*. Berkeley: University of California Press.
Rescher, Nicholas 1977, *Methodological Pragmatism: A Systems-Theoretic Approach to the Theory of Knowledge*. New York University Press.
  1988, *Rationality: A Philosophical Inquiry into the Nature and the Rationale of Reason*. Oxford: Clarendon Press.
  1992, *A System of Pragmatic Idealism*, Vol. I. Princeton University Press.

1993, *A System of Pragmatic Idealism*, Vol II. Princeton University Press.

Richardson, Henry S. 1994, *Practical Reasoning About Final Ends*. Cambridge University Press.

Ripstein, Arthur 1993, "Preference," in Frey and Morris 1993, pp. 93–111.

Rorty, Richard 1982, *Consequences of Pragmatism*. Minneapolis: University of Minnesota Press.

1989, *Contingency, Irony, and Solidarity*. Cambridge University Press.

1990, "Truth and Freedom: A Reply to Thomas McCarthy," *Critical Inquiry* 16: 633–643.

1991a, *Objectivity, Relativism, and Truth: Philosophical Papers*, Vol. I. Cambridge University Press.

1991b, "Solidarity or Objectivity?" in Rorty 1991a, pp. 21–34.

1991c, "The Priority of Democracy to Philosophy," in Rorty 1991a, pp. 175–196.

1991d, "On Ethnocentrism: A Reply to Clifford Geertz," in Rorty 1991a, pp. 203–210.

1993, "Putnam and the Relativist Menace," *Journal of Philosophy* 90: 443–461.

Sayre-McCord, Geoffrey 1996, "Coherentist Epistemology and Moral Theory," in W. Sinnott-Armstrong and M. Timmons (eds.), *Moral Knowledge? New Readings in Moral Epistemology*, pp. 137–189. Oxford University Press.

Scanlon, T. M. 1982, "Contractualism and Utilitarianism," in Sen and Williams 1982, pp. 103–128.

1998, *What We Owe to Each Other*. Cambridge, Mass.: The Belknap Press of Harvard University Press.

Sen, Amartya, and Bernard Williams (eds.) 1982, *Utilitarianism and Beyond*. Cambridge University Press.

Shafer-Landau, Russ 1997, "Moral Rules," *Ethics* 107: 584–611.

Shklar, Judith N. 1984, *Ordinary Vices*. Cambridge, Mass.: The Belknap Press of Harvard University Press.

Smith, Michael 1994, *The Moral Problem*. Oxford: Blackwell.

Stich, Stephen 1990, *The Fragmentation of Reason: Preface to a Pragmatic Theory of Cognitive Evaluation*. Cambridge, Mass.: MIT Press.

Stout, Jeffrey 1988, *Ethics after Babel: The Languages of Morals and Their Discontents*. Boston: Beacon Press.

Sumner, L. W. 1987, "Justice Contracted," *Dialogue* (Canada) 26: 523–548.

Taylor, Charles 1979, "The Validity of Transcendental Arguments," *Proceedings of the Aristotelian Society*, 1978–1979: 151–165.

1985a, *Human Agency and Language: Philosophical Papers*, Vol. I. Cambridge University Press.

1985b, "What is Human Agency?" in Taylor 1985a, pp. 15–44.

1985c, "Self-Interpreting Animals," in Taylor 1985a, pp. 45–76.

1989, *Sources of the Self: The Making of the Modern Identity*. Cambridge, Mass.: Harvard University Press.

1991, "Comments and Replies," *Inquiry* 34: 237–254.

1993, "Explanation and Practical Reason," in Martha C. Nussbaum and Amartya Sen (eds.), *The Quality of Life*, pp. 208–231. Oxford: Clarendon Press.

Thomas, Laurence 1988, "Rationality and Affectivity: The Metaphysics of the Moral Self," *Social Philosophy and Policy* 5: 154–172.

Tietz, Udo 1993, "Faktizität, Geltung und Demokratie. Bemerkungen zu Habermas' Diskurstheorie der Wahrheit und der Normenbegründung," *Deutsche Zeitschrift für Philosophie* 41: 333–342.

Vallentyne, Peter (ed.) 1991a, *Contractarianism and Rational Choice*. Cambridge University Press.

1991b, "Contractarianism and the Assumption of Mutual Unconcern," in Vallentyne 1991a, pp. 71–75.

Velleman, J. David 1989, *Practical Reflection*. Princeton University Press.

Wallace, R. Jay Forthcoming, "Moral Responsibility and the Practical Point of View," in T. van den Beld (ed.), *Moral Responsibility and Ontology*. Dordrecht: Kluwer Academic Publishers.

Ms., "Principled Agency."

Walzer, Michael 1990, "A Critique of Philosophical Conversation," in Kelly 1990, pp. 182–196.

Watson, Gary 1975, "Free Agency," *Journal of Philosophy* 72: 205–220.

Weale, Albert 1993, "Justice, Social Union and the Separateness of Persons," in Gauthier and Sugden 1993, pp. 75–94.

Wiggins, David 1991a, *Needs, Values, Truth: Essays in the Philosophy of Value*, 2nd. edn. Oxford: Basil Blackwell.

1991b, "Truth, Invention, and the Meaning of Life," in Wiggins 1991a, pp. 87–137.

1991c, "A Sensible Subjectivism?" in Wiggins 1991a, pp. 185–214.

Williams, Bernard 1978, *Descartes: The Project of Pure Inquiry*. Harmondsworth: Penguin.

1981, "Internal and External Reasons," in Williams, *Moral Luck:*

Philosophical Papers 1973–1980, pp. 101–113. Cambridge University Press.

1985, *Ethics and the Limits of Philosophy*. Cambridge, Mass.: Harvard University Press.

1995a, "Replies," in Altham and Harrison 1995, pp. 185–224.

1995b, "Internal Reasons and the Obscurity of Blame," in Williams, *Making Sense of Humanity and Other Philosophical Papers 1982–1993*, pp. 35–45. Cambridge University Press.

Wingert, Lutz 1993, *Gemeinsinn und Moral: Grundzüge einer intersubjektivistischen Moralkonzeption*. Frankfurt-am-Main: Suhrkamp.

Wittgenstein, Ludwig 1984, *Bemerkungen über die Grundlagen der Mathematik*. Ed. G. E. M. Anscombe, Rush Rhees, G. H. von Wright. Frankfurt-am-Main: Suhrkamp. English: *Remarks on the Foundations of Mathematics*, revised edn. Trans. G. E. M. Anscombe. Oxford: Basil Blackwell, 1978.

Index

Index

Index

frameworks, 173–176

Gauthier, David, 7, 215n
  on agency, 77–79, 80, 82–83
  and the categorical force of morality, 11
  and the moral skeptic, 12–14, 19–20
  as a rationalist, 9–10, 12–13, 19–20, 55,
    58–60
  and the rationality of morality, 10–12,
    17–20, 54–55, 58–63
  and Rawls, 7, 58–59
  on reflective equilibrium, 7
  as a subjectivist, 10, 55–57, 134,
    138–141
  see also basic choice problem: and
    Gauthier; contractarianism:
    Gauthier's; current situation; false self-
    assessment: Gauthier's test for;
    Gauthier's non-moral justification;
    initial situation; moral alternatives
    problem: Gauthier's solution to;
    rationality: Gauthier's conception of;
    renegotiations argument: Gauthier's;
    utility maximizer: Gauthier's; value
Gauthier's non-moral justification, 9–12,
  58–70, 73, 77
  criticism of, 71–85, 138–141, 158–163
Gert, Bernard, 248–249, 248n, 250n,
  252–255, 257n
Gewirth, Alan, 8n
goals, epistemic, 244–246
Goodman, Nelson, 233

Habermas, Jürgen, 7, 201n
  and Apel, 14n, 16n, 17n, 101n, 262–265
  as an empiricist, 262–263
  on hypothetical reconstructions,
    106–107
  and Kuhlmann, 14n, 16n, 17n, 101n,
    262–265
  and the moral skeptic, 16–20, 99–104,
    100n, 106–107, 110
  as a rationalist, 17–20, 99–108
  and the rationality of morality, 16–17,
    98–99, 102–104
  and Rawls, 7, 91, 95–97
  on reflective equilibrium, 7, 105
  on up-justification, 14n, 262–265
  on the validity of legal norms, 88, 90
  on the validity of moral norms, 88, 90,
    93–94
  see also categorical force of morality:

according to Habermas; coherentism:
and Habermas; contingency of
morality; discourse: Habermas'
understanding of; discourse: rational/
ideal; discourse ethics; ethnocentricity,
the problem of; fallibility; Habermas'
democracy principle; Habermas'
principle of universalization;
impartiality: according to Habermas;
justification: transcendental-pragmatic;
justification: universal-pragmatic;
moral alternatives problem: Habermas'
solution to; rationalism: indirect
discourse-ethical; rationalism: weak vs.
strong; reason, communicative;
relativism, moral: and Habermas;
substantive approach: and Habermas;
validity, universal
Habermas' democracy principle, 95n
Habermas' moral principle, see Habermas'
  principle of universalization
Habermas' principle of universalization,
  102
  criticism of derivation of, 110–125
  derivation of, 97–106, 109–112,
    120–123
  first formulation of derivation of,
    109–110
  interpretation of, 89–90
  premises of derivation of, 101–106,
    114–119, 121
  Rehg's formulation of derivation of,
    123–125
  second formulation of derivation of,
    120–123
  statement of, 88–89, 109
Hare, R. M., 232n
harm, 255–256
humanity, 181–182, 189–190

identification, see identity
identity, 180
  and exploitation, 81
  Outsider's concept of, 176–177
  and self-assessment, 133–138
  Taylor's concept of, 174–176, 175n,
    183–184, 186–187
impartiality, 113–114
  according to Habermas, 88
impossibility arguments, 171–172,
  177–178, 183
  see also Taylor's impossibility thesis

281

Index